School Desegregation

Shadow and Substance

School Desegregation

Shadow and Substance

Edited by
Florence Hamlish Levinsohn
and Benjamin Drake Wright

The University of Chicago Press
Chicago and London

The contents of this volume originally appeared as the May 1976 issue
of *School Review*. The book was partially funded by a grant from the National Institute of Education.

The University of Chicago Press, Chicago 60637
The University of Chicago Press, Ltd., London

Library of Congress Cataloging in Publication Data
Main entry under title:

School desegregation.

Originally published in the May 1976 issue of School
review under title: Is school desegregation still a good
idea?
Includes bibliographies and index.
1. School integration—United States. I. Levinsohn,
Florence Hamlish, 1926-   II. Wright, Benjamin Drake,
1926-
LC214.2.S36   370.19'342   76-17291
ISBN 0-226-47575-1
ISBN 0-226-47577-8 pbk.

What an unheard-of thing it is, in fine,
To love another and be equally loved!
What sadness and what joy! How cruel it is
That pride and wit distort the heart of man,
How vain, how sad, what cruelty, what need,
For this is true and sad, that I need them
And they need me. What can we do? We need
Each other's clumsiness, each other's wit,
Each other's company and our own pride. I need
My face unshamed, I need my wit, I cannot
Turn away. We know our clumsiness, we cannot
Forget our pride, our faces, our common love.

DELMORE SCHWARTZ

Contents

Introduction

Since the end of the Civil War, the education of Blacks has been surrounded by controversy and marked by the same forms of discrimination that characterized access to jobs and housing.[1] In the period immediately following the war, church groups and others of good will went into the South to open schools and teach the freed slaves to read and write. The white resistance to Reconstruction finally brought about its demise and with it much of the education that Blacks had been provided. Gradually, the southern states followed the lead of some northern cities and established segregated schools. By 1896, the Supreme Court, in *Plessy* vs. *Ferguson,* had legitimated the separate school laws passed in the South. Not only were schools for Black children segregated but for the most part they did not satisfy the other part of the *Plessy* decision that required that education be equal; schools for Black children received far less financial support than did those for whites in the same districts. In these years between the end of Reconstruction and the First World War, when the northward movement of Blacks had been steady but slow, it was common for Blacks to walk to a centrally located school designated for their use. As immigration rose, and Blacks were forced to live in segregated sections of the towns and cities of the North, the pattern changed. Black schools were located in Black neighborhoods. *De jure* and *de facto* segregation operated in both South and North to isolate Black children in schools of inferior quality.

These patterns did not develop without resistance from both Blacks and sympathetic whites. And that resistance, often met with violence by whites, culminated in the *Brown* vs. *Board of Education of Topeka* in 1954. As might have been predicted, that decision met with the same negative reaction as had the earlier attempts to equalize educational opportunity. But it was the first decision to have both the force of the federal government and a supporting group of Blacks and whites behind it. It seemed to many of us that within a "reasonable" time the Black children of this nation would have equal access to education.

But the struggle continues even now, more than 20 years later. It is not the same struggle that forced Booker T. Washington to adopt a compromise position, one that he thought would provide some assistance to those so badly deprived. It is not the same struggle that

1

resulted in the National Association for the Advancement of Colored People's fight to provide buses to children who were walking miles to attend Black schools. Nor is it the struggle that resulted in the development of Black colleges in the South.

It is a new struggle, one that we can see an end to. For there are judges, lawyers, and lay people in our land who are determined to finally bring to Black children the full benefits of equal access to schooling, to obey the law as it was interpreted by the Supreme Court in 1954 and strengthened since.

In 1975, as the school year was ending, and as we anticipated the renewal of the struggle for desegregation in the next school year, we decided it was time to take stock, to put the question boldly to some of the people who had been thinking over the matter with great seriousness. We sent to a selected group of people a brief statement summing up the school desegregation controversy to date and inviting them to write a reply to the highly complex question, "Is School Desegregation Still a Good Idea?" With one exception, we did not write to those whose positions had been publicly stated recently, nor to people whose positions we could predict. The exception was Robert Crain who had participated in the early discussions about this volume.

Despite the impression we had gained that there was great division on this issue, all of the responses we present here strongly, at times even passionately, support the continued desegregation of the schools. It seems to be, for most of these people, a matter of "simple justice." Most of our contributors appear to assume that there is no possibility that the nation will reverse its long-range goal to eliminate racial isolation in the schools. Having made this assumption, they go on to discuss how this goal can be implemented more effectively and what the barriers are to that implementation.

It is possible that the few people who declined our invitation may have taken an opposing view. But given the overwhelmingly positive answer by those who did respond, and given the fact that those who declined numbered so few among those invited, that possibility is unlikely. What is more likely is that the political climate has been such, as Alvin Poussaint and Toye Lewis point out, that those who support desegregation have been less vocal lately, that the political climate has encouraged those who oppose integration to be more vocal. It may also be true that the early support for ending racial isolation may not have been, as Betty Showell says, as strong as some of us thought. That the opposition has gained strength has become quite clear in the last couple of years. Or at least it appears to have become clear. Florence Levinsohn's essay on the nature of television reporting of the news about desegregation, however, raises a question about how much actual opposition there is. Perhaps the opposition that we note in the press regularly is actually matched by an equal amount of support that is less visible. Certainly the essays in this volume that offer means by which the opposition can be overcome—by law, social pressure, or fiscal means—combined with those essays that attempt to comprehend the opposition—expressing the clear hope that understanding can help to overcome that opposition—are a passionate statement of support by academics, school teachers, and others whose lives are in one way or another touched by the issues.

The most significant fact that emerges from these essays is that while academics and other researchers have given a good deal of time to looking at the effects of desegregation on test scores—a highly traditional means to study school effects—and while school planners have developed a variety of traditional means to mix racial populations—buses have after all been used to transport children to school for a long time—there has not been much imagination and foresight brought to the problem. In the rural South, as Bullock and others point out, it was easy enough to desegregate simply by altering school attendance lines and using different bus routes. But in large complex cities where housing patterns have traditionally isolated both racial and ethnic groups, simply putting children on a bus to send them out of their own neighborhoods is not enough. This solution has been, in many cities, less than adequate because it has not been planned carefully, as Finger describes, and because it has not been accompanied by in-school efforts to improve educational offerings and make integrated classrooms and activities comfortable for all the children. Busing has thus created fury in some cities, which has inevitably brought us to the point, as Charles Willie tells us, where we overlook the real problems and focus on "the phony issues" of busing.

Perhaps any other effort to desegregate schools would have met with opposition from some quarters. Lillian Rubin's description of the people in the opposition in Richmond, California, raises this specter. But it is just as likely that some of the approaches suggested by Bullock, Finger, Gottlieb, Meadows, Rist, and Willie offer viable means to accomplish desegregation without arousing the small pockets of violent opposition that create severe tension throughout a city.

It is also possible that if those engaged in the evaluation of school desegregation looked beyond test scores they would find, instead of so many failures, some success stories that would then encourage rather than discourage those who are making decisions. Robert Crain and Stanley Robin and James Bosco raise serious questions about the role of academic research in the study of desegregation that cannot be easily dismissed. At the heart of much decision making, both in the courts and in school system planning offices, and in the offices of the National Association for the Advancement of Colored People where so many cases of litigation begin, is at least a strong nod to the tales told by academics about the effects of segregation and desegregation upon schoolchildren. The implications of most of this research are debatable, and we are grateful to Crain for raising the lid on that box.

The other type of research, which Robin and Bosco discuss, that deals with race relations in cities, with the effects of the movement of Blacks and whites on the cities and on the schools, is also of questionable value, though its impact has not been as strong as the first yet.

Embedded in the question, is school desegregation still a good idea? is the larger question, what has happened in the last few years to our concern for racial equality, to our concern for improving relations between the majority and minority peoples that inhabit our land? Following the great strides of the sixties, when so many majority people rallied to the cause of Blacks, Indians, Chicanos, and other minorities, there was a hiatus, a period variously described as "benign neglect," or "retreat from progress." Perhaps we longed to return to the "good old days." But overall, the movement toward equality cannot be stopped, only temporarily derailed. There has been in this nation, alongside its harsh and often brutal treatment of its native American Indians, its Blacks, Irish, Jews, Poles, and other minorities, a steady movement forward, very slow perhaps, but nevertheless over history nearly continuous, of differing people gaining together a secure place in a young insecure nation. It is possible that the ugly treatment accorded minorities resulted in part from the crassness of youth—nations are young just as people are (though it may be questionable whether young people are as brutal as their elders. And it may be questionable whether young nations are as brutal as older ones). Maturity doesn't always bring charity and kindness. But history tells us that, in the long span of time that we have survived on this earth and especially since the advent of the democracies, though there have been and continue to be horrible cases of brutality —Germany in the thirties and forties, Hiroshima and Nagasaki, Vietnam, the Soviet prison camps, South African apartheid, Chilean repression—there has also been a steady movement forward to abolish the forms of brutality that marked the earlier stages of our history. We no longer make slaves of half the people on earth. We no longer hang children for stealing bread, we no longer put the insane in chains. Though we take horrible steps backward into the Dark Ages periodically, we move inextricably toward a more humane world.

And so it is likely that the problems of school desegregation will finally be resolved not in courtrooms, though we will continue to take legal and other measures to bring about the end of racial isolation in the schools, but in the larger context of improved race relations in the society, though there is also the likelihood that race relations in the society will improve as a result of school desegregation. Nellie Brodis, a long-time teacher in the Detroit schools, suggests that the best place to start desegregation is when the child enters school. She is one who believes that school desegregation will lead the way to improved race relations.

Certainly it is safe to say that the two are inextricably bound together, that the opposition to ending racial isolation in the schools is at least partly the result of racial prejudice and that the placing of minority and majority kids side by side in schools is bound to eliminate some of this prejudice. If the process of desegregation were undertaken with this goal in mind, there would undoubtedly be different methods used than simply busing children in and out of neighborhoods. The teachers writing in this volume, and interestingly only the teachers, show their deep concern for what is done in the schools once the children arrive there. We are grateful to our contributors for having so clearly and forthrightly written in reply to our question. We hope that the merit of the remedies they offer will be recognized and that they will be tried by those who are making decisions and applauded by those who are influencing decisions.

We want to express our gratitude to Robert Dreeben, John Glidewell, and William J. Wilson for their encouragement and for their assistance in the planning and putting together of this volume. We want also to thank the National Institute of Education for its financial support.

Florence H. Levinsohn
Benjamin D. Wright

Note

1. Most of the material in the next few paragraphs is from Richard Kluger's *Simple Justice* (New York: Knopf, 1976), which describes the long struggle of Blacks to attain equal access to education.

Racial Balance or Quality Education?

CHARLES V. WILLIE
Harvard University

In 1954, the *Brown* v. *Board of Education of Topeka* decision of the Supreme Court described an equitable educational process as one in which a student of one racial group is able "to engage in discussion and exchange views with other students." Obviously, racial segregation prohibits this kind of exchange between Black and white students so that the Court therefore declared it to be unlawful in public education.

The fact that the desegregation decision was intended to foster education seems to have been forgotten. The focus has shifted, instead, to balanced racial ratios in public schools. The arguments of both liberals and conservatives in the Boston school desegregation case (*Morgan et al.* v. *Hennigan et al.,* June 21, 1974) demonstrate this. In a letter to the editor of the *Boston Globe,* John W. Roberts of the Civil Liberties Union of Massachusetts said, "[Judge W. Arthur Garrity's] task is to evaluate plans as they are placed before him not on the basis of the educational quality of the plan, but rather on the basis of whether or not they meet the standards for school desegregation developed by the Federal Court in a series of cases over the past 20 years."

Because of the complexity of the various plans filed and the need for speedy determination of a plan to be effected in September 1975, Judge Garrity of the United States District Court in Boston appointed a panel of four masters in February 1975, with authority to conduct hearings and make recommendations to the court. Four of us comprised the panel: Edward J. McCormack and Jacob J. Spiegel, lawyers, and Frances Keppel and I, educators. We were multiethnic, interracial, and interdisciplinary. We worked with two court-appointed experts, Robert Dentler and Marvin Scott, also educators.

Attorneys for the Black parents and their children claimed that the plan we developed did not provide the "greatest practicable actual desegregation" because we had given "legally improper weight" to certain criteria such as the preservation of community lines and the conciliation of resistance to desegregation (Worsham 1975). What our plan did provide was described by some observers, however, as a quality educational program for Boston.

But this aspect of the plan seemed, for many people, less important than white, Black, and other minority ratios in each school district. In his initial comment upon Garrity's final school desegregation order (issued May 10, 1975), the president of the Boston chapter of the National Association for the Advancement of Colored People (NAACP) said that the order, in general, was a good one, but that he would examine it carefully to determine whether it desegregated all segregated schools. He said he would examine the order to determine "whether there are any schools left which are predominantly Black." He implied that there should not be any such schools and stated that this was the requirement that must be met (Wilkie 1975).

The NAACP response to the judge's final order focused on the method rather than on the purpose of desegregation. This focus of the NAACP and of the plaintiff parents on racial ratios in 1975 was in accord with state action taken 10 years earlier. In 1965, the Massachusetts legislature passed the Racial Imbalance Act that declared as racially unbalanced any school with more than 50 percent nonwhite students. The law itself could be described as racist because it declared illegal, and therefore not in the public interest, any school which had a majority Black student body. The principle enunciated is that it is not in the public interest for whites to be a minority in any Massachusetts schools, hardly a valid educational principle.

Thomas Pettigrew has reminded us that "many relatively unprejudiced whites engage in [racial discrimination] virtually every day of their lives," and that one need not be a racist to contribute to and

---

CHARLES V. WILLIE is professor of education and urban studies, Harvard Graduate School of Education. He was one of four court-appointed masters in the Boston school desegregation case and has conducted desegregation research which is reported in two books —*Race Mixing in the Public Schools* and *Black Students at White Colleges.* Former president of the Eastern Sociological Society, Professor Willie is a member of the Social and Behavioral Sciences Assembly of the National Research Council and has served on the board of directors of the Social Science Research Council. Dr. Willie has lived in both the North and the South and has attended predominantly Black and predominantly white schools.

perpetuate institutional racism (Pettigrew 1973, p. 272). On June 21, 1974, Garrity found that the Boston School Committee "intentionally and purposefully caused or maintained racial segregation in meaningful or significant segments of the public school system in violation of the Fourteenth Amendment." He further said that such segregation "need not have been inspired by any particular racial attitude in order to be unconstitutional." The same can be said of the Racial Imbalance Act.

Because laws are statements of social norms they affect the behavior of minority as well as majority members of society. Indeed, the Supreme Court decision, *Plessy* v. *Ferguson,* delivered in 1896, which declared that state laws may sanction separate facilities for Black and white citizens as long as the facilities are equal, became normative and influenced the actions of Americans for more than 50 years.

With the Racial Imbalance Act in the background, it is not difficult to understand why powerful opinion molders such as state legislators focused their attention on the method rather than the purpose of school desegregation, making it difficult to overcome a preoccupation with racial ratios and forcing a concern with quality education to be sidestepped.

Nevertheless, as the court-appointed masters in Boston, we tried to link school desegregation with quality education. Many, but not all, of our proposals were included in the final court order to desegregate the city public schools. Some of the highlights of these proposals are presented here as a guide to the future—to a new approach to school desegregation which focuses on purpose as well as method.

We began by deciding that busing is a phony issue. Our conclusion was based, in part, on information provided by the Massachusetts commissioner of education. He said, "Thirty thousand kids were being bused in Boston before there was any desegregation plan" (Anrig 1974–75, p. 11). This number was about one-third of all students enrolled in Boston public schools and was less than the number of students who would be required to use transportation in our plan, which proposed busing for only 15,000, half the number being transported to school even before court-ordered desegregation. The estimated number of students to be bused in the final court order was 21,000–24,000—still less than the number that used transportation before court-ordered desegregation.

Our plan for the reorganization of the school system into community districts and for the redrawing of district boundaries to promote a sense of community and minimize busing was an effort to refocus attention from transportation to education.

Before our draft plan was issued, the superintendent of schools for the City of Boston said, "It is the issue of busing . . . , which, whether correctly or not, has assumed major importance to a considerable segment of Greater Boston's population" (Leary 1974–75, p. 13). It was in light of this that we attempted to have the citizens of Boston examine the issue of how children go to school in relationship to why they go to school. We assumed that children attend school to obtain an education and that how they go to school is of secondary importance.

Our plan included an invitation to local colleges and universities to cooperate with the city school department in a long-term project to improve educational quality and promote excellence in the public schools. Judge Garrity's order of May 10, 1975, noted that these institutions (21 in cities and suburbs of the metropolitan area) had "committed themselves to support, assist and participate in the development of educational excellence" in the public schools. In his court order he directed the members of the Boston School Committee "to use their best efforts to negotiate a contract" with each of the colleges and universities. The contract would set forth the scope of authority of the parties and the role to be played by each. The president of Boston College (one of the 21 schools) said he was encouraged by the new superintendent's attitude toward college and university participation (McCain 1975).

Under the plan, colleges and universities are expected to do more than provide tutoring assistance and develop research projects, traditional ways of involvement. These institutions are to be paired with specific schools, to work out appropriate cooperative relationships that are mutually beneficial.

The original idea to foster excellence in the public schools as a way of making desegregation more acceptable was contained in the plan prepared by the Boston School Committee. While we rejected most of the plan of the School Committee as inadequate, we were impressed by that portion that indicated that some schools should be magnetized by extraordinary educational opportunities. We were intrigued by this idea, impressed by the array of excellent colleges and universities in the Boston metropolitan area, and believed that if links between educational institutions could be effected, some public schools could be transformed into magnets of educational excellence. Thus, the idea of magnet schools which was advanced by the School Committee was strengthened by the masters who proposed specific means to magnetize a few schools.

The colleges and universities are not expected to serve as altruistic lords or benevolent despots, determining unilaterally what ought to be done to and for the public schools. The turbulence at Columbia

Charles V. Willie

University in the 1960s was due, in part, to the absence of a good-neighbor policy toward Harlem, and has lingered in the corporate memory of colleges and universities.

While we assumed goodwill and willingness to assist by the colleges and universities, we, in addition, based our request to them on the idea that their own self-interest would be served by helping to promote domestic tranquillity in the Boston area. Student enrollment has become a significant component in the stability and even viability of some private colleges and universities. Potential students might be disinclined to come to a burning Boston. So, it was in the self-interest of most private schools to help defuse the desegregation issue and keep Boston cool and calm.

Since some of us serving as masters had many years of experience working with faculty and administrative personnel of colleges and universities, we knew that an appeal to these institutions for their assistance during these troubled times merely on the basis of altruism might obtain a short-term, but no long-term, commitment or follow-through. Our clue to appealing to their self-interest came from the activities of several local businesses.

Even before the court began to formulate its final school desegregation order, several businesses, through the National Alliance of Businessmen and the Greater Boston Chamber of Commerce, formed the Tri-Lateral Task Force with the Boston School Department to create partnerships between specific businesses and specific public schools, with the hope of contributing to peaceful desegregation. Several businesses participating in the partnership program —retail sales, mortgage banking, insurance, and public services —would suffer greatly were Boston to go up in smoke. They recognized their self-interest in maintaining a cool and calm Boston in volunteering to do whatever they could. Their activity led us to believe that others might be motivated by similar self-interests.

What made us enthusiastic about the possibility of cooperation between colleges and universities and elementary and secondary public schools within the context of a court order was that it provided the opportunity to unite the method—desegregation—with the purpose—quality education. This arrangement, we believed, could serve as a model for major metropolitan areas throughout this nation. Such an arrangement is not new in Boston or elsewhere, but the unique feature of this plan is to pair public schools with colleges and universities.

In the past, local Boston communities such as Roxbury, a Black community, worked with more colleges and universities than it wanted or needed, while Italian or Irish sections, such as East Boston

11

or Charlestown, were more or less ignored. Our plan recommended the pairing of a college or university with each high school and with several middle and elementary schools. For many of these schools, a cooperative relationship with an institution of higher education is a first-time experience.

It is important to bear in mind that a desegregation plan which followed the guidelines of the 1965 State Racial Imbalance Act was legal but racist. A decade ago, school desegregation was believed to basically benefit Blacks, but public law that is believed to benefit Blacks is rarely, if ever, examined for racist content.

The attitudes that contributed to the enactment of the racial imbalance law in Massachusetts were similar to the attitudes of those who interpreted the data from the survey of educational opportunity mandated by Congress in 1964. James Coleman, the senior researcher of that study, said, "There is evident, even in the short run, an effect of school integration on the reading and mathematics achievement of Negro pupils, [and that] in the long run, integration should be expected to have a positive effect on Negro achievement . . . (Coleman et al. 1966, p. 7). He concluded that "the achievement of minority pupils depends more on the schools they attend than does the achievement of majority pupils" (p. 22). Thus, the push toward integrating Blacks with whites in predominantly white schools was accelerated because of this expectation that the higher achievement level recorded by whites would somehow improve Black achievement. This was the wisdom of the mid-1960s out of which the State Racial Imbalance Act emerged.

But the Coleman Report (1966) had other findings that were given less attention: (1) "it appears that differences between schools account for only a small fraction of differences in pupil achievement," (2) "minority pupils . . . have far less conviction than whites that they can affect their own environments and futures," (3) "when [minority students have a belief that they can affect their own environments and futures], . . . their achievement is higher than that of whites who lack that conviction," and (4) "those blacks in schools with a higher proportion of whites have a greater sense of control" (p. 23). Elaborating upon the latter point, Coleman said, "Black children in an integrated school come to gain a greater sense of their efficacy to control their destiny. It is very likely due to the fact that they see that they can do some things better than whites . . . a knowledge which they never had so long as they were isolated in an all-Black school" (Coleman 1968, p. 25). Thus, a significant variable which ought to be considered is the sense of efficacy which school desegregation might stimulate among

Blacks. Most school desegregation plans have tended to ignore these findings.

In the light of these findings, we veered from the requirement of a similar ratio of Black, white, and other minority children in each school and proposed that the student bodies of Boston schools be diversified rather than strictly balanced. Whites need not always be the majority in good schools. If a sense of control is significant educationally, some schools should have a majority of whites in the student body with a sufficient minority of Blacks to have educational impact upon the total system. Other schools should have a majority of Blacks with a sufficient minority of whites to have a meaningful influence.

The concept, sufficient minority, is relative and could vary from 49 percent to 20 percent. My own studies of community organizations suggest that minority participation of less than one-fifth in a democratic and free organization tends to have little effect upon institutional decision making. A school desegregation plan should attempt to have a racial majority (Blacks, browns, or whites) in each school of not more than two-thirds of all students; this proportion can accommodate population changes in the future without requiring the drawing of new district boundaries too often. The important point is that the size of a minority population necessary to influence an institution or organization and its programs or policies may be different from the size of the minority population within the total community. The critical mass of a racial or ethnic group necessary for effective input in democratic decision making may be larger or smaller than its proportion in the total population. The concept of diversity as a guideline for desegregation would do two things: (1) prevent racial isolation in education, and (2) facilitate conditions for the development of a sense of control by Blacks as well as by whites in schools in which either race might be a majority.

Our concept of diversity in the composition of student populations in specific schools and districts instead of adherence to a strict racial ratio introduced another idea which seldom has been discussed in litigation for school desegregation. The idea is that there is educational benefit in being a member of the minority. Being in control is something of value. But learning how to depend upon others, to trust others, to receive and accept assistance when needed, is something of value, too. Minorities have had to learn these things, and some have been strengthened by enduring their minority status, persevering, and triumphantly transcending adversity. The recent studies of self-concept by Gloria Johnson Powell (1973) and Morris Rosenberg and Roberta C. Simmons (1972) indicate that minority children have de-

13

veloped positive concepts of themselves, sometimes more positive than the self-concepts whites or majority children have developed. By recommending the creation of student bodies and school districts in which Black and brown populations would be a majority, we were creating an opportunity for some whites to experience the beneficial effects of being a minority.

Years ago, Robert Merton recognized the potential contribution of the minority to the total society when he wrote, "It is not infrequently the case that the non-conforming minority in a society represents the interest and ultimate values of the group more effectively than the conforming majority" (1949, p. 367). In a pluralistic and cosmopolitan society in which everyone may be in a minority in one context or another at some period of time, it is well that, in school, whites should learn not to fear the consequences of minority status; and Blacks should learn to be comfortable with the responsibilities and requirements for majority status. Such would be effective education for life in a pluralistic society.

We developed a novel plan to locate magnet schools, those with extraordinary educational programs designed to attract to them racially diversified student bodies. Some parents insisted, through a legal representative retained by the Home and School Association, that desegregation would be more acceptable if students could have a choice regarding school of enrollment. We knew that "open enrollment" plans had been used in the past to circumvent desegregation rather than to promote it. Yet the desire for choice in a free society is compelling and should be accommodated if it can be done in a way consistent with the requirements of desegregation.

Thus, we proposed that the entire Boston school system should be organized into nine community districts and one citywide district. Magnet schools with extraordinary educational opportunities were located in various sections of the citywide district and would be open to all students as long as the composition of their total student bodies was similar to the citywide school population of 51 percent white, 36 percent Black, and 13 percent other minorities. Students could choose any specific magnet school in the city and be guaranteed a desegregation experience with a student body at a fixed ratio, or they could choose to enroll in their community district. In the community district, however, students would be assigned to a school for the purpose of achieving desegregation according to the ratios of whites, Blacks, and other minorities in that district. Each school would be similar to the racial ratio of the district, with variations being permitted within a range of 25 percent. Most districts had a majority of white students, but some had a majority of Blacks. While desegregation of

14

the district might prevent a student from being assigned to his or her neighborhood school, the distance to be traveled to and from school would be less within a district than the one to a magnet school. The choice would be between a magnet school with extraordinary educational offerings at a considerable distance from home and a less illustrious school relatively close by. But the first would have fixed racial ratios while the second would vary with the district, so that some districts would have largely white populations and others largely Black ones.

According to folklore, whites will not attend schools in neighborhoods that are predominantly Black. We examined the facts and determined that this folklore did not have an empirical base. A few Boston schools such as Trotter Elementary and Boston Technical, with extraordinary programs, located in areas densely populated by Blacks were attended by whites from all sectors of the city. Moreover, similar experiences had occurred in other communities such as the Martin Luther King, Jr., Elementary School in Syracuse, New York, when it was under the principalship of William Wayson.

In fact, we determined that the most appropriate locations for magnet schools were in neighborhoods to which persons might not be attracted unless the educational programs were extraordinary. Schools in such locations could truly become magnets for desegregation as well as for quality education. Thus, we recommended that some of the schools to be magnetized—Roxbury, East Boston, Charlestown, and South Boston High schools—be ones located in predominantly Black, Italian, and Irish areas. Their educational programs were to be enhanced by linking them with Harvard University, Massachusetts Institute of Technology, Bunker Hill Community College, the University of Massachusetts in Boston, and several major businesses in the city.

The ethnic and racial communities surrounding these high schools were relatively isolated. Since students had already demonstrated that they would go into neighborhoods in which the racial population was different from their own if the quality of education at the school was outstanding, we believed that students also would go into ethnic neighborhoods in which the population was unlike that of their own if the education was extraordinary. Magnetizing schools in the major racial and ethnic communities of the city would overcome their isolation and at the same time provide a unique cultural context within which to achieve desegregation, while upgrading the quality of education.

To guarantee space for outsiders in the four high schools—that is, students not resident in the Black, Italian, or Irish communities—we suggested an experimental Freshman Studies Program for ninth graders from the four communities to be located in downtown Boston. These first-year high school students who probably had previously had only limited interracial and interethnic contact were to be educated together in a neutral location outside their home communities and away from the negative reinforcing influences of friends who were accustomed to their isolation, and justified it with many rationalizations.

Even if the magnet-school concept failed to attract outsiders into the more or less closed and isolated ethnic communities, the experimental Freshman Studies Program guaranteed that a desegregation experience would begin for some of the students from these communities. The twofold process of recruiting students to the high schools in the ethnic communities because of the extraordinary quality of their educational programs and sending the freshman class to a neutral territory where an interracial experience was guaranteed was a custom-tailored approach we designed to achieve racial desegregation as well as to defuse potential violence. We believed, with Judge Garrity, that "no amount of public or parental opposition will excuse avoidance by school officials of constitutional obligations to desegregate and the constitutional principles which mandate duty to desegregate cannot be allowed to yield simply because of disagreement with them." We attempted to design a special approach for the special racial and ethnic areas in Boston, which would recognize this principle of the court while stimulating the least amount of resistance and violence. The approach was tailor-made for Boston, but it could be used in other major cities that have multiple racial and ethnic areas that are relatively isolated.

Because of the need to limit the number of magnet schools to maintain their unique attractiveness, the number was cut back, and our final report recommended only East Boston and Charlestown High Schools as citywide magnet high schools. These, unfortunately, were not included in the final court order. The experimental Freshman Studies Program was also eliminated because of the unavailability of a facility in downtown Boston where students from the four communities could have been educated together.

As we analyzed the testimony received in public hearings and talked with official and community leaders, two themes for recommended action emerged—one a populist theme and the other an elitist. While these two seem contradictory, they were often expressed by the same person. Careful analysis of these two themes—one supporting inclusive and the other advocating exclusive educational arrangements—reveals the intersection of social class with school desegregation.

Populist advocates encouraged us to get the people involved, particularly parents. They supported our recommendation that a citywide committee of leading citizens monitor the desegregation process. They were also enthusiastic about the proposed community district councils. Some even felt that machinery should be established for electing parents to the community councils so that they would represent all the people. We hesitated about recommending an election, fearing that this might become one more issue over which to wrangle and divide the community, and fearing further that the energy consumed in the electoral process might leave the winners spent and unable to mobilize sufficiently to deal with the real issue of desegregated quality education. Notwithstanding these doubts, our final plan recommended community district councils to which parents could be elected to serve with teachers, students, public officials, and others. Thus we embraced the populist goal of getting the people involved.

But this orientation, we discovered, was limited largely to citizen participation in an advisory capacity to the school administration. We proposed that the populist view of getting everyone involved should also extend to the involvement of poor white students in the METCO (Metropolitan Council for Educational Opportunity) program sponsored by the state board of education, which each day bused approximately 2,400 Black students from Boston to relatively affluent suburban communities. The suburban schools participated in the program on a voluntary basis but received state support that varied with the number of students accepted. We hoped to extend the beneficial effects of METCO for overcoming racial isolation to poor whites who might thus overcome socioeconomic isolation, particularly whites enrolled in Title I schools. The response in general was unsympathetic. It seemed that the community wanted to keep poor whites as invisible as all Blacks. There was little desire to provide extraordinary opportunities for whites who were poor. And so the proposal to make Title I poor whites eligible for the METCO program was not included in the final court order.

We also attempted to implement the populist view with reference to the "examination" schools, including the two Latin schools and the technical high school. Our goal was to maintain the excellence which has characterized these schools, whose graduates have tended to go on to college, while making them available to a broader range of students of different racial and ethnic backgrounds. Students had

17

been admitted to these schools on the basis of their performance on standardized examinations. We proposed that previous performance, such as rank in class, might be a fairer criterion for admission than performance on a specific test given on a particular day, although examination scores might be used to provide the lower limit for an eligible pool of applicants.

We believed that if the examination schools were the greatest of the Boston schools they should be willing to serve all students, since the greatest of all is first the servant of all. To accomplish this, we proposed that the Latin schools should add a post–high school or precollege year in which any city resident not sufficiently prepared for college could enroll. Becuase of the excellent record which these schools have accumulated in sending their graduates on to higher education, they were especially suited to make available to the total community a special college preparatory program. Such a program at the Latin Schools would meet an important need. Some families now send their children to private academies for a precollege year to make up for deficiencies in their high school education. Others without the means to do this find that their children must miss out on college.

All of the proposals for the examination schools were rejected. "Don't tamper with the examination schools" was the prevailing attitude in the Boston community. We discovered that the populists were also elitists and wished to eliminate any influences which might contaminate the exclusivity of these extraordinary schools. In general, populism seemed to be acceptable as long as it did not require a rearrangement of the educational opportunity system with reference to the social classes.

Our concept of diversity, with neither whites nor Blacks always predominating, rather than a fixed racial ratio was abandoned in the final court order. Some parties to the Boston school desegregation case argued that the responsibility of the court was to achieve the greatest practicable actual desegregation and that this could be achieved best by requiring all community districts to approximate the citywide school population of Blacks, other minorities, and whites. The attempt by the court to achieve this goal resulted in the elimination of a predominantly Black school district which we proposed.

Only our concept of establishing community districts as a method of organizing the school system, and the idea of linking public schools with colleges, universities, and businesses to promote educational excellence was retained in the final court order. Indeed, the possible linkage between schools and other organizations and institutions in the community was extended to include labor unions and museums.

In summary, we proposed a new approach to school desegregation which attempted to unite method and purpose. Some of our proposals were rejected in favor of advancing racial quotas, method without its purpose.

Ultimately, desegregation is to achieve quality education. In a pluralistic society, there can be no quality education where there is not desegregation. But desegregation can go forth in a constitutional way without facilitating quality education. How to prevent separation of method from purpose in education is a problem in need of serious study. An editorial in the *New York Times* summed up the issue quite nicely: "Integration must be made synonymous with better education" (May 20, 1975).

References

Anrig, Gregory. "Our Goal: Elimination of Racial Isolation." *Harvard Graduate School of Education Association Bulletin,* vol. 59 (Winter 1974–75).

Coleman, James S. "Equality of Educational Opportunity." *Integrated Education,* vol. 6 (September–October 1968).

Coleman, James S., et al. *Equality of Educational Opportunity.* Washington, D.C.: Government Printing Office, 1966.

Leary, William J. "Boston: The Way It Is and the Way It Might Be." *Harvard Graduate School of Education Association Bulletin,* vol. 59 (Winter 1974–75).

McCain, Nina. "College Heads See Role More Realistic under Garrity's Plan." *Boston Globe* (May 13, 1975).

Merton, Robert K. *Social Theory and Social Structure.* New York: Free Press, 1949.

Pettigrew, Thomas. "Racism and the Mental Health of White Americans: A Social Psychological View." In *Racism and Mental Health,* edited by Charles V. Willie, Bernard M. Kramer, and Bertram S. Brown. Pittsburgh: University of Pittsburgh Press, 1973.

Powell, Gloria Johnson. "Self-Concept in White and Black Children." In *Racism and Mental Health,* edited by Charles V. Willie, Bernard M. Kramer, and Bertram S. Brown. Pittsburgh: University of Pittsburgh Press. 1973.

Rosenberg, Morris, and Simmons, Roberta G. *Black and White Self-Esteem: The Urban School Child.* Washington, D.C.: American Sociological Association, 1972.

Wilkie, Curtis. "Phase 2 Order Raises Many Questions, Fears." *Boston Globe* (May 12, 1975).

Worsham, James B. "School Plaintiffs Renew Charges against Masters." *Boston Globe* (May 10, 1975).

School Desegregation: A Synonym for Racial Equality

ALVIN F. POUSSAINT
Harvard Medical School

TOYE BROWN LEWIS
Freedom House Institute for Schools and Education, Boston

The issue of school desegregation has become so explosive that some areas in the country have literally drawn "battle lines." If these trends continue, the nation may be threatened with division as severe as that during the Civil War. Unfortunately, in the heat of controversy over desegregation strategies, the basic principle under which desegregation policy was established has been lost.

The 1954 Supreme Court decision which outlawed "separate and equal" schools advanced the notion of equality in a society which had operated largely under institutionalized racism. The new law introduced a radically different notion of social and psychological functioning among Americans. It challenged the behavior of whites toward Blacks and mandated a change. The basic aim of desegregation is to have people function in a manner that reflects a principle of equal opportunity. White Americans were ordered to respect the rights and dignity of Black Americans in the same way they are ordered to pay taxes, obey traffic laws, and send their children to school until age 16.

The Issue of Equality

The basic issue raised by the decision of 1954, remains with us today: full equality for Blacks. David Gil (1973) offers a lucid presentation of the principle: "All humans everywhere, in spite of individual and cultural differences and uniqueness, are intrinsically of equal worth, and are hence entitled to equal social, economic, civic, and political rights. The political goal derived from this value premise is the estab-

20

lishment of a social order on local, national, and world-wide levels, based on the principle of full equality."

We believe that school desegregation is inextricably linked to the problem of race in America. No discussion of the need for "quality" education or even of the economic problems of the urban poor can long obscure this relationship. If school desegregation should be abandoned, the nation's racial policy is likely to drift in the direction of resegregation, for it is clear that the largest effort made so far to alleviate the inequality of race has been the one made in education, while policies in economic development, housing, criminal justice, and other fields have been given much lower priority in the enforcement of equal opportunity. Perhaps it is unfortunate that the burden for achieving racial equality in the nation has fallen so heavily upon public education, but until appreciable gains are made in other areas, we must not abandon this policy, though there certainly are negative factors associated with placing so large a burden on the educational system. While some people argue that, despite the resistance to desegregation, this policy has received less opposition than efforts to redistribute opportunity in the job market or in housing, the exodus from the inner cities to the suburbs as a white protest against school desegregation has contributed to the economic destruction and social imbalance of our cities. Racial isolation has become intensified in some cities. Nevertheless, there have been enough instances of successful desegregation to convince us that the policy remains viable.

Kenneth Clark views the debate about desegregation as evidence of the inequality in our society. The fact of segregation, he says, is the

---

ALVIN F. POUSSAINT, M.D., is associate professor of psychiatry and associate dean of students at Harvard Medical School. His articles have appeared in *Ebony, Redbook,* the *New York Times Magazine,* and major scientific journals. He is the author of *Why Blacks Kill Blacks* and coauthor of the book *Black Child Care* with James P. Comer.

TOYE B. LEWIS is senior consultant to the Freedom House Institute for Schools and Education in Roxbury, Massachusetts. She has worked in the area of public education policy development since 1966, serving as chairperson on the educational policy committee of the New School for Children, an alternative community school in Boston, 1968–73. She has also consulted on educational planning with the National and Boston Urban League; Boston Model Cities Program; METCO, Boston's voluntary interdistrict school transfer program; and the Mayor's Plan for Decentralization of the Boston Public Schools.

argument against equality. If equality prevailed, there would be no argument (Clark 1975). The appeal in the school fight must be to the morality of the nation—to its commitment to democracy, equality, and justice.

Segregation which deprives Blacks of equal opportunity is grounded primarily in two institutional systems: economic and educational. Blacks have been denied land ownership and capital, and the dual education system has favored whites. As long as a society segregates children either on the basis of race or class in its major institution for human socialization, the schools, it discriminates against these citizens. This form of discrimination becomes systematic, an accepted way of life, and results in rigid race and class isolation.

From this perspective, no system of separate quality education regardless of its quality, can alter the basic economic segregation of Blacks any more than the public school system can compete with the private school system to rearrange the social class rankings which maintain the rich at the top. The issue is greater than education; it has to do with the access routes to which education systems lead. Furthermore, talk of racially segregated public schools in the 1970s obscures even further the issues of class segregation. Questions are rarely raised about the inequality perpetuated by the existence of the dual system of public and private schools in the nation.

Equality, then, is the critical issue. It is the moral issue which all critics of desegregation must face. The increase in opposition to desegregation strategies among social scientists and politicians reflects a decline of morality in the society. If equality of opportunity is no longer a good idea, then whites will suffer as much as Blacks because once the precedent is set that equality is not needed for Blacks then the value premise becomes weakened for everyone. Other oppressed groups, such as white women, risk a narrowing of the opportunity structure which has only recently begun to open for them. It is unfortunate that the women's liberation movement has not taken up the fight for desegregation of the schools and directed their mobilization to the "sisters" who actively or passively oppose school desegregation strategies.

Factors Leading to the Current Crisis: Psychological Reasons for White Resistance

One deep psychological residual of slavery and racism is the view so many whites still hold that Blacks are not their intellectual equals, deserving equal educational facilities. This view may underlie the concern of whites who fear the decline of their schools if the facilities and resources are shared with Blacks.

In a sense, busing is a superficial issue in the desegregation controversy. But resistance to it as a means to achieve school desegregation has demonstrated that many whites are anti-Black. Busing is an administrative issue in any school operation and cannot be as complex a problem as it has been made to seem. The underlying racial prejudice of white parents and the fear of harassment and injury to their children that Black parents have are the real issues underlying the "busing problem." White parents do not want to be ordered by the law to send their children to school with Black children. And Black parents fear white retaliation directed at their children. It seems ironic that busing is described as "forced" by even responsible national leaders and the news media while few would ever consider using that term for schooling, though school attendance is compulsory and is so in decaying and irrelevant public school systems while technology has so surpassed classroom instruction that a youngster can often gain greater literacy and learn more about survival by watching TV at home.

The Shift from Desegregation Policy

Continued segregation of schools is being explained by social scientists as a response to the need to reduce racial violence exacerbated by school desegregation efforts or as appropriate until economic conditions among Blacks and whites are more equalized.[1] To say that desegregation is no longer a good idea because a disruptive minority of Americans resist the idea is to succumb to a racism which will only further divide the nation. The nation's internal stability and security will be in jeopardy until its citizens accept the notion of racial equality. It is ironic that we spend billions of dollars attempting to establish a principle of democracy in Southeast Asia, despite massive resistance by the people of those nations, and fail to give similar priority to achieving the democratic principle of racial equality in our own nation.

There is also the attempt to draw a distinction between commitment to school desegregation and racial integration (Novak 1975). Increasingly, ambivalent whites claim to favor racial integration as a principle, but oppose busing as a strategy for desegregation. These are the same people who opposed community control of schools in the 1960s, school pairing, campus-school designs, and other plans for school desegregation. They also gave little support to the alternative

schools movement by parents where attempts were made to develop
integrated, high-quality schools outside the traditional public school
system.

We learned in the South from both the movement to achieve open
public accommodations and school desegregation that whites will
obey the law if it is vigorously enforced. Therefore, the burden for
achieving racial equality ultimately rests with political leaders at the
federal, state, and local levels; officials in the police and school departments; teacher organizations; labor union leaders; and religious
leaders. Where these leaders take stands firmly against bigotry and
explain the importance of desegregation to the nation, those parents
who act out of ignorance and fear are less likely to resist school desegregation orders.

The Social Responsibility of Leadership

The apprehension, fear, and frustration among parents and other
citizens associated with school desegregation are further complicated
by bigoted and opportunistic stands on the issue taken by politicians.
Instead of attempting to educate the American public about the right
of minorities to equal schooling, these politicians respond to the ignorance and fear of the voters and take stands against busing as a
desegregation strategy rather than assuming responsible leadership
and favoring measures to reduce racial isolation in the schools.

The loudest voices against busing are from public officials whose
legislative records have shown long-term opposition to public policies
that promise social and economic progress for Blacks. Other officials
who previously supported desegregation, now more concerned about
winning elections, have abandoned earlier stands and today talk of
"needed change in the law." Only a few still support busing; most
have simply become silent on the issue, avoiding the negative repercussions of being in the spotlight as busing advocates.

Until recently, politicians, including our unelected president, were
making statements against court-ordered busing, but once they were
reminded that their positions were essentially against the law (Supreme Court decision on busing, April 20, 1971) they switched to the
position that court-ordered busing is the law of the land and must be
obeyed *until the law is changed.*[2] But talk of changing the law is talk of
reversal of the intent, as a nation, to guarantee equal opportunity to
Blacks.

This new strategy was probably precipitated by the fact that earlier
stands against court-ordered busing were providing ammunition to

the more militant anti-busing factions. Though these resistance groups are predominantly white, public officials cannot condone their disruptive tactics any more than they did the less extreme civil rights movement strategies. If massive disorder is given too much support, it can surge out of control of the ordinary police forces. Thus, the anti-desegregation movement has forced a demonstration that the law-and-order doctrine of the current national administration is meant for all Americans, not just Blacks.

Many politicians (and social scientists dependent upon federal contracts for research) have been more concerned with popularity than equal opportunity. During Phase I of Boston's court-ordered school desegregation plan (1974–75 school year), the mayor and city council were openly against school desegregation, and some city council and school committee members were openly organizing groups against the policy. The mayor refused to request federal troops through the governor to demonstrate to the city that racial violence would not be tolerated. Some proponents of school desegregation in Boston point out that the court order would have been more readily complied with had there been federal troops deployed to Boston at the onset of massive violent resistance which closed the schools in troubled white areas. Whether their actions were prompted by their own beliefs or their need to gain popular support we cannot know, but it is clear that Boston's political leaders did not provide leadership on the side of justice and equality.

Quality Education and School Desegregation

Those who insist on discussing the importance of quality education over and above school desegregation often fail to draw the necessary distinction between issues of service delivery, quality of educational services offered in the public schools, and the fundamental right to attend the schools. School desegregation policy relates to the basic right to attend schools throughout the public system. Program development, planning, and improvement are the service issues which must be simultaneously addressed, not used as diversionary issues to avoid desegregation. The quality of public school education should be constantly monitored by both providers of the educational service and the consumers (students and parents) as a matter of course. But when the school desegregation issue is drawn into the question of quality, it tends to foster the myth that Blacks are not and cannot be educationally equal to whites.

25

Those who speak of alternatives to integrated education or more incremental approaches to achieve integration advocate that we work to improve Black schools first with the expectation that the rise in quality will attract white students. The problem with this proposition is twofold: first, at a time when public education faces a serious fiscal crisis, there will be little or no commitment to providing the funds necessary for improving the quality of education in separate Black schools.

Second, whites will probably not relinquish control over Black schools, and white control in itself may perpetuate inferiority in these schools. The inferiority of Black schools in the past was generally a condition occurring under white control. Furthermore, many advocates of this alternative fail to realize that the public education system is primarily an employment system for whites. These whites are unlikely to be willing to relinquish their jobs in schools in Black neighborhoods and, thus, their control over the education of Black children. White control of education in predominantly Black schools does not bode well for quality education for Blacks. There is historic evidence of neglect and discrimination, and the lack of Black input and control over educational socialization has been established as a negative factor in Black motivation, identity, and self-esteem. One key ingredient to improve education of black children must be Black adults in positions of power, authority, and decision making within the educational system.

In the late 1960s, we witnessed tremendous battling for control over Black schools when many, disillusioned with failure of integration strategies in northern schools, opted for control of the schools in the inner cities. The teachers' unions, mayors, social service systems, and other interest groups in the white community coalesced to defeat this movement. Attempts to establish alternative schools with high-quality curriculum innovation and development were shattered by failure of the government or private sector to support and adequately fund Black attempts to control and improve alternative schools, and Black leaders were unable to mobilize enough resources to create their own separate schools. Some demonstration monies were given to the community schools effort by major foundations and the U.S. Office of Education, but when the community control/Black education issue became identified as a political issue in America's big cities, most of these funds were withdrawn. At the height of the movement for community control of schools, especially in New York, the question arose: who governs the schools? The answer seemed clear enough: the white power structure (public officials, teachers' unions, and school contractors). These groups appeared determined to prevent Blacks from controlling the schools even in their own neighborhoods.[3]

The untenable situation of Blacks pushing for control of predominantly Black schools while whites try to hold the line will merely be reactivated if there is a resurgence of the idea of improving schools within the Black community as an alternative to busing. In fact, with the continuing depressed economic situation, white reaction could be even more resistive.

Past experience with community control and the current realities of union control and the current realities of union control of schools suggest that it will be more difficult to secure the manpower and resources to improve education in predominantly Black public schools than for Blacks to work for integration of facilities and curriculum within newly desegregated schools. Desegregation need not negate the opportunity for Blacks to work in the schools wherever *their children are assigned,* to integrate the staff and curriculum, and generally see that the learning environment reflects full participation of the Black community and input of Black culture.

Many advocates of "quality" Black schools understandably want to protect Black children from overt acts of white opposition to desegregation. In fact, school desegregation offers no promise that Black children will be spared the cruelties of racism. But are these immediate and short-term consequences of racist resistance to school desegregation greater than the long-term cruelties of educational inequality and denial of upward mobility perpetuated by continued segregation of the races?

In Boston, many Black parents desired desegregation because they believed in equal opportunity. Despite the continuing violent resistance to school desegregation during the 1974–75 school year, there was no organized move on the part of Boston Black parents to resist school desegregation. At the height of the violence in September 1975, Freedom House Institute on Schools and Education received numerous calls from parents urging persistence in getting their children on the buses and to their newly assigned schools. The common comment was: "They will not keep our children out of those schools. Black people have the same right to those public schools as whites."

Economic Issues

Some critics of desegregation seek to shift the attention from school desegregation strategies to a discussion of the economic problems in the society. The proposition is usually formulated as: the basic prob-

27

lem is not education, but economic. Peace will be restored to our cities if the enforcement of desegregation policies is simply relaxed and suspended in critical areas of the country until the economic status of Blacks and whites can be more equalized. Then, it is predicted, Blacks will be more acceptable to the white working class.

This proposition is specious. Close examination of the Black youth on school buses reveal that a good number of them do, in fact, come from well-scrubbed, clean, God-fearing, disciplined, working-class families. The true economic issue is that the timing is poor for enforcing any type of strategy to support desegregation. Desegregation implies redistribution of resources. The nation is undergoing an economic depression. Goods and services are scarce, and whites fear losing the few gains they've made in the past four decades since the Great Depression of the thirties. Further, whites do not merely see Blacks coming to their schools but fear that, once they are in the schools, Blacks will also desire to move to their neighborhood. There are really two problems associated with inequality in the nation—race and class. Black children are concentrated at the least advantaged end of the economic scale. Therefore, any discussion of the economic problem in the nation will logically lead us back to the necessity of a policy for equal opportunity in the economic as well as the public school system.

Too little has been said in the school desegregation controversy about desegregation at the teaching and administrative levels. School desegregation at this level means increased economic opportunity for Black adults in a variety of jobs and services. This issue was at the heart of the movement for community control of schools. The concept of school desegregation must expand to include greater participation of Blacks in teaching, decision making, and service positions in the desegregated systems.

Economic realities present an even stronger case for school desegregation because they suggest needed redistribution of opportunity in very tangible terms, not only as access to schools for Black youth, but also for jobs for Black adults. As long as there is a free market system, there will be a percentage of poor people, and a sizable percentage of those will be white. Thus, to suggest that desegregation strategies in the schools be relaxed until poverty is abolished suggests abandonment of the concept of desegregation.

The Challenge of Desegregation

Achievement of school desegregation and racial equality remains a critical problem. The emotional and psychological toll that resistance to it will have on Black children and their families will be as great as the toll the struggle for integration and liberation has had on Black families since slavery. Yet, Blacks must pursue their constitutional rights. The strategies to achieve desegregation must be deliberately speedy. Any relaxation of these strategies will give aid to forces seeking a reversal of school desegregation policies and the continued subjugation of Blacks as a institutionalized practice.

Black parents must be willing to submit themselves and their children to the stresses of confrontations as well as to the opportunities for increased options that come with desegregation. Black educators must be willing to organize and push for greater job equality in the educational system. Politicians, Black and white, must be willing to provide aggressive leadership in Congress and at state and local levels to see that Black interests are represented. Whites who believe that an open opportunity structure and the goal of equality are the best system for *all* citizens must continue to support school desegregation policies.

The challenge is to maintain a persistent stand for school desegregation and also to push for desegregation in other arenas such as business, employment, housing, and criminal justice.

School desegregation will not come easily. It was resisted in the South with cries of "never," and it is resisted in the North with the same alarm. If school desegregation, the only enforceable racial policy in this nation, is no longer seen as a good idea, then the ideal of racial equality may soon become irrelevant.

The irony of the school desegregation struggle highlights a historic contradiction. Whites resisting school desegregation procedures are proclaiming that these procedures are a denial of their rights and freedom of choice. In reality, these dissenters seek to maintain a *privilege,* not a right—the privilege of private access to the better resources based on the denial of these resources to Blacks.

We are far from resolving the problem of school desegregation because we have not agreed upon the definition of the problem. Too few of us are willing to admit that the school issue is really the race issue in America. If the anti-"forced-busing," anti-Black advocates continue to gain support, Blacks can expect the bleak outcome of forced resegregation.

Notes

1. James Coleman, one-time proponent of school desegregation, has indicated through public statements a shift from his earlier position because of

concern for the massive white resistance desegregation strategies have generated ("Dr. Coleman's Evidence," 1975).

2. Vice President Nelson Rockefeller is reported by the *New York Times* as having said "court-ordered busing is the law of the land and must be obeyed until the law is changed" (*New York Times*, September 13, 1975).

3. The movement for community control of schools reached its peak with the I.S. 201 Ocean Hill–Brownsville controversy in New York City which ultimately led to decentralization of the New York City public schools. This reorganization, however, has not changed the power situation. Whites continue to maintain control over the school system.

References

Clark, Kenneth B. Presentation to Freedom House Institute for Schools and Education, Boston, February 22, 1975.

"Dr. Coleman's Evidence." *New York Times* (July 13, 1975), sec. 4.

Gil, David G. *Unravelling Social Policy.* Cambridge, Mass.: Schenckman Publishing Co., 1973.

Novak, Michael. "Blacks Need Jobs First to Achieve Full Equality." *Boston Globe* (August 28, 1975).

Why Academic Research Fails to Be Useful

ROBERT L. CRAIN
RAND Corporation

In what way has social research helped the nation resolve the issue of school desegregation? The answer seems to be in no way. A great deal has been written on school desegregation, but it has not been useful, and it is the purpose of this paper to consider why this has been the case.

Research on school desegregation (Weinberg 1975*b*, St. John 1975, Schwartz 1975) seems beset by three problems:

1. Almost none of the research has been concerned with determining how desegregation should be done, locating techniques which minimize public opposition or maximize student benefits. Instead almost all of it has been concerned with asking whether some desegregation was better than none, a question relevant to the national controversy over busing but of little relevance to policymakers.

2. When research has asked whether desegregation was good or bad, it has almost always asked the question in the wrong way —namely, in terms of short-run achievement tests rather than long-run effects on students or the impact of desegregation on the whole community.

Most researchers will agree with the two statements above; but those who do not share my prointegration bias may not agree with this next statement which I think is also correct: when researchers have focused on the short-run effects of desegregation, they have been far too quick to conclude that desegregation has not been beneficial.

I will argue that the explanation for this state of affairs lies in the nature of the federal role in research and in the character of academic social science.

31

The Federal Role in Policy Research

A local school district considering school desegregation will not embark on the sponsorship of a major program of research. It would cost too much in time and money, and local government decisions are made by "political" men, not "rational" men, anyway. Almost all policy research on school desegregation has been funded by the federal government and by large foundations. Federal research money is spent in two ways: for unsolicited grants in which researchers propose research on a topic of their own choice, and solicited contract research in which the government chooses the topic and searches for a "contractor" to do the work. It is only in this second type of funding that the government controls the research agenda, and very few such government contracts have been let to study school desegregation. There is a simple reason for this: almost all contract research moneys are for evaluation of federal programs. School desegregation is a federal policy, but not a federal program. No funds are appropriated annually to finance school desegregation; consequently no funds are appropriated to evaluate the effectiveness of that funding. In contrast, something on the order of $10 million to $15 million are spent annually to evaluate the impact of federal compensatory education efforts. There are exceptions to this rule, and these exceptions have produced some important research. Presidential commissions, especially the Eisenhower and Kerner Commissions, have funded important research on questions of national importance which are not directly related to existing federal programs. In the case of school desegregation, the three most important studies were funded by contract: the Coleman Report (1966), through a direct legislative mandate by Congress; the only study of the long-term impact of desegregation on students (Crain and Weisman 1972), by the United States Commission on Civil Rights; and the most important study of white

---

ROBERT L. CRAIN has been writing research reports, articles, and books on school desegregation since 1964. A southerner, he attended segregated schools in Louisville, Kentucky, and worked as an engineer and social worker before becoming a sociologist. He taught at the University of Chicago and Johns Hopkins University before going to RAND to head a team designing a national study of school desegregation for the U.S. Commission on Civil Rights, which the commission did not carry out.

flight as a response to southern school desegregation (Cataldo 1975), through the policy-oriented RANN (Research Addressed to National Needs) division of the National Science Foundation. The only existing "how to do it" manual on school desegregation (Smith, Downs, and Lachmann 1973) was funded by federal program evaluation moneys.

These studies have been useful, but they represent only a fraction of what needs to be done. The federal government has not contracted for more research because the government does not routinely contract research on basic policy questions. The other federal funds spent on school desegregation research have been dispersed through the unsolicited research grants system used to fund basic science.

Federal policymakers have, however, influenced research in another way by providing an audience for school desegregation research. As research consumers, Congress and the administration view the evaluation of school desegregation in terms of the achievement test scores of minority students. This version of "academic achievement" plays a critical role in a politically useful proposition: minority poverty results not from majority prejudice nor from institutional bias but from "deficits" in minority adults, which in turn result not from their ethnicity but simply from the experience of poverty in childhood. Thus, the race problem is defined as a poverty problem, to be solved by a war on poverty for which the effective strategy is to intervene in childhood. This proposition has obvious appeal to political conservatives and those in charge of existing institutions. Applied to school desegregation it takes away the moral sting and replaces it with the appeal that desegregation is only a device to provide equality of educational opportunity. But as Christopher Jencks has pointed out: "The case for or against desegregation should not be argued in terms of academic achievement. If we want a segregated society, we should have segregated schools. If we want a desegregated society, we should have desegregated schools" (Jencks et al. 1972, p. 106).

It seems to me that school desegregation has been advanced as a social program partly for moral reasons—desegregation is bad—and partly in the hope that desegregation would change either the attitudes of white Americans or cause a change in the racial behavior of other social institutions. It seems to me very hard to argue that the test scores of Black students were the critical reason motivating the *Brown* plaintiffs. Certainly the evaluators of school desegregation cannot use a dubious criterion for the evaluation of school desegregation without defending its suitability. If desegregation has been evaluated in the wrong terms, the federal policymakers, as the clients of that research, deserve a share of the blame.

The Role of the Academy

Perhaps we have already identified the reason why research on school desegregation is inadequate—because the federal government has failed to fund it. Research is expensive. Nearly all of the studies on school desegregation were done on skeleton budgets. But the fact remains that to the extent these small funds provided an opportunity for policy-relevant research, it was not done. In the remainder of this paper I will argue that this happened because of the constraints imposed by the structure and culture of academic social science.[1] I want to make clear, however, that when I criticize my colleagues and friends for being insensitive to policy issues I do not exempt myself.

With that said, let us analyze the behavior of social scientists. In doing so we will be guarded by two harsh propositions: first, that human beings, even those with brilliant minds, often use a surprisingly simplistic logic in ideological debate; and second, that even the most humanitarian of us are influenced more than we like to admit by the consequences, in money and prestige, of our decisions. The discussion below divides the constraints on academic researchers into three categories: those imposed by the reward structure of the university, those resulting from the culture of contemporary social science, and those resulting from the role of ideology.

The Reward Structure of the University

Nancy St. John (1975) has completed the awesome task of reviewing over 100 studies of the effects of school desegregation on children. Thirty-seven of these are pretest/posttest studies of the impact on Black student achievement; of these, 25 measure its impact over only a one-year period, usually the first year of desegregation. Surely the effects of desegregation cannot be assessed adequately in the first year; why is it that so many studies have such a glaring methodological weakness? One reason is the pressures from school boards and funding agencies for "timely" results. Another may be the regulations regarding tenure. Most assistant professors are hired on three-year contracts, and an "up-or-out" decision on tenure is usually made in the fifth year of one's professional career. Given the time lost making the adjustment to college teaching and the long delays between completion of research and publication, this means that contract renewal decisions are based on only one year of work, tenure decisions on about three.

The "publish or perish" incentive system requires that research papers be written for academic audiences, and especially for departmental colleagues. But few research-oriented social scientists are in departments of education. Most appointments in education are considered low status. Since the audience for papers on school desegregation neither knows nor cares about educational practice, it is understandable that these papers seldom deal with the practical details of how to make desegregation work. Rewards in social science departments go to papers dealing with "basic scientific problems," not to applied research. The result is that research which begins as a study of school desegregation may end up as a refining of reference group theory or the contact hypothesis, or as an application of new techniques for analyzing quasi-experimental designs. My colleagues' and my work on the politics of school desegregation (Crain 1968; Kirby, Harris, and Crain 1973) is an excellent example; it makes contributions to theories of community decision making (and has been well received by academic political scientists), but is useless to a school superintendent or federal judge faced with questions of how to make desegregation work.

The perverse incentives of the academy would not prevent the achievement of elegant and valuable research if it were only possible to do it quickly and cheaply. Unfortunately, measuring the effects of school desegregation is an extraordinarily difficult, time consuming, and expensive task. Genuine experimental design is usually not possible. The effects of desegregation may take a decade or longer to appear, and a useful study should utilize data from a number of different desegregation plans. An unsolicited research proposal, even if it had sufficient methodological rigor and met the approval of an academically oriented review panel, would still not be funded at a level sufficient to do the work. Consequently it is not surprising that of the 67 studies of Black achievement cited by St. John, only two gathered data from more than one city. Given that desegregation, like other educational innovations, can be implemented well or badly, one simply cannot generalize from a single case.

Add to this sheer technical difficulties and the fact that there are many things that social science does not know how to do. We can measure achievement reasonably well—but we have been working on that problem for nearly 100 years and have spent literally millions of dollars in refining achievement testing. In contrast, the first large-scale measurement of attitudes dates only to World War II. We do not have a set of conceptual categories for the measurement of "non-cognitive" characteristics, let alone an agreed-upon set of measures.

Why Research Fails to Be Useful

The Culture of Social Science

Academic social science is a social system, with its own norms and value system and a set of system maintenance defenses to protect its integrity. It is a system whose function is to advance pure research, and it is not well suited to answering practical questions. The scholarly value system recognizes the conflict between pure and applied research and defends itself by downgrading the latter's value. One study of the criteria used to evaluate journal articles offered 10 criteria to the social scientists of a major university; of the 10, applicability to practical problems was ranked dead last (Chase 1970).

In a field dedicated to the slow accumulation of scientific knowledge, methodological conservatism—preventing a discipline from going astray—is useful. Thus, the arbitrary $P < .05$ rule: if there is more than one chance in 20 that the results are a statistical artifact, they should not be published.

Methodological conservatism is even more rigidly enforced when the social scientist engages in applied research. In some cases this is highly appropriate; one would not want to embark on a multimillion-dollar program of social intervention because of research which reported a false positive impact. But social scientists are reluctant to admit that human need usually cannot wait for a decisive experimental validation of a program, or a complete theoretical understanding of the underlying process. Social science made a valuable theoretical contribution to the creation of the community action program but, had the program's inventors waited for incontrovertible evidence of its potential, they would be waiting still.

Methodological conservatism may also be inappropriate in the case of evaluation of an ongoing program. The criteria of statistical significance can easily become twisted into what appears to be a recommendation that a *new* social policy—approval of school segregation—be adopted because we cannot prove with certainty that the existing policy of approval for school desegregation is superior.

The methodological traditions of social science also fail to prepare us to answer questions about whether the impacts of a particular program are large enough to warrant its costs. Social science has very little experience with evaluating the size of an effect. In its single-minded concern for developing social theory, the research question is usually "does x affect y, or does it not affect y?" We impose an Aristotelian dichotomy in an effort to establish a theoretical structure of relationships among variables. In experimental psychology, the statistical procedures used to measure the impact of a factor often do not even compute a measure of the size of the impact, only determining

36

whether its existence is statistically significant. In sociology, we use measures of the size of impact—mainly regression coefficients—but have developed no criteria to help us understand how much of an effect should be considered large or small. One of the main reasons why the Coleman Report (1966) is interpreted as showing that "schools don't make a difference" is because of our lack of experience in interpreting the particular statistic used to measure the effect of school resources; the unique percentage of variance explained is usually a very small number, and the inexperienced social scientist is likely to jump to the conclusion that this means that the effect itself is very small.[2] Finally, social science method is based on a norm of conflict. Papers read at professional meetings are subject to immediate criticism. Disagreements are interesting and valuable. But policymakers have difficulty coping with advice from academics who disagree with one another. If social science cannot provide useful policy advice until academics have exhausted all possible ways of disagreeing, the utility of social science is limited.

The Significance of Ideology

Powerful though the incentives may be to remain within the ivory tower and limit oneself to the pursuit of pure science, there are also strong incentives to encourage many of us to make excursions into the real world. One such incentive is publicity. I hope my colleagues are better than I am at coping with the heady experience of being quoted in the *New York Times*. For the incentive structure of mass-media journalism is much more perverse than that of the academy: it is the routine and relentless application of man bites dog to all social issues. We are rewarded not for saying what is true but for saying what is startling, not for contributing to the solution of a problem but for our contribution to the reader's next cocktail-party argument. Academics, like other intellectuals, are easily seduced into grand ideological debates, and one of the main problems with research on school desegregation is that it has been used as a pawn in debates over the meaning of social inequality and the moral worth of Blacks and whites. One should not underestimate the importance of these ideological issues in structuring both the questions which are asked and the answers that are given. The scholarly literature frequently contains references to the Black-white achievement gap similar to this one from an analysis of the effects of desegregation on Black student verbal ability: "But if the relationship is significant from a statistical point of view, its absolute magnitude must also be kept in mind . . . [the analysis] implies that assigning Negro students to mostly white classes would raise their verbal ability about 1.94 points. That is less than one-sixth of the difference between average Negro and white achievement in these schools at grade twelve" (Cohen, Pettigrew, and Riley 1972, p. 358).

This effect can be made to look large or small, depending upon the choice of units of measurement; for example, the effect described above as "less than one-sixth of a difference" is also more than a half year in grade equivalents. But what do the magnitude of the effect of an educational intervention on Black achievement and the size of the Black-white "gap" have to do with each other? Is the quoted assertion meant to imply that we should not divert precious resources toward school desegregation but rather conserve them in the search for the single great reform which will eliminate this racial "inequality"? Or is it just that the author is more intrigued with the question of social inequality than with the question of whether school desegregation is beneficial?

Of course desegregation as a social policy cannot be all "good" or all "bad." Some students benefit while others do not. Some plans are executed well and others poorly. Students and communities benefit in some ways but not in others. Yet just this sort of moral simplification often seems to lie behind popular writing by academics. It is easy for me as a prointegrationist to see this in antidesegregation arguments; I assume that someone from the other camp would have no difficulty finding the same fault in my work. Here are some of the rationales which I suspect lie behind the writing of some conservatives:

Desegregation must be ineffectual, since its success would provide evidence that educators are guilty of providing unequal education in segregated schools.
Desegregation must be ineffectual, since its success would provide evidence that Blacks are not genetically inferior.
Blacks must prefer segregation, otherwise whites would be guilty of white racism in segregating them.

Equally moralistic arguments are made by pro-Black writers:

Desegregation must be ineffectual; its success would provide evidence that the white teachers in integrated schools are not racists.
Desegregation must be ineffectual; its success would provide evidence that Blacks are incapable of autonomous social development.
Desegregation must be ineffectual; its success would imply a social process in which something "rubs off" from superior white students onto inferior Blacks.

38

Desegregation must be ineffectual; its success would imply that the
federal government has practiced a policy in the South which is
beneficial to Blacks, and this would be evidence that the government is not racist.

Overstated so baldly, these arguments seem ridiculous. But I do not
mean to ridicule: these issues burn with an uncontrollable fury, especially in Blacks and white southerners like myself. (It is no accident
that white sociologists studying the race question are more likely to
have been born in the South [Gaston and Sherohman 1974].) We are
trying to do dispassionate scientific analysis of an issue which has led
to slavery, lynching, murder, and civil war.

Although the Black person on the street has remained mildly sympathetic to desegregation, more and more Black intellectuals have
become critical of it. I hypothesize that this is because of the drive to
create a theory of the Black experience consistent with the belief that
Blacks are capable of creating an autonomous social system. One can
see this change in the contrast between the writings of Franklin
Frazier (1939) and Joyce Ladner (1971) on Black family structure.
For Frazier, Blacks were the helpless victims of racism which had
destroyed the Black family; for Ladner, the absence of family stability
was not a sign of helplessness but evidence that Blacks had succeeded
in retaining elements of African culture.

There is another source of moralism in writings on school desegregation: this is the widespread cynicism and criticism of federal policy from the left, particularly by social scientists. Lipset and Ladd
(1972) show that social scientists describe their politics as to the left of
other academics and far to the left of the general public. In 1948,
when segregation was official policy in the United States, a poll of
social scientists showed overwhelming agreement that segregation
was harmful (Deutscher and Chein 1948). In fact there was almost no
research on the question, and certainly none that would meet today's
standards of scientific evidence. Yet when desegregation became federal policy after *Brown,* there was no round of applause from the academy, and today when the evidence (such as it is) seems to suggest that
desegregation has favorable effects there is more academic opposition
to it than there was in 1949. Perhaps this is based on greater scientific
knowledge; perhaps it is mere faddishness, but I think it is in part just
an expression of opposition to the status quo.

The question remains why ideology should be of such importance
in scientific analysis. One answer, a direct result of the incentive system and federal funding policies, is that there are only a handful of
social scientists in the United States who are involved full time in

39

research on school desegregation. For most of us, school desegregation is a part-time research interest, perhaps only an avocation, sandwiched between more "serious" scientific concerns.

There is one more incentive which sometimes entices academics into writing on school desegregation and which also leads to bias in our research; this is the desire to exert influence over the policy process. A scientist who has spent even a short time watching the process of school desegregation must invariably feel "if only they would listen to me." Perhaps they should, but whether they should or not, it seems to be against human nature (or at least my own nature) to resist the impulse to give advice. Unfortunately, when a researcher is intent upon giving good advice, it is difficult to avoid leaning on the data to make sure they agree. This problem is the flaw in St. John's otherwise very useful review of desegregation research.[3] A fair summary of St. John's policy advice seems to be that she is opposed to compulsory desegregation, meaning that it should be replaced with voluntary desegregation and increased concern both with housing desegregation and with making sure that existing desegregated schools become truly integrated. I certainly agree with at least the latter part of her advice, and I am glad she has said it. In partial support of this view, she summarizes 65 studies of Black achievement: "As implemented to date, desegregation has not rapidly closed the black-gap in academic achievement, though it has rarely lowered and sometimes raised the scores of black children. Improvement has been more often reported in the early grades, in arithmetic, and in schools over 50 percent white, but even here the gains have usually been mixed, intermittent, or nonsignificant. . . . Bi-racial schooling is apparently not detrimental to academic performance of black children, but it may have negative effects on their self-esteem . . ." (p. 119).

I don't know what this paragraph says to most readers, but I think it says something different than what the data themselves say. St. John cites 64 studies which use standardized achievement testing: of these, four show some negative effects, 37 show some positive effects, 15 show no statistically significant effects, and seven show a mixture of positive and negative effects. Of course, the 64 studies vary considerably in quality. St. John examines this and writes (p. 31), "It is also evident that the tighter the design the more often is no difference found between segregated and desegregated minority group children." She cites 11 studies as meeting acceptable standards of research; five of these studies show statistically significant positive effects on one or more tests, usually along with nonsignificant findings on other tests; one study shows a mixture of positive and negative effects, and five studies show no differences. But I would read her data differently. For example, she classifies the work of Alan Wilson (1967) as showing no desegregation effects, when what she means is that Wilson shows no effects of school racial composition over and above the positive effects due to the fact that white students have higher socioeconomic status than Blacks. The policy implication is that desegregation could be expected to have positive effects on Black achievement only if the white students involved were of higher socioeconomic status than the Blacks. But since I know of very few communities where whites do not have higher status than Blacks, it seems incorrect to conclude, as St. John does, that this study demonstrates that desegregation has no effect. Studying her appendix, I judged 19 studies to meet her criterion of research quality.[4] The most common result in these studies is a significant positive gain on one achievement test in one grade, coupled with no significant gain on a different test or in a different grade. This occurred in 10 cases. In two others, all results for all grades were positive and significant; in four, no results were positive and significant; and in three, significant positive results occurred simultaneously with significant negative results. None of the 19 studies showed results which were more often negative than positive.

St. John recommends against compulsory desegregation, but the achievement data which she has compiled do not support her in this view. Nine studies are pretest/posttest, control-group designs in cities which embarked on large-scale compulsory desegregation; two of these showed positive results on all tests for all groups; four a mixture of positive significant results for some groups and nonsignificant results for others; and three showed a mixture of positive and negative results. St. John may be correct in recommending against compulsory desegregation plans, but her data cannot be used as evidence for her point of view.

The same problem—allowing one's excitement about giving policy advice to color interpretation of data—seems to me at the heart of Coleman's writing on desegregation and white flight (1975). He was intent upon making two points: first, that in the cost-benefit calculus of federal program impact the private actions of individual citizens in response to a federal program must be considered along with the direct effects of the program; second, that desegregation planning must be sensitive to local conditions and reflect sociological wisdom as well as judicial correctness. Both points are sound ones and need to be made. Unfortunately, Coleman attempted to bolster his opinion by arguing from data that school desegregation has had a considerable impact in driving whites into the suburbs—a conclusion which has been roundly attacked and which disagrees with analyses done by

41

other good researchers.[5] In studying Coleman's data, I concluded that white flight as a response to desegregation is not as serious a problem as he has argued.

The political problem with the work of both St. John and Coleman is that once data are overinterpreted, they can be cited by anyone. My concern is that both works will be used as arguments not for improving desegregation plans in the way that St. John and Coleman intended, but as arguments against desegregation of any kind.

What Is to Be Done?

The reader who grants even a fraction of my thesis may despair. To call for a moratorium on social research on policy matters would be precisely the sort of frivolity I have criticized. Policy research is here to stay, and I think that such research could prove useful. But in order to be useful, it will have to do two things: first, it will have to evaluate school desegregation in terms of its intended consequences rather than by criterion of our own choosing. Second, it will have to ask the question, how can desegregation be done better? Neither one of these objectives will be easy. It is an obvious, but still important, fact that evaluation using one set of criteria for success may produce results very different from another using different criteria. A good example of this is the research on the programs of the War on Poverty. The Community Action Program was often accused of failing when its goal was defined as "eliminating poverty." When OEO commissioned an evaluation which used the Community Action Program's true goals—increasing the local political power of minorities and the poor—a large-scale evaluation drew quite positive conclusions (Vanecko 1969).

Scientific evaluation of school desegregation on its own terms must begin by announcing that some of its goals cannot be evaluated by science. For example, if segregation is immoral and desegregation is favored in order to eliminate immorality, science has nothing to say. Scientists evaluating desegregation on its own terms must also recognize that policymakers may not appreciate the effort. For example, it seems likely that one goal of the school desegregation movement was to drive a wedge into the institutional structure of southern segregated society, hoping to create a chain reaction of institutional reform. Did this happen? The question is for a historian, not a sociologist. But my point is that if it did happen, pointing this out will not please Congress nor encourage conservatives to favor desegregation. But, regardless of what Congress may think, social scientists have the obligation to do value-free policy research when it is needed. There are other criteria which can be used to evaluate school desegregation which do not have these problems and which have not been adequately explored. For example, Audrey Schwartz's (1975) review of the school desegregation literature finds only three studies which ask whether desegregation has affected the number of Blacks going on to higher education after graduation: all three studies seem to point to positive desegregation effects in this important area. To my knowledge, the only study which has looked at the effects of school desegregation on the adult behavior of Black alumni is my own (Crain and Weisman 1972). Morris Rosenberg (1974) summarizes its findings as follows: "Those black adults who attended integrated schools were more likely to complete high school, to attend college, to earn somewhat more money, to enter higher status occupations, to have stable marriages, to own their own homes, to be financially responsible, to have steady jobs, to live in integrated neighborhoods, to have white friends and acquaintances, and to say they are happy. They are less likely to get into fights, to have been arrested, and to be anti-white" (p. 424).

As Rosenberg points out, the analysis is hardly methodologically pristine, and I am sure that I am not above introducing bias into my analysis. However, Rosenberg writes, "this study is thus not the last word on the subject, but it is the only word and an extremely important one—more important certainly than school achievement scores."

The study needs replication. But, unfortunately, there is no way to repeat the study with good methodology for a reasonable cost and in a reasonable period of time. But it certainly seems reasonable that we allocate a small amount of resources toward research which asks the right questions even with a methodologically imperfect design, rather than saving all our funds for elegant research which answers the wrong questions.

I am optimistic that social science can make a useful contribution in telling federal and local officials how to handle desegregation most effectively. Research can tell us a lot about how to draw a desegregation plan, how to cope with public opinion, how to prepare a school staff for desegregation, and how to modify the curriculum to make desegregation succeed. In this there are no great methodological problems. Competent case studies of desegregating districts are sufficient for much of this. But the federal government must fund this research.

The problems of the poor fit between social science and policy research on controversial issues apply to more than just school desegregation, and it is not obvious that any significant reform is possible.

43

Two favorable signs: the creation of the National Science Foundation's policy arm (RANN), which attempts to combine the policy focus of contract research with the strengths of the unsolicited proposal system, is one. The other is the movement to create departments and schools of applied social science (although these are in danger of being taken over by a new academic discipline searching for grand theories of policy). If policy questions and social science techniques are to be successfully married, it will require the creation of a new profession whose incentive system, methodology, culture, and ideology are consistent with its mission.

Notes

I wish to acknowledge the contribution of Gregg Jackson, U.S. Commission on Civil Rights, and Gary Orfield, The Brookings Institute, for providing some of the ideas for this paper.

1. For a similarly pessimistic, and well-written review of the relationship between academic sociology and policy, see Mack (1975).

2. For a detailed discussion of this point, see Crain (1973).

3. I would be remiss if I did not point out that St. John's work is superior to most academic writing on the effects of school desegregation. First, although she limits herself to the short-run effects of desegregation on students, she notes clearly that this is a value judgment on her part. (Others have written up achievement test results as if there was no other question worth asking.) In addition, she uses a variety of student outcomes, not just achievement.

4. She required pre- and posttests and SES controls, deleted two studies which controlled on school SES, and added studies with pre- and posttests with either IQ controls or randomized assignment.

5. See Weinberg (1975*a*) and Rossell (1975). In addition, Reynolds Farley of the University of Michigan's Institute for Population Studies is currently analyzing school desegregation data and reports finding no significant amount of white flight as a result of desegregation.

References

Cataldo, Everett; Giles, Michael; Athos, Deborah; and Gatlin, Douglas. "Desegregation and White Flight." *Integrated Education* (January 1975).

Chase, Janet M. "Normative Criteria for Scientific Publication." *American Sociologist* 5 (August 1970): 262–65.

Cohen, David K.; Pettigrew, Thomas F; and Riley, Robert T. "Race and the Outcomes of Schooling." In *On Equality of Educational Opportunity*, edited by Fredrick Mosteller and Daniel P. Moynihan. New York: Vintage Books, 1972.

Coleman, James S. *Recent Trends in School Integration*. Washington, D.C.: Urban Institute, 1975.

Coleman, James S., et al. *Equality of Educational Opportunity.* Washington, D.C.: Government Printing Office, 1966.

Crain, Robert L. "How Large Is the Effect of School on Achievement Test Performance?" In *Southern Schools: An Evaluation of the Effects of the Emergency School Assistance Program and of School Desegregation.* Vol. 1. Chicago: National Opinion Research Center, University of Chicago, 1973.

Crain, Robert L., et al. *The Politics of School Desegregation.* Chicago: Aldine Publishing Co., 1968.

Crain, Robert L., and Weisman, Carol Sachs. *Discrimination, Personality, and Achievement.* New York: Seminar Press, 1972.

Deutscher, Max, and Chein, Isidor. "The Psychological Effects of Enforced Segregation: A Survey of Social Science Opinion." *Journal of Psychology* 26 (October 1948): 259–87.

Frazier, E. Franklin. *The Negro Family in the United States.* Chicago: University of Chicago Press, 1939.

Gaston, Jerry, and Sherohman, James. "Origins of Researchers on Black Americans." *American Sociologist* 9 (May 1974): 75–82.

Jencks, Christopher, et al. *Inequality.* New York: Harper & Row, 1972.

Kirby, David J.; Harris, Robert; and Crain, Robert L. *Political Strategies in Northern School Desegregation.* Lexington, Mass.: D. C. Heath Co., 1973.

Ladner, Joyce. *Tomorrow's Tomorrow: The Black Women.* New York: Doubleday & Co., 1971.

Lipset, Seymour Martin, and Ladd, Everett Carl, Jr. "The Politics of American Sociologist." *American Journal of Sociology* 78 (July 1972): 67–104.

Mack, Raymond W. "Four for the Seesaw." In *Sociology and Policy,* edited by Mirra Komarovsky. New York: American Elsevier Publishing Co., 1975.

Rosenberg, Morris. Review of Robert L. Crain and Carol Sachs Weisman's *Discrimination, Personality and Achievement. Social Forces* (March 1974).

Rossell, Christine. "The Political and Social Impact of School Desegregation Policy: A Preliminary Report." Paper read at the annual meeting of the American Political Science Association, September 2–5, 1975, San Francisco.

St. John, Nancy. *School Desegregation: Outcomes for Children.* New York: John Wiley & Sons, 1975.

Schwartz, Audrey James. "Social Science Evidence and the Objectives of School Desegregation." Los Angeles: University of Southern California School of Education, 1975.

Smith, Al; Downs, Anthony; and Lachman, M. Leanne. *Achieving Effective Desegregation.* Lexington, Mass.: D. C. Heath Co., for the Real Estate Research Corp., 1973.

Vanecko, James J. "Community Mobilization and Institutional Change: The Influence of the Community Action Program in Large Cities." *Social Science Quarterly,* vol. 50 (December 1969).

Weinberg, Meyer. "A Critique of Coleman." Paper distributed at the 113th annual convention of the National Education Association, July 3–8, 1975, Los Angeles. (*a*)

Weinberg, Meyer. "The Relationship between School Desegregation and Academic Achievement: A Review of the Research." *Law and Contemporary Problems* (Duke University School of Law) 39 (Spring 1975): 241–70. (*b*)

Wilson, Alan. "Educational Consequences of Segregation in a California Community." In U.S. Commission on Civil Rights, *Racial Isolation in the Public Schools.* Vol. 2. Washington, D.C.: Government Printing Office, 1967.

Coleman's Desegregation Research and Policy Recommendations

STANLEY S. ROBIN
Western Michigan University

JAMES J. BOSCO
Western Michigan University

Busing schoolchildren for desegregation is clearly unpopular. A 1974 Gallup poll (Gallup 1974) showed that a majority of Americans would prefer that busing for desegregation be ended. The resistance to busing has crystallized around two issues: (1) busing promotes white flight, destroying the cities, jeopardizing the fiscal base of school systems, defeating the attempt at desegregation; and (2) busing does not increase the quality of education and may be detrimental to it.

One of the central figures in the development of the rationale which served as a basis for desegregation was James Coleman. His study, *Equality of Educational Opportunity* (1966), was used as a basis for the U.S. Commission on Civil Rights recommendations in *Racial Isolation in the Public Schools* (1967), in which is stated, "The conclusions drawn by the U.S. Supreme Court about the impact upon children of segregation compelled by law—that it affects their hearts and minds in ways unlikely ever to be undone—applies to segregation not compelled by law" (p. 193), thus paving the way for critical litigation to bring about the desegregation of schools that had been racially isolated not by Jim Crow school laws but by the racial segregation of cities.

In the seventies, having become a central figure in the desegregation controversy, having appeared to be a proponent of busing, Coleman announced new research results and policy recommendations that seemed to reflect a drastic alteration of his views. At the national meetings of the American Educational Research Association in 1975, in press conferences and before the Congress, Coleman stated his opposition to mandatory busing. Inevitably his pronouncements were widely broadcast by the media. *Time* (1975) reported that Coleman "recently cooled his enthusiasm for busing"; CBS News (October 28, 1975) referred to him as a "convert" in describing his testimony to the Senate Judiciary Committee chaired by Senator Eastland. These representations of Coleman's "conversion" may have been unfair, for in his earlier study he had not endorsed mandatory busing, and his research did not deal with the impact of desegregation upon the racial composition of cities. However, it is important to examine Coleman's latest research in desegregation and his policy recommendations because of his visibility.

In the October 1975 issue of the *Phi Delta Kappan,* in an article entitled "Racial Segregation in the Schools: New Research with New Policy Implications," Coleman presents the findings of his most recent research on school desegregation and white flight. He reports his findings on trends in segregation within schools, trends in segregation among or between school systems, and white flight from central city school districts. He found that as of 1973 de jure segregation had been largely eliminated, leaving only de facto segregation. This pattern occurred primarily in large cities, in the South as well as the North, and resulted from a large absolute decline in segregation in the South but virtually none in the North. A second finding was that the racial differences between cities and suburbs had increased. The

---

STANLEY S. ROBIN is professor of sociology and director of the Center for Sociological Research at Western Michigan University. He is currently working in the areas of teacher role, female occupational mobility, and mental health. He has collaborated with Dr. James Bosco on a series of studies of white flight and court-ordered busing. This collaboration has also produced a series of studies on stimulant drugs for children and a forthcoming special issue of *School Review* on this topic.

JAMES J. BOSCO is professor of teacher education and director of the Center for Educational Research at Western Michigan University. His interest in desegregation research was a result of experiences with litigation regarding desegregation in the Grand Rapids School System where he served as director of a cooperative research center sponsored by Western Michigan University and the Grand Rapids Public Schools. In collaboration with Stanley Robin he has done research on white flight and court-ordered busing. His other research activities involve research on the social context of the use of behavior modifying drugs for children and individualization of instruction.

proportion of Blacks in city schools grew while the suburbs remained white.

This resulted in a third set of findings of which the major one was that "the loss of whites did increase when there was a reduction of school segregation" (Coleman 1975, pp. 76–77). This general finding was modified by four qualifications: (1) the loss of whites was smaller in smaller cities than larger ones; (2) the loss of whites was intensified when the city had a high proportion of Blacks; (3) the loss of whites was intensified when there was a high disparity in racial composition between city and neighboring suburbs; and (4) the loss of whites, due to desegregation, appears to be a one-time effect, confined to the year of desegregation. Coleman concluded: "Ironically, 'desegregation' may be increasing segregation. . . . Eliminating central city segregation does not help if it increases greatly the segregation between districts through accelerated white loss" (p. 77).

On this basis, Coleman drew "implications" that school desegregation policy should center on slowing the exodus of whites from central cities; that the courts should confine their actions to the elimination of de jure segregation; that communities should decide how much desegregation they wish in their schools and how they will achieve it; that mandatory within-district busing should be discontinued; that mandatory cross-district busing not be initiated; and that school desegregation might be accomplished by allowing children in metropolitan areas to attend any school in the area that has a lower proportion of the child's race than the neighborhood school.

Confusion among the Terms "Desegregation," "Busing," and "White Flight"

Throughout the *Phi Delta Kappan* paper, Coleman fails to clarify critical concepts. While "de jure" and "de facto" are commonly used to describe different types of segregation, they may be equally useful to describe desegregation. Customarily, desegregation refers to a process that results from the implementation of law or policy. This can be considered de jure desegregation. However, desegregation can also occur as a result of individual decisions not mandated or directly influenced by law or policy. This can be regarded as de facto desegregation. In describing his study, Coleman speaks in terms of de jure desegregation when, for example, he states, "Since elimination of all racial segregation within school systems—through compulsory busing when necessary—seems on the way to becoming national policy, it is especially important to ask what the policy accomplishes" (1975, p.

75). Yet the data that he uses do not apply. Interracial school contact, the mean number of children of one race in proportion to the average number of children of another, is the independent variable Coleman uses to measure desegregation. But desegregation as a result of policy action (the desegregation about which he draws conclusions) and the proportions of Blacks and whites in a school (the desegregation he measures) are not the same. The proportion of Blacks and whites can change without any implementation of policy or law pertaining to desegregation. Desegregation, as defined by Coleman, is certainly an interesting phenomenon, but the demographic occurrence that he uses to measure it cannot be used to draw conclusions about the deliberate desegregation through law and policy. Since he indicates clear concern about desegregation policy, we might expect that he would have examined the impact of policy by identifying cities which had de jure desegregation—which he did not do.

Since well before 1968, demographers have noted that the proportion of Blacks in cities was growing because whites were leaving. But it is not possible to link this white movement to the introduction of desegregation law and policy in Coleman's school districts since Coleman does not offer evidence of de jure desegregation. It is not a variable in his study. He simply defines white flight as "the proportionate change in white students in the districts since the preceding year . . ." (1975, p. 76). What Coleman is demonstrating actually sheds little light on the consequence of desegregation but is rather an artifact of the racially changing residential patterns.

Furthermore, desegregation is not synonymous with busing. Busing is only one approach to the problem. Although Coleman generalizes conclusions about desegregation policy to busing, he only measures de facto desegregation, which is that desegregation which is not traceable to policy or law. Most of the cities used in Coleman's research have not experienced mandatory busing for desegregation.

De Jure and de Facto Segregation

The distinction between de jure and de facto segregation plays an important part in Coleman's analysis. First, this distinction provides the rationale for the study and the policy recommendations. He says: "It is proper and necessary, when school segregation arises from segregating actions of school administrators, to require administrations to undo the effects of those actions, for the actions constituted a denial of equal protection guaranteed by the Fourteenth Amendment. But it is neither proper nor necessary to require the elimination

49

of school segregation that arises from individual action (principally via residential segregation) without asking what the policy accomplishes" (1975, p. 75).

Second, the distinction provides the rationale for the data base of the study: "School segregation in large cities coincides principally with residential segregation, but this is less true of smaller cities, towns, and rural areas. Redrawing school attendance lines can and often does reduce segregation sharply in smaller cities" (p. 76). Thus, the data which Coleman et al. analyze are only from *large* cities.

It is unfortunate that Coleman leans so heavily on the weak distinction between de jure and de facto segregation. He asserts that "once equal protection is assured, then school desegregation must be justified in terms of its consequences" (1975, p. 77). But the promulgation of this distinction raises a complex of issues he does not come to grips with. First he accepts, without reservation, this questionable and complex distinction. Then he elevates it by asserting that de jure segregation should be abolished because it is an evil in and of itself, but that the elimination of de facto school segregation "must be justified" in terms of some other consequences. Were we to accept this distinction, we would then need to determine which *consequences* are the important ones. While it may seem obvious to Coleman which factors are important, it is not at all obvious to us. We must ask, "proper" on what basis, "necessary" for what? Once the factors are identified, research needs to be conducted to see if those consequences which justify the abolition of de facto segregation occur and are enduring. This sort of analysis is a logical precondition for policy creation.

The specification of segregation in large cities as de facto and as de jure in the smaller ones provides the rationale for Coleman's analysis of the data from the 46 largest cities in the United States. He observes that "redrawing school attendance lines can and often does reduce segregation sharply in smaller cities" (1975, p. 76). This observation ignores the long history of gerrymandering for racial homogeneity in large cities and ignores, further, the fact that such gerrymandering also occurs in smaller cities and towns to the same ends. Proceeding with research on desegregation as if it coincides with residential segregation, is at least questionable.

Coleman's Attribution of Motivation

The term "white flight" contains concealed attributions of motive. To eliminate this connotation of motive, we will use the term "white emigration." Critical to the relevance of data about white emigration to desegregation policy is an understanding of the reasons why whites emigrate. Different assumptions about why whites emigrate lead to different conclusions about desirable policy. Coleman maintains: "This increase in between-district segregation, as I have said, results principally from the movement of whites to districts with fewer Blacks" (1975, p. 76). Since he offers no data to substantiate such motives, Coleman might simply have said that the increase results from the movement of whites from central city areas to suburban area. Data gathered by Molotch (1969) do allow such interpretation. He found that no imputation of "flight" could be found in a Chicago community of rapidly changing racial composition (white to Black). Coleman suggests motive in emigration, but he presents no data from which he can determine motive; the data he presents are gathered from cities which generally have had no formal policies of desegregation.

In a footnote where he discusses the motive for white emigration from Washington, D.C., he states that it is not primarily racial prejudice of federal officials that leads them to choose to live in Montgomery County, Maryland, rather than Washington, but rather their desire for quality education. But the extent to which those most concerned about their children's education are also inclined to move from the central city is an empirical issue about which Coleman has no data. It could be as well that those who are avid for their children to get a good education are also those whose racial attitudes and feelings toward desegregation inspire a resistance toward white emigration. There is a contradiction between this footnote and Coleman's conclusion that desegregation promotes white "flight" and causes schools to become more segregated. If it is not racial prejudice but concern for quality of schools which causes parents to move to suburban school districts, then why does he assert that whites flee desegregation? Does Coleman believe that desegregated schools are inherently poor schools, or that it will inevitably appear that way to concerned parents?

Further, his assertion that whites will move even farther away in the face of between-district desegregation is without supportive data. There are other constraints on parents. Few families plan their residential location solely on the basis of school attendance. Important considerations in residential selection are income, cost of housing, and the proximity to place or places of employment. Coleman observes that in cities such as Detroit, Atlanta, San Francisco, New Orleans, St. Louis, and Indianapolis, "the segregation between city and suburbs is already as large, or nearly as large as segregation among schools within the central city district" (1975, p. 76). But in these cities the emigration of whites occurred without busing. Thus, Coleman seems to contradict his own proposition that busing alone is motivating the emigration of whites from central city school districts.

Qualifications Observed and Discarded: The Rush to Conclusions

Coleman notes qualifications in his findings about the effect of desegregation upon white emigration, but they are not reflected in his policy recommendations. The qualifications are: white emigration was substantial for the group of large cities but was much smaller for the smaller cities; white emigration was intensified when the city had a high proportion of Blacks; white emigration was intensified when there was a high disparity in racial composition between suburbs and city; and the accelerated loss of whites appear to be a one-time effect (see also Bosco and Robin 1974). A policy recommendation based on such findings, if they were valid, might be that busing would be appropriate in some instances and not in others. But there seems to be no awareness of these variations in Coleman's policy recommendations. He seems more disposed to try to answer the question: is busing, in general, desirable or undesirable for desegregation? This effort to generalize hides an important reality: communities vary widely in their reaction to busing. Why is it necessary to take an unequivocal stand? Busing is only one of a variety of approaches to achieve desegregation. The important issues are when, where, and how busing can best be used to achieve desegregation in the schools. The important and intriguing question with regard to busing is how to explain the variation ignored in Coleman's conclusions.

Coleman's Example: Or How to Stack the Deck and Still Lose the Game

Coleman attempts to dramatize the acceleration of segregation between city and suburb by estimating the racial composition 10 years hence of a hypothetical city which is 50 percent Black, which already has a high degree of segregation between city and suburbs, and which has 50 percent desegregation in the central city district. He predicts that, without "desegregation" in the schools, this hypothetical city would, in 10 years, have a "65 percent Black population by one estimate and a 67 percent Black population by another." With "deseg-

regation" he predicts a "75 percent Black population with one estimate and a 70 percent Black population with the other" (1975, p. 77).
It is, he asserts, possible to conclude that, by one estimate, school
desegregation increases the Black proportion of the population by 10
percent and by another 3 percent in a 10-year period.[1] (Estimates of 5
percent and 8 percent increments in Black population are apparently
also possible by juxtaposing the figures differently.)[2] He concludes,
"Thus, in the long run (that is, 10 years), substantial desegregation
does, on the average, hasten the shift of the city to being predominantly Black; but the impact is not enormous, simply because it is (as
best we can tell), a one-time acceleration which does not continue in
subsequent years (ibid.)

For this example, Coleman chose a city with characteristics highly
associated with white loss, with or without "desegregation," that also
experienced 50 percent "desegregation" in one year. This last condition fits only two of the cities in his 22-city sample. Thus, though
Coleman has "stacked the deck," his conclusion is that "the impact is
not enormous." He adds a further qualification that this loss in white
population is much the same as would have occurred without school
desegregation and would, of course, be smaller in smaller cities. Unfortunately, his example does not seem to effect his general conclusions that white "flight" is a result of school desegregation. If desegregation is "not solving the problem of segregation" in his own
selected example, it cannot be said to exacerbate it to any appreciable
extent.

Coleman offers Detroit (75 percent Black) as another example
about which he concludes: "The contact of Blacks with whites in the
cities' schools would be *less* after one year than if no desegregation
had taken place (1975, p. 77). Yet he is quick to caution that cities vary
in reactions to desegregation and that using the data derived from all
cities to make a prediction about a single city is likely to be wrong. It is
difficult to understand why, given this acknowledgment, he goes on to
use the examples as a basis for contending that desegregation would
produce white "flight." He tends to overlook the acknowledged variation from city to city from his data (see also our comparison of
Kalamazoo and Pontiac, Michigan [Bosco and Robin 1974]) in his
policy "implications" that mandatory busing should be discontinued.

Recommendations as "Implications"

The final section of Coleman's *Kappan* paper is entitled "Policy Implications." However, since the links between the policy recommenda-

tions and empirical findings are tenuous, his statements reveal values which are extraneous to and independent of the research or any of the variables in his research. The term "implication" is not deserved.

Two difficulties attend the convergence of his policy recommendations with the research reported: the exclusion from the research of variables which are salient to the policy, and the inclusion of factors (such as traditional rights of parents, and distinctions between de jure and de facto segregation) in the policy formulation, for which no research has been provided. Coleman limited his research to a consideration of demographic trends in the racial composition of school districts; it did not involve other questions of achievement levels, interracial attitudes, or what goes on in schools once they are desegregated. These consequences are of more than tangential interest in assessing the impact of "desegregation." Thus his policy recommendations have little to do with the findings of his research but rather are based upon a series of additional values which are inserted post hoc into the argument: that de facto school desegregation must be justified in terms of its consequences; that de jure and de facto segregation are mutually exclusive; that community residents do not like to have their children bused to schools over which they have no neighborhood control; that neighborhood control over schools is a time-honored right. The insertion of other values reaches its culmination in the statement that "the policy implication, according to the second point of view, is for the courts to limit themselves to remedies which undo the segregation actions of school administration, but also to undo state actions which have increased residential segregation, and for local communities to address the question of just *how much segregation they wish to eliminate from their schools and how they shall do so*" (1975, p. 78; emphasis added). Such considerations, not touched upon by his research, play a strong role in his policy "recommendations."

Logical Difficulties in the Policy Recommendations

Coleman's ultimate policy recommendation is made after setting forth an alternative and then discarding it. He notes that his research results could provide a strong argument for metropolitan-wide school desegregation through the courts: "Since the emerging form of segregation is across district boundaries then clearly the actions to address this must be actions that reduce segregation across district lines. ... This approach ... would attempt to overcome its [white emigration] effects on school segregation by metropolitan wide school desegregation, i.e., through busing children to bring about a racial balance over the metropolitan areas" (1975, p. 77). Having made this statement without evaluating it in relation to his findings, he then goes on to say, "From a second and different point of view, these results raise the question of just how far in the quest for racial integration of school it is wise to go" (p. 77).

The alternative that Coleman does propose is comprised of a series of suggestions that do not logically cohere. He says, "The appropriate means of reducing school segregation that results from residential segregation is to reduce the residential segregation itself, or if there is substantial community support for eliminating school segregation through busing to bus in the face of residential segregation" (1975, p. 78). He thus proposes residential desegregation as the alternative to busing. But if the more limited and conservative approach to reducing segregation in schools by changing school attendance patterns is the source of intolerable community dissatisfaction, then how could a community be expected to support the notion of modifying residential segregation? Coleman is concerned about the consequences of school desegregation when it is de facto, but he seems oblivious to the possible consequences of residential desegregation when it is de facto. If whites are leaving because of school desegregation, would they be more willing to stay, given residential desegregation?

Coleman also states, "The focus in school desegregation should be on doing whatever possible to slow the exodus of whites from central cities and to facilitate the movement of Blacks to the suburbs" (1975, p. 78). To stem the tide of whites to the suburbs it would seem necessary to understand the reasons why they leave the city. Since the trend of white emigration from central cities predates desegregation efforts, the motive cannot simply be an escape from desegregation. Indeed, Coleman suggests this early in his discussion. However, for his recommendations, that observation seems to be lost. What needs to be asked is: since he suggests that reducing residential segregation is the preferred approach to achieving school integration, should he then not logically need to support legal action against de facto residential segregation by the same mechanisms which he maintains are in violation of the individual's historical and traditional rights in school desegregation? He notes that "the aim should be to reduce residential segregation, because it is this segregation which is particularly difficult to overcome since it requires policies like busing which engender great resistance" (ibid.). It is difficult to understand how a task that will engender great resistance can be justified because it avoids a task which generates less resistance.

Coleman contends that the policy of busing eliminates a parent's right to choose his child's school through the choice of residence. But is this so? Even with mandatory busing parents choose their children's school through residence patterns. Bused school attendance is not random. If it is possible to determine which schools will be attended via busing, it is possible to choose school(s) by virtue of residence. While it is true that school systems that use busing do not necessarily offer parents the option to have their children attend a neighborhood school, there is a distinct difference between denying parents the right to choose a school for their children and the right to choose a school near their home.

Coleman's major recommendation is that desegregation should be accomplished by a plan that *allows each child in a metropolitan area* to attend *any school in that area* so long as the school he chooses has no higher proportion of his race than his neighborhood school. This policy of voluntary busing preserves, Coleman says, the traditional rights of the parents to select their child's school by residential selection and adds the right of school selection under specified circumstances. But there are difficulties with this position. Were it implemented, schools considered better would receive an influx of students and become overcrowded,[3] which would then require that these schools be enlarged in order to resolve the conflict that would arise between the right of a child to attend a neighborhood school and his or her right to attend a preferred one. In an era of community resistance to school bonds and millages, it is hard to imagine the superintendent of schools and the school board going to the more affluent in the community, those whose children probably attend the desired schools, to request monies to expand these schools so that they can be further desegregated and so that the underused educational facilities, which are not so desirable, can be increasingly left vacant. This defies political and fiscal reality.

If state legislatures adopted Coleman's proposals (enabling legislation), there would arise a logical inconsistency with his position that local communities should address the question of how much segregation they wish to eliminate from their schools and how they will do so. The logical difficulties are resolved only by avoiding any attempt to desegregate.

Thus, Coleman's research and policy recommendations reported in the *Phi Delta Kappan* and the Urban Institute publication (Coleman, Kelly, and Moore 1975) are seriously flawed. His research contains conceptual errors. His "policy implications" are actually recommendations, but are logically inconsistent. Yet, his name lends visibility, importance, and credibility to these recommendations. His pronouncements may be agreeable to those whose views coincide with his, but they will not advance understanding of the issues. Indeed, ground will be lost; time and effort better invested in needed research will be spent in refutation; later findings, perhaps more appropriate to policy guidance, will inherit the resistances created by these efforts.

In the foreword to the report by the Urban Institute which sponsored the 1975 study by Coleman et al., William Gorman says, "Internal and external review of this paper leads us to conclude that clear answers on the effects of school desegregation have not yet been found and that research on the issue should continue." We agree.

Notes

1. Gregg Jackson (1975) in adding other variables to Coleman's data (population, density, per pupil school expenditures, etc.) reduces the ability of "desegregation" to predict white loss considerably below the .05 level of significance.
2. See Coleman et al. (1975, pp. 49–81). This exercise can produce widely varying estimates under differing conditions and using somewhat different dependent variables, such as loss of white students in the school systems.
3. Coleman et al. (1966) note this problem in commenting about the voluntary busing program in New Haven. They state, "The most important defect in the plan as a desegregation device is that it apparently depends upon the availability of space at the receiving school and overcrowdedness at the sending school" (p. 474). This observation is not present in the more recent work.

References

Bosco, James, and Robin, Stanley. "White Flight from Court-ordered Busing?" *Urban Education* 9, no. 1 (April 1974): 87–98.

Coleman, James. "Racial Segregation in the Schools: New Research with New Policy Implications." *Phi Delta Kappan* 57, no. 2 (October 1975): 75–78.

Coleman, James; Kelly, Sara; and Moore, John. *Trends in School Segregation, 1968–73.* Washington, D.C.: Urban Institute, August 1975.

Coleman, James, et al. *Equality of Educational Opportunity.* Washington, D.C.: Department of Health, Education and Welfare, 1966.

Gallup, George H. "Sixth Annual Gallup Poll of Public Attitude toward Education," *Phi Delta Kappan* 56, no. 1 (September 1974): 26, 30.

Jackson, Gregg. "Reanalysis of Coleman's 'Recent Trends in School Integration.'" *Educational Researcher* 4, no. 10 (November 1975): 21–25.

Molotch, Harvey. "Racial Change in a Stable Community." *American Journal of Sociology* 75, no. 2 (September 1969): 226–38.

U.S. Commission on Civil Rights. *Racial Isolation in the Public Schools.* Vol. 1. Washington, D.C.: Government Printing Office, 1967.

Why Busing Plans Work

JOHN A. FINGER, JR.
Rhode Island College

The year 1975 has seen a rising opposition to busing for school integration. Advocates of busing are placed in the position of defending the initiation and continuation of busing. Those opposed to busing can have their opposition widely accepted despite the complete lack of analysis of the consequences. Historical injustices against Blacks and minorities are widely known, but much of the public seems unaware of or unconcerned about present injustices and the official acts of discrimination which are still perpetuated.

I have come to the conclusion that there is a categorical truth in the United States: Black children attending predominantly Black schools are attending schools which are inferior in every dimension. If the injustices of racial isolation, segregation, and unequal opportunity are not to be perpetuated, desegregation is a necessity. The issue is not whether or not to bus, but whether or not to integrate, for there is no way to achieve integration except by busing. Busing need not be a calamitous event which tears cities apart and drives those who can leave to the suburbs, but to avoid calamity requires procedures which deal with the issues and problems involved.

In this paper I want to examine some of these problems and to look at the procedures used in carrying out desegregation and suggest why some desegregation plans have been successful and some have not.

Perspective on Advocacy

Many people who seem willing to accept integration as a goal are unwilling to accept busing as a means of achieving it. If busing is to be an acceptable procedure, the desirability of integrated schools must be made strong enough so that the hardship of busing will seem worthwhile. Many laws and regulations impinge on individual freedom or beliefs. Taxation, compulsory school attendance, conscription, and 55-mile per hour speed limits have varying degrees of opposition, but citizens speak to the need for taxes, military service, and such, and the purpose becomes widely accepted. People seem willing to undergo hardships and adversities when the purpose is accepted. Some causes, such as abortion, have ardent opposition and support, but integration by busing does not seem to be a cause with much support.

In today's climate, advocacy for integration by busing is difficult to obtain from the political leadership. Much of Congress apparently sees that terminating busing will lead toward separatism, or consignment of children in blighted neighborhoods to stunted development, for antibusing legislation has encountered considerable opposition in Congress. Nonetheless, speaking openly in favor of integration by busing is not expedient, and thus the most advocacy that can be obtained is silence or lack of opposition.

There is probably a balance between how strongly people believe in the desirability of a particular outcome and the adversity which will be tolerated in order to achieve it. Increasing the commitment to integration is very much needed, but the balance could be partially rectified by attending to some of the hardships that accompany busing and desegregation. It is not trivial to begin by noting that there are both short-term and long-term hardships in desegregation. Some cities have suffered because attention was paid to the short-term effects rather than the long-term ones. It is the long-term effects for which there must be a balancing of goals and purposes with adverse effects.

Short-term effects include such items as reassignment to a different school; apprehensions of what the new school assignment will be like; moving graduating seniors to a different school; breaking up an athletic team. With effective planning and management the short-term adversities may have almost no residual effects after a few months.

Long-term effects are different. Long bus rides or long walks to school don't go away, but continue year after year. Even if a student believes in the desirability of integration, that goal may not be sufficiently strong to provide justification for a long bus ride. On the other hand, riding a bus to a better school provides its own

---

JOHN A. FINGER is professor of education at Rhode Island College. He has been consultant to several state agencies and federal courts concerned with developing plans for desegregation and has worked extensively in problems of educational assessment. He is the author of numerous papers relating to problems of assessment and, in 1972, co-authored with P. Merenda and G. Migliorino a series of monographs reporting the results of research conducted in Sicily.

justification. Attention needs to be directed toward assuring that for every student on a school bus the inconvenience is justified by the result. Some of the adverse events which occur in busing for desegregation can be controlled. The transportation system can be well managed with on-time buses and fast, efficient routes; sufficient, but not excessive discipline on buses, comfortable seats, and a relaxed mood. Included should be efficient systems for busing for after-school activities and emergencies. To reduce adverse effects, students should not be required to walk excessive distances, especially if there is a school nearer to their residence than the one to which they are assigned. If reassigned students do not view the new school assignment favorably in comparison with the previous assignment, or if students are bused to an integrated school which has segregated classrooms, ineffective teachers and programs, which lacks discipline, or has excessive racial hostility, then the adverse effects are increased. Students in integrated schools continually evaluate as part of their daily experiences the outcomes being achieved with the inconveniences of achieving them.

Desegregation Plans That Work

Perhaps some of the difficulties in developing desegregation plans result because Charlotte, North Carolina, has been used as a model. The Charlotte plan is fine for Charlotte, but other cities need plans which will meet their particular situations. North Carolina has a county organization of schools, thus the desegregation plan involved the entire county. Since Mecklenberg County is approximately 40 miles long and 20 miles wide and Charlotte is centrally located within the county, one could not easily work in Charlotte and live outside the school district. Integration in Charlotte has been successful not only because white flight was difficult, but because of teacher and citizen effort, because the court took immediate corrective action when one area changed in its population, and because there were built-in safeguards in the desegregation plan to assure residential stability.

The Charlotte plan was buttressed by walk-in schools in integrated neighborhoods, an important feature in any desegregation plan for it makes an integrated neighborhood the place to live to avoid busing.

I can recall a planning session where someone suggested that people might buy trailers and locate their trailers after the school assignments were made. A quick solution to that problem was jokingly offered. Make all the schools portable and have a rule: first put down the houses, then the schools. During the planning for Charlotte it became clear that the major problems in developing the desegregation plan, once the court gave its directive of what must be done, were how to prevent white flight and how to provide stability in housing. The grade assignment plan for elementary schools which located the fifth and sixth grades in Black neighborhoods and the first four grades in white neighborhoods provided residential stability, because, except for those residing in integrated neighborhoods, all white elementary level children were bused two years for the purposes of integration. There was no place to move, except to an integrated neighborhood or outside the county to avoid busing.

The Charlotte plan had some equity since equal numbers of Black and white elementary children were bused, although each Black child was bused four years while his white counterpart only two, and the primary school–age Black children were bused while the white children bused were older. The plan could not, however, easily evolve so that the artificiality of the schools serving grades 5 and 6 would disappear. Subsequently, in three cities, Waco and Austin, Texas, and Boston, Massachusetts, I proposed a plan in which the school organization would be 4-4-4 or 5-3-4. In these plans there would be middle schools, all of which would be located in the Black or minority neighborhoods. Although recognizing that such a plan would have inequities, perhaps even too much inequity to be tolerated because young Black children but not young white children would be bused, such a plan might make bus riding purposeful if Black children felt that riding to an integrated elementary school was worthwhile and if white children felt that the middle-school programs and facilities were good. Complete equity may be less important than feelings of satisfaction and acceptability by children and parents, improved educational experiences, and stabilized city populations. No city has adopted such a plan, probably because too much school plant alteration and construction is required, although high costs would seem a small price to pay for a successful school desegregation plan.

Cities are different, and a plan which is suitable for one city may be quite inappropriate for another. In Denver, for example, anyone who has the financial means can avoid busing by moving to Denver's outskirts. This is possible because Denver is bordered by other cities, and the Supreme Court in the Detroit case ruled that except under certain circumstances the suburbs could not be included in a desegregation plan. The Denver plan, however, has many features which provide residential stability within the city. Denver, like Charlotte, has walk-in

61

schools in integrated neighborhoods and integrates as many schools as possible, when integration can be accomplished with a short bus ride. In the part of the city most distant from minority neighborhoods and possibly most prone to white flight, white students are bused either to junior or senior high school, but they are not bused at elementary level. Instead, they attend elementary schools which receive minority children who have long bus rides for six years. Those minority children are selected because they live within walking distance of both junior and senior high schools.

As originally designed, Denver had a unique pairing feature whereby some 10,000 of Denver's 40,000 elementary pupils attended schools which were part-time paired. A child went to his neighborhood school for half the day and thus was not in an integrated classroom. The child would spend the other half of the day in an integrated class, either in his own school or in one to which he was bused. Every child attended and was a member of two schools, had two teachers and two sets of classmates, one integrated, one not. Children in the paired schools were rotated so that for a semester a child would remain in the neighborhood school, and then for a semester would be bused. The part-time feature of the Denver plan was recently overturned by the higher courts. However, the plan was designed in anticipation of this possibility, so that, even though Denver intends to use a grade assignment plan for those schools for September 1976 no major realignment of paired schools will be required. The part-time feature probably lessened some of the apprehensions about desegregation, and this may well have been one of the features that resulted in Denver's success. Another major contributing factor was undoubtedly attributable to the diligent efforts of the school administration, principals, and teachers, and to the very effective work of the Community Education Council that the Court appointed to monitor the desegregation program.

The Denver plan has been at least somewhat successful in meeting a goal, which should be an important part of every desegregation plan. A prospective purchaser of a home or a prospective renter finds that the desegregation plan does not have much influence on the choice of home location within the city, except that the influence is to maintain integrated neighborhoods. Meeting this criterion does more than prevent within-city movement. It assures that the citizens will be aware that the procedure is as fair as it can be. Parents will not discover that some friend has been lucky and avoided busing, or that some political string has been pulled and a preferred assignment obtained.

Cities are different. What may be appropriate in Charlotte and

Denver may be completely inapplicable in Boston with its discrete ethnic groups, or in Detroit with its school population now 73 percent Black with a trend showing a very regular 2 percent yearly increase in Black population for the past 15 years.

Desegregation Plans That Don't Work

Some desegregation plans have followed practices that seem destined to fail. In Dade County, Florida (Miami), elementary children have been reassigned, and large groups of children residing only a short distance from one school are required to walk as much as two miles to a different school. Requiring walking, rather than providing a bus, not only creates initial resentment by parents and children, but the resentment continues because the long walk continues. In any desegregation plan, children should be provided with as much convenience as possible in all aspects of any new school assignments, not just as a matter of equity since the children are not guilty of any transgressions, but also because hardships such as long walks create resentment which is frequently directed at desegregation and the court, rather than at the school department which has failed to provide the transportation.

Atlanta is one of the cities which has become resegregated. The procedures adopted there were such that resegregation was inevitable. Dallas in 1971 used similar procedures with similar results. In both cities the children in a neighborhood or area in which whites resided were assigned to a Black school simply because the area was the nearest area to the Black school, while other areas of the city remained untouched. The procedure avoided busing, or at least long busing, but the affected areas were quickly depopulated of school-age children. The procedure may not have produced much educational benefit anyway since areas close to Black neighborhoods frequently are of low socioeconomic status, but that is a moot issue because, by one means or another, the white population disappeared. People with children don't rent or buy in the area, and those who can do so, move elsewhere. Where movement out of the area does not occur, children are sometimes listed as living with relatives, or parents simply give false addresses.

Oklahoma City provides another example of a plan which may not work in the long run. Oklahoma City uses the Charlotte model, but, since the plan has been implemented, new housing tracts have been developed that are in areas annexed to Oklahoma City but incorporated as separate school districts before annexation. Oklahoma City could lose much of its white population to these areas, and if they are not made part of the Oklahoma City school district the city schools will become increasingly Black.

One of the reasons that desegregation plans fail is because some children are bused but others are not, for this creates residential instability.

In Raleigh, North Carolina, the school board submitted a preliminary plan using grade assignments similar to the Charlotte plan but in which children from some areas of the city were not bused because the plan had some defects in its design. Before the plan was considered by the court, real estate advertisements appeared which indicated where houses could be purchased so as to avoid busing.

The Boston plan is also residentially unstable. Boston faces many problems which probably result from the tediously slow process by which that city has finally been required to fully desegregate, a process which allowed the opposition to busing to become fully and completely organized and the animosities and ill will to become intensified and hardened. If Boston should survive these problems, it is doubtful that it can surmount the consequences of its present pupil assignment procedures, which create preferential home locations and, as a consequence, residential instability.

Assigning students to desegregated schools by computer has been attempted, but all the computer programs that I know of create residential instability and for this reason will not work effectively. A preliminary plan was prepared but rejected for Denver. I attempted unsuccessfully to use a computer program for Stamford, Connecticut, developed by the Desegregation Center at the University of Miami.

A computer program which assigns students to schools and provides transportation routes would seem to be very desirable because it could simultaneously minimize number of students to be bused, travel time, and number of buses required. Unfortunately, minimizing these parameters results in some extremely undesirable outcomes. If students are selected on the basis of race and proximity to school, students residing in integrated neighborhoods would sometimes be assigned to Black schools if they are white and white schools if they are Black. Sending Black and white students in an integrated neighborhood to different schools is not a desirable outcome of a desegregation plan. This problem could be avoided by an alternative procedure which assigns all the students in a city block or some other geographic aggregate to a school. However, both procedures create residential instability for several reasons. Some children of the same

64

race will be bused all 12 years and others not bused at all. The residents of some areas of the city will be bused and other areas will not be bused. This in itself would result in residential instability, but could be exacerbated if influential people succeeded in having their residential area not selected for busing or if people believed that this occurred. The computer-program procedure results in a pattern throughout the city of bused and nonbused areas.

Concluding Comments

It is the courts that are carrying out desegregation procedures because the president of the United States and the Congress do not have the courage to rectify the constitutional offenses identified by the courts. Political leaders are perfectly aware of the problems of blighted cities, problems which include poverty, crime, and violence. It is deplorable that they often do not direct their support toward those remedies that would help to eradicate the sources of difficulty. The integration of schools is a primary example of such a remedy.

The courts may not be the most effective agency for carrying out such broad social remedies as desegregation, for courts do not have administrative capabilities in their structure. Lawyers are designated as officers of the court, because courts rely upon them through the advocacy system to bring the facts, the law, and the precedents before the court. A judge's task is to determine whether the facts in a case are of sufficient similarity to some previous cases to justify relying upon precedent. Characteristics of cities are so different that a judge providing remedial procedures consistent with what has been approved by higher courts may have difficulty selecting procedures that are both appropriate and equitable.

Judges are human too. Because of public sentiment against busing, a judge may adopt undesirable practices or fail to undertake steps he knows are needed, desirable, or just. For example, too few buses may be ordered or inadequate school facilities may be tolerated, or students may be reassigned from a school with excellent facilities to a substandard school lacking everything, or some students may be bused many years and others not at all. A court, even while enforcing the equal protection clause of the Constitution, may violate that very section by not assuring that students, innocent of any transgressions, are accorded every possible convenience to compensate for the inconvenience of reassignment or busing.

There is no way to achieve desegregation except by busing. Those who oppose busing but favor integrated schools are advocating an unattainable outcome. Their cozy platitudes of "Integration, yes! Busing, no!" could bring this nation to racial isolation and separatism.

Perhaps I am a dreamer. Perhaps racial prejudice and hostility are too deep-seated ever to be rectified. Perhaps I was naive in believing that integrated schools could bring effective education to all students. Perhaps, because desegregation has not proceeded smoothly, prejudices have been renewed and kindled, and the possibility of reconciliation and brotherhood is gone. I hope not! I hope there will soon come a day when political expediency will give way to leadership, and with it will come fulfillment of the American ideal of equality.

White against White: School Desegregation and the Revolt of Middle America

LILLIAN B. RUBIN
Wright Institute

This is a story about Richmond, California[1] (and the cities and neigh-borhoods adjacent to it that make up a single school district) during the years 1967–72—the years when those communities suffered the agonies of a struggle to desegregate their schools. It might as well be Boston, 1974. For wherever and whenever these struggles occur, whether in Pontiac, Michigan, Boston, Massachusetts, or Richmond, California, the issues and the actors are the same—poor and working-class whites pitted against Blacks, the latter usually a little poorer, usually a little lower down on the working-class scale.

In Boston, much is made of the ethnic factor. Gerry Nadel, writing in *Esquire* magazine in February 1975, notes, "The city itself belongs to the Irish, the ones who didn't make it to the suburbs." In Rich-mond, neither the ethnic factor nor the urban-suburban division is important. The West is newer; ethnic enclaves have not had genera-tions to take root—often do not exist with the tenacity and cohesive-ness of the East; and the city and the suburbs were brought together in a single school district a decade ago. Yet from Boston and from Richmond the response is the same—a cry of outrage and pain. The reason, I believe, is that, despite differences between life on the east coast and the West, between the life-style of the Catholic Irish of Boston and the Protestant migrant from Oklahoma, Arkansas, or Texas or Richmond, there is an even more basic similarity. These are the women and men of America's working class and lower middle class—the people who have worked hard all their lives and have little to show for it; the people whose dreams of a better life for themselves and their children have been dashed on the realities of limited educa-tional opportunities,[2] unemployment, underemployment, and spiral-ing inflation; or the people who, with a mighty effort, have managed to haul themselves up from the bottom but who know how precariously they hang onto their newly acquired status.

The Difference Is Class

> Let 'em send their damn buses; no kid of mine 'll ever ride 'em. Not
> if I have to get out there and stop those buses myself.

So spoke a conservative who led the struggle against desegregating the Richmond schools. "Racist bastards" is the typical angry liberal integrationist retort. But the answer is not so simple. The conservative opponents of busing in the Richmond Unified School District (RUSD) are, indeed, racists, but then so are the liberal proponents—not so overt, not so virulent, not so irrational, more in struggle over it, but racists nevertheless. The question in this case is why significantly more members of the liberal group were able to overcome their fears, or at least to set them aside, than among the conservatives. The answer, I believe, is that the difference in their class position results in both subcultural and ideological differences which together interact to motivate their behavior.

The protagonists in this desegregation struggle occupy different places in the social structure—that is, the conservative opponents are largely working class and lower middle class, while the liberal proponents are professional middle and upper middle class. They do dif-

---

Dr. Rubin returned to school in adulthood after having been active in California politics for many years—activities that included the professional management of several major political campaigns. She received her Ph.D. in sociology from the University of California at Berkeley, is presently a Research Associate at Scientific Analysis Corp. in San Francisco, and a member of the faculty of the Wright Institute Graduate Division, Berkeley. Her study of a community in conflict over school busing entitled, *Busing and Backlash: White against White in an Urban School District,* was published in 1972 by University of California Press. She has recently completed work on a study of life in working class families funded by the Behavioral Sciences Research Branch of NIMH. The product of that research will be published in October, 1976 by Basic Books under the title, *Worlds of Pain: A Study of Working Class Families.* Her next research project is a study of middle-aged women entitled, "Women in the Middle Years: Rejects from Life?"

ferent kinds of work, have different levels of education and different educational experiences, and hold different places in the power and status hierarchy of the society—differences that lead to disparate orientations to political issues, to work, to the meaning and purpose of education, to the family unit; and which in turn condition their hopes, their fears, their aspirations, and set the course of their collision once the issues became salient. To understand the meaning of their political behavior, one must understand these differences.

Rather than relying on notions that suggest some psychological predispositions or aberrations such as an authoritarian personality as an explanation for the behavior of the working class and lower middle class, my analysis suggests that the behavior on both sides of the struggle stems from that complex of rational and nonrational, conscious and unconscious, self-interest and false consciousness, that motivates human behavior and belief in all places and at all times.

The data to be presented here derive from field observations over a period of two years, election data analysis, analysis of school district documents, and from 31 lengthy, in-depth interviews (lasting from two to six hours) with both the elected and lay leaders on each side of the conflict—a sample that represents the total leadership population of the two major contending organizations.

Education and Educational Philosophy

When we look at the disparity in educational background and experience between the two groups, it hardly comes as a surprise that they have divergent expectations of the schools and define their ideal educational system in wholly different terms.

Median years of education among the conservative leaders is 13; among the liberals it is 18. Only three conservatives are college graduates, while 15 of the 16 liberals have at least a bachelor's degree, and of those nine have advanced degrees. The exception is the lone Black man on the executive board of the integrationist organization who has only a fifth-grade education.

When a lower-class conservative is asked what he ideally expects from an educational system, the first phrases that almost invariably spring to his lips are "the 3 R's," "more discipline in the classroom," "end sex education," and "get rid of sensitivity training and of liberal teachers who are trying to brainwash my kids." They want a no-frills, no-nonsense education; schools that will train their children to be moral and upright citizens, teach them to be patriotic, "put some starch in their spines," and avoid filling their heads with notions that parents do not understand. As one conservative board member put it during one of many sex education debates, "The parents can answer any questions the children have, and what they can't answer there's no need for the kids to know"—a remark that met with lusty approval from his large and sympathetic constituency in the audience.

Responding to the same question, the upper-middle-class liberals answer that they expect the schools to encourage "spontaneity," "innovativeness," "initiative," "flexibility," "independence," and, above all, not to stifle "the natural curiosity and creativity with which children come to school."

There was no point at which the responses merged, or even came close together. The liberals in this study are almost all professionals whose work allows them great freedom and requires innovation, independence, and initiative. Expecting that their children will follow in their footsteps, they call for education that encourages those qualities above all else. But of what use would those qualities be to a factory worker, a clerk, or a petty bureaucrat where the conditions of work are largely unfree, monotonous, and repetitious, and where a free spirit would endanger the job? Such dull, routine jobs may require more than anything else a kind of iron self-discipline just to get to work every day. If so, then most of those holding those jobs could be expected to wish for a disciplined child rather than an innovative one since they probably have little ability to project to a work situation that is free or to imagine its requirements.

Consonant with the educational philosophy they expressed, not a single liberal spontaneously indicated a belief that the schools should focus more on teaching the basic skills. When I asked why, they often shrugged carelessly and said that they were not worried about their children learning to read or write; they simply took for granted that they would. And, indeed, that is an apt assumption for, by and large, their children read well and, in fact, attend schools showing the highest reading test scores in the district.

On the other hand, one of the primary demands of the conservatives is that the schools place more emphasis on the "3 R's", a response to the fact that the schools their children attend do not place well on standardized tests. Analysis of school achievement scores in Richmond shows that among white students the lower the SES, the lower the reading scores—a finding that is not unique to that area.

Many lower-class parents were quite well aware that the children in the upper-middle-class hills schools do much better than their own, and several of my respondents seemed to accept that fact as part of the "natural" order of things. More than once I was told that they thought it quite natural that their children would not achieve as well as the children of "those professors and other people with lots of education up there on the hill." If that is natural, then why, they ask quite logically, isn't it natural that Black children will perform even more poorly? And what sense does it make, they want to know, to integrate schools with each other where both sets of children come from the lower classes and already perform poorly?

Through two election campaigns (in 1967 and 1969) and as often as they had an audience in between (which was at least twice a month at school board meetings) conservative anti-integrationist leaders hammered away at the relationship between SES and school achievement. They cited the Coleman Report to support their argument that the problem was socioeconomic status, not race, and gave wide publicity to the Report's conclusion that the most important variables related to school achievement are the family background of the child and the social class of the school. (Of course, they left out any mention of the Report's finding that Black children achieve better in integrated settings without deleterious effect on the whites.) Given their racial hostilities and fears, and given that they were quickly and persuasively informed that integration would provide no benefit to their children (no serious plans were made to upgrade the quality of education, of teachers, or of school plants in the Black or the poor white neighborhoods), it is hardly surprising that these lower-class parents resisted so tenaciously.

At the same time, the integration of the upper-middle-class children from the hills was scheduled for the third year of a three-year plan. Not only were those children to be spared the worst trauma of the transition period, but, when they finally were put on buses, they were to be integrated into the only ghetto school that had a brand new plant, that was being developed as a demonstration school with a specially selected staff, and that already had several federally-funded special projects offering academic enrichment and innovation, with more promised. Thus, the upper-middle-class parents could foresee an immediate payoff—a vision that made integration more palatable. I quote from one interview at length since it tells the story most compellingly.

I: Why did you support two-way busing?
R: Because I believe in integrated schools as being good for all kids ultimately, and good for education. I was bused as a child all my life in what people would consider very unsafe conditions—that is, in middle western winters—and we were bused home for lunch, too, so we rode the bus four times a day. So I don't have the fears.

71

I: Were you concerned about the possibility that academic standards would be lowered?

R: It was my impression that King School would not be one bit less academically oriented than Kensington.

I: Would you have been willing to send your child to Verde?

R: (Emphatically) No! I'm not willing to experiment with my children. They have only one chance to get educated.

I: Then how could you have taken the position that the Broadway and Dover [white working-class schools in San Pablo] parents should send their children there?

R: (She hesitated, reddened with confused embarrassment, and finally spoke lamely.) Well, I mean I wouldn't send my child to Verde if it were 97 percent Black and with such poor facilities. But if I felt that under the plan the school had potential, that would be different. Then (very defensively), I was willing to send my child to an integrated school; those people down there weren't even willing.

It is also of some significance that the anti-integration leaders largely live in fringe neighborhoods where interracial exposure exists because both groups are too poor and too powerless to do anything about it, and where contacts are more likely to be abrasive and to provoke hostility, or have only recently escaped them. One respondent spoke of his struggle to escape such a neighborhood with great feeling. "I know what it's like to live in a tough neighborhood where the kids take turns beating you up every time you walk around the corner. I fought desperately to better myself and to get out of that neighborhood. Then all of a sudden they were talking about busing my children back there to the school where I went. If they think they can do that to me, they're crazy."

On the other hand, most of the district's upper-middle-class proponents of integration live in a quiet, peaceful, hills area, high above the turmoil of Richmond's Black ghetto. The few Blacks who are their neighbors share their middle-class values and life-style. They hardly ever see a ghetto Black; the menace of a ghetto rising is an abstraction far from home; and the specter that their children might be accosted, perhaps beaten, by an angry band of Black youths has little reality in their lives.

Occupation, Income, and the High Cost of Living

The occupational picture of the two groups reflects their educational differences. Of 16 liberals 13 are professionals, while only two of the

15 conservatives fall into that category. Only one liberal leader—the only Black man—is a blue-collar worker, compared with nine conservatives.

As would be expected, income differences are equally striking. The modal income of liberal families in the study is "over $25,000"; among conservatives it is "$10,000–$14,000." Ten of the liberals earn over $20,000, while only three conservatives do. (All three are presently members of the school board.) But the differences are more profound than these figures would indicate, for with the exception of the one Black man in the $10,000–$14,000 bracket, all the liberals who earn less than $25,000 a year are young professionals who have not yet reached the peak of their earning potential. Among the conservatives, on the other hand, most are at or close to the peak of their expected lifetime earning curves and can expect only such increments in earnings that will come from cost-of-living increases or union negotiation.

When considered in conjunction with the fact that these are largely young families, the importance of the last point cannot be overestimated. In their middle thirties, these working-class and lower-middle-class men reach their maximum earning potential at the very stage in the family life cycle when family pressures for spendable income escalate—that is, when the number of children at home is highest, when housing needs are most pressing, when household consumer durables become a necessity rather than a luxury, and when the wife is least able to leave the home to help. To cope with the squeeze, these men may moonlight or work overtime; they may live in a state of helpless outrage and frustration over the high cost of living and taxation—or both. That to some the rage is displaced to the handiest scapegoat in American life—the Blacks—should come as no surprise.

Thus, the conservative school board and its constituency attack the Work Incentive Program—a state-sponsored program to encourage high school–aged girls who are welfare mothers to complete their degree requirements, and which allows each student up to $75 for such expenses as graduation announcements, class ring, and college-admissions applications. And liberals who earn $20,000 and more each year shout "racist." While racist feelings certainly are one factor motivating the conservative attack on this program, there are other objective factors that are equally important. Consider that the efforts of these hardworking people bring them relatively few comforts and probably no luxuries. They are in a continuing struggle to feed their families and to keep up the mortgage payments on the modest house. Those with older children either are unable to afford to supply the expensive high school graduation amenities or do so at considerable sacrifice to family needs. As they see it, the taxes they pay buy privileges for others that they cannot afford for themselves. Not much of a bargain, they conclude.

Educational Aspirations

The differences in occupation, income, and education between the two groups lead to differences in the way parents perceive school and value education, and in their aspirations for their children's future.

Every upper-middle-class liberal parent in this study aspires to some form of higher education for his children. While no doubt they are concerned about their children's ability to make a living, that is not central. More than anything else, they talked about wanting their children to do "what would make them happy," or "would offer them fulfillment," and there was an implicit assumption that without education that goal could not be achieved. Thus, education is valued not for instrumental purposes, but as an end in itself.

The working-class and lower-middle-class conservative families were much more ambivalent about higher education. The few who unequivocally said they saw a college education in their children's future were decidedly vocationally oriented and referred only to their sons. Only one talked about learning in some broader sense as the goal of a college education.

Education for women?—While it is hardly news that boys and girls are subjected to differing socialization processes and differing role expectations within the family, it was surprising to find the sharp differences between classes in attitudes toward women and their role. When talking about higher education for their children, it never occurred to the upper-middle-class group to leave their daughters out, while it rarely occurred to a working-class mother or father to include the daughter in. The only working-class father who talked about wanting his daughters to go to college said it was important because "in college they can meet a better-type man who can support them better." A more typical comment came from a conservative board member who said, "For my girls, they don't need to go to college. I want most of all for them to get married and have homes of their own."

These views are congruent with the differences in the education and status of the women in the families of the two groups and with the range of alternative roles each group permits to its women. The conservative women have substantially less education than their liberal counterparts—a median of 12 years compared with 16. The conserva-

74

tive women married younger—median age of 19 at marriage compared with 23 among liberals—and are younger when they bear their first child. There is an average of 1.2 years between marriage and the birth of the first child in the conservative families, 3.2 years among the liberals.

While most women in both groups are housewives, the proportions differ substantially—80 percent among the conservatives compared with 56 percent among the liberals. Of the seven liberal women who are employed, five are professionals and two are secretarial workers, while of the three conservative women employed, only one is a professional—a teacher—and the other two are part-time secretarial or clerical workers.

Nevertheless, the recent ferment among women has made itself felt in both classes. A question about the occupation of the women of the household was met with a defensive reaction from both liberals and conservatives, men and women. On the liberal side it took the form of an almost shamefaced discomfort over the need to reply "housewife." The women generally shifted uncomfortably in their seats, lowered their eyes, and muttered the word. A few rushed to assure me that it was "only until the children get a little older," and presented some evidence of preparation for that future day. Their husbands were almost equally discomfited by the question, and almost always volunteered some information about the professional status of their wives before their children were born. One man answered, "Housewife, liberated."

On the conservative side, however, with few exceptions the women seemed to draw themselves up to their full height, to sit straighter, and to respond clearly, "Housewife." One young woman took the opportunity to express her outrage with the women's rights movement. Several others volunteered the information that they are "proud of my job," "doing the most important job there is," "wouldn't be anything else." And their husbands agreed. "I wouldn't have it any other way. What kind of a man would I be if I couldn't support my family," was one typical comment. "I don't believe in career women," was another.

This vehement response in support of a traditional role for women—so out of tune with the times, with my own experiences, with the large literature on the discontent of modern American women—was deeply puzzling. I could understand the value that a working-class or lower-middle-class family places on the financial ability to allow the mother to stay at home; to have both parents out of the home when there are young children and where adequate child care is not available can be catastrophic to the family. Moreover, women of the working class who are also in the labor force generally have the doubtful privilege of doing two full days' work in one—one on the job and the other after they get home at night—a way of life that few women would look forward to. Thus, for the working-class or lower-middle-class wife to be able to afford to stay at home is a valued advantage and a significant step up. But the anxiety I was hearing seemed to be saying more than these rather ordinary things, and none of the replies sounded very convincing. Rather they had the air of an extreme defensive reaction, fearful responses to the erosion of traditional values. It was as if by reaffirming those values more loudly, by clinging to them more tightly, they could keep the world from changing before their eyes.

But what, my reader may ask, does this discussion of the woman's role in the family have to do with the conflict over school integration? The answer, I suggest, is that the difference in the way the woman's role is defined in the two groups contributes to different family responses on the question of neighborhood schools.

The professional upper-middle-class family represented here values independence among all its members and encourages them to seek to maximize personal development. Thus, even though still only in a limited way, women are expected to orient to a world outside the family. The choice of a professional career may be a difficult one for a woman in this stratum, but it is no longer unthinkable. The result: a woman is not solely dependent for validation upon her role within the family; ancillary roles are legitimately available to her. She does not desperately need to make motherhood and housewifery a full-time career in order to justify her existence.

The working-class and lower-middle-class subculture, on the other hand, is dominated by an inner-family orientation; members are expected to find both social and emotional gratifications within its bosom. No woman worthy of the title "mother" would wish to do otherwise. In fact, it is she who is counted the failure if some member of the family turns outward to have his or her needs met. In such a family, nurturing it and raising the children become a woman's only meaningful functions. The result: the child-centered family and the family-centered role of women become mutually reinforcing. Take any part of that job away prematurely and the woman will fight like a tiger, not, as is so often thought, to protect her little ones, but to preserve for herself as long as possible the only legitimate role identity that her social world permits.

The difference in attitudes toward nursery school between the two groups lends support to these speculations. While almost all the children of the professional upper middle class attend nursery school, none of the working-class and few of the lower-middle-class children have any nursery school experience. Because of my own upper-middle-class bias, I assumed at first that was because it would have been a financial burden, but, as I talked to family after family, it dawned upon me that the reasons were more closely related to family role definitions than to finances. (After all, the difference in the annual income of a teamster who makes about $14,000 a year and an assistant professor at the university is not great.) With that realization I began to ask why they did not send their children to nursery school. The almost unanimous reply was that young children belong at home with their mothers, that "they get sent out into the world young enough and we should be willing to protect them as long as possible." Quite aware of the disparity between her beliefs about nursery school and those of the upper middle class, one working-class mother remarked, "We know our children are going to have to grow up but we're not going to push them out of the nest because we're too lazy to take care of them like those people up there in the hills."

Ironically, then, the notion that "woman's place is in the home" may have unintended social consequences, for it seems possible that it is one of the structural sources of the conflict when the needs of school integration call for busing children from their neighborhood schools.

Participation History

The differences in community and political participation histories between the liberals and conservatives are also great. Most of the liberal integrationists had a rich participation history before entering the school conflict; they reveal high rates of community activity and a wide range of interests. But on the conservative side, participation histories are almost barren—a fact that may partially explain their lack of responsiveness to any but their own adherents when they finally came to power. These men and women had not been visible in the larger political community before the school crisis. Since they came to prominence within the framework of a special purpose organization whose mission was to prevent school desegregation, they faced few or none of the constraints of maintaining a previous community position. Since they belonged to few, if any, other organizations, they felt none of the cross-pressures that derive from multiple-group affiliation. Finally, since they came into public life at a time when the district was profoundly polarized, their continued isolation from those of different persuasion was ensured. Except for the public exchanges, which too often turned out to be hostile shouting matches,

77

members of the opposing forces almost never met on a person-to-person basis.

Rationality and Irrationality

I started out by saying that the behavior of the conservatives in the RUSD is a complex of rational and nonrational, conscious and unconscious, self-interest and false consciousness, that motivates human behavior and belief in all places and at all times. Until now I have argued for the rationality of the conservative position—that is, from their perspective, self-interest demands opposition to integration. In the short run it makes sense for the working class to try to stem the tide of Black gains since they are the most immediately threatened by them—their jobs, their neighborhoods, their schools. Tragically for America, such racist behavior is not a phenomenon given to the lower classes alone. For now that significant numbers of Blacks, Chicano, and other minorities are knocking at university doors, we keep hearing the cry, "We can't lower academic standards. Would you want a less than perfectly qualified doctor to take care of you?"—a cry that sounds very little different to my ear than the carpenter who stoutly maintained on a television broadcast recently, "I'm not prejudiced, but we can't have guys who don't know anything about construction on the job. Would you want to live in a house built by guys who don't know where to put the nails and the beams?"

But there is also a profound irrationality in the single mindedness of the conservative position. they vehemently attack any program of assistance for the Black poor, but quiescently accept the public policy that dispenses favors to the already well favored—charity in the form of tax loopholes, subsidies to private, profit-making industries, construction of roads and highways for the benefit of private industrial development, and the like.

I wondered, for example, why my conservative respondents were not demanding free medical care for themselves rather than wishing to deprive those who were poorer. Since that particular matter came up spontaneously very often, I asked about it. The answers I got were an aggregate of nonrational notions related to the American creed of individualism and personal achievement. "This country was built on every person pulling himself up by his bootstraps," said one man. And another, "How could I respect myself if I couldn't take care of my family?"

When I replied that the government not only helped the poor but the rich as well, and pointed out that Standard Oil (the most important industry in the district) was "helped" through such devices as oil-depletion allowances, most often they said that was all right with them. After all, "Standard supplies a lot of jobs around here, don't they? S'pose they went out of business, then what would we do?"

If we think in terms of the Marxian notion of false consciousness —that state of consciousness in which people, responding to the ideological and social superstructure that surrounds them, are no longer able to perceive their own self-interest, let alone to act upon it—both the conservative anger at benefits to those who are worse off than they, and their passivity and acquiescence in the face of far greater benefits to those who are better off, become comprehensible. The system has taught them to believe in a highly individualistic notion of achievement, assuring them that each man gets his just rewards. Why, then, should somebody get something for nothing? For those who have to run so hard just to stay in place, it must be especially galling. On the other hand, they have also been taught that without the American corporate structure the country would fall upon evil times. Thus, in their own interest, the people must sacrifice to protect those corporations. They believe their own self-interest is bound to the corporations. As the man I quoted earlier said, "S'pose they went out of business, then what would we do?" Therefore, they accept the subsidy of aircraft manufacture as part of the national interest, and when in the midst of rising unemployment and spiraling inflation the president offers a program of tax relief to industry in lieu of programs that are directed at alleviating some of the most immediate pain of the unemployed, that seems right and natural —especially to those who are not yet unemployed.

Is it any wonder that these working-class and lower-middle-class people who are caught in so many binds are so angry and so ambivalent that they displace their hostility downward and scapegoat Blacks? They have failed to make the connection that the appropriate target of that anger is not those poor people whose misfortunes are even greater than their own, but a social system that breeds such inequities and whose ideology so distracts its citizens that they are unable to perceive them.

Racial Stereotypes and the Power of Preconceptions

To the question, "Are they racists?" the answer must be an unequivocal, "Yes," for both liberals and conservatives. But there is a difference; for among the former, the most overt manifestations are missing. The liberal integrationists acknowledge that America is a racist society and that whites have discriminated unjustly against Blacks for centuries. While they are not quite sure how, they are guiltily aware that they have been complicit in these injustices, and they wish to redress them. But the stereotypes and fears run deep, and they are difficult to overcome.

Despite the evidence to the contrary, even the most committed integrationists in the RUSD could not shake the fear that the presence of Black children in the classroom would have a deleterious effect on the quality of education, a fear that made their commitments very ambivalent and that was a central determinant in the course of the struggle. They wanted integrated schools, but as one mother said, "My children have only one chance to get educated, and I'll not sacrifice that."

And while the integrationist board members can be justly proud that when they had the opportunity they appointed the first (and to this date, the only) Black man to serve on the RUSD board, *what* they chose to tell me about him was curious, indeed. After informing me that he is a lawyer and a graduate of "fine eastern schools," each in turn ran down this Black man's family background as if giving me a dog's pedigree. Each in his own way told me that he comes from a "fine family of lawyers and judges," that there is a "long line of educational professionals" in his background, and that his wife is also "a cultured and educated person." Moreover, the minutes of the public meeting at which the appointment was announced show one board member making the statement: "Mr. Hatter's parents both are university graduates and practicing attorneys, and all four grandparents are university graduates who completed graduate work." It was as if his parentage were somehow meaningful in evaluating the adequacy of their choice or his performance as a school-board member. Look, they seemed to be saying, we didn't appoint just any ordinary "nigger." One respondent, answering my question about whether the board members knew anything about their other colleagues' families, looked surprised and said, "Why no. I don't think so; at least I don't."

Since racial fears and stereotypes are more prevalent, more overt, and more gross among the conservatives, distorted perceptions and projections of their own feelings and anxieties are more common. They generally refuse to admit that white society has any responsibility for the plight of the Blacks. They grant that "we have a problem," but it stems, they say, from the fact that "the colored just can't seem to get along." Nothing stands in their way but their own deficiencies, they insist. If Black children do not do well in school, it is only because their parents do not value education, because they are undisciplined, and because they do not "talk proper English"; the last being argued especially forcefully by a man who, in another context, assured me that "we haven't went to forced two-way busing and we've made great strides."

Indeed, it is one of the ironic observations of this study that the very people who mistreat the English language most are the quickest to criticize the language and dialect of Blacks. One reason they resist sending their children to ghetto schools, they insist, is because Black children speak poorly. Yet the language deficiencies among their own friends and colleagues are unheeded. When one of their number argues that he ought to be free to send his children to any school he chooses just so long as "it's credentiated," and another says, "I always have spoke my mind," they apparently are unaware that anything is wrong with the language. It leads one to wonder whether the very perception of language inferiority is related to the fact that the words (or dialect, or cadence, or all three) are coming from a person whose skin is Black.

Reflecting their racial fears and tensions, these conservative whites are inclined systematically to overestimate the proportion of Blacks in the community and in the schools. Thus, despite statistical evidence to the contrary, several conservative respondents put Richmond's Black population at well over 50 percent, one suggested that it was as high as 80 percent. In fact, Blacks presently represent just over 36 percent of Richmond's inhabitants, and they are only 27 percent of the school population.

These observations are not new, nor are the people in the Richmond school district unique. Williams and Ryan (1954) observed the same phenomenon in Cairo, Illinois, where, in spite of official census figures showing that the Black population never exceeded one-third of the total, the belief persisted among white residents that Blacks made up one-half to three-quarters of the city's population. More recently Reginald Damerall, writing of a desegregation struggle in Teaneck, New Jersey (1968), also documented the stereotyping of Blacks. There, where the Blacks were all very substantial middle-class families, Teaneck whites "saw" them as "slum dwelling and culturally deprived." And there, where the elementary school that was 50 percent Black had higher achievement scores than three all-white schools in a district of eight, neighborhood-school adherents insisted that integration would diminish educational quality.

Conclusion

This, then, is a sketch of the two groups who squared off to fight the battle of desegregation in the Richmond schools. Given their different places in the social system, and the different perspectives that derive therefrom, it is little wonder that they were unable to talk to each other in ways that would facilitate understanding. While the upper-middle-class liberals had some ambivalence about the impact of integration in their schools, both their place in the system and their belief in their ability to control their own fate gave them some assurance that whatever school their children would attend, they could make it a good one. And they probably were right. Conversely, the working-class conservatives also probably were right when they felt less secure about their children's fate under the plan to integrate, and less sure that they would be able to influence that plan or their children's destiny. For the lower-class conservatives, the threat—both real and imagined—was more immediate and palpable; any payoff was so distant as to be unimaginable. If we are ever to integrate the American society successfully, that balance will have to be redressed.

In sum, the question ought not to be "Is school desegregation still a good idea?" Rather, we need to ask, what has made it seem like such a bad idea? Why has it been so difficult to realize? To answer those questions, we need to examine the context in which school desegregation plans are made—who benefits, who loses, who has no real stake, and why? We need to look squarely at discrimination in other institutions in our society—jobs and housing, for example—that support school segregation. And perhaps, most important of all, we need to understand the dimensions of social class as well as racial discrimination and segregation—to lay to rest the myth of a contented and affluent white working class, to acknowledge the imbalance between classes in our society. Those things done, we will have no need to ask whether school desegregation is a good idea. We will ask, instead, how to spread the burdens of social change—in schools, in jobs, in housing—more equitably throughout the class structure of America.

Notes

1. For a more complete analysis of the problems discussed herein, see *Busing and Backlash: White against White in an Urban School District* (Berkeley: University of California Press, 1972).

2. In Boston, as well as in Richmond, like the Blacks, the children of the white poor and working class also go to schools where achievement levels are well below state and national norms.

References

Damerall, Reginald. *Triumph in a White Suburb.* New York: William Morrow & Co., 1968.
Williams, Robin M., and Ryan, Margaret W. *Schools in Transition.* Chapel Hill: University of North Carolina Press, 1954.

TV's Deadly Inadvertent Bias

FLORENCE HAMLISH LEVINSOHN

Looking back over the past 20 years of television, we see what appears to be an extraordinary mirror of the changes in our society vis-à-vis the Black community. One searched nearly in vain 20 years ago for a Black face on the screen.[1] In the popular media—the newspapers, magazines, radio—there were, 20 years ago, separate Black outlets. In every large city with a sizable Black community, there was a separate newspaper, there were a few Black radio stations, and *Ebony,* a Black imitation of *Life,* had begun to reach a national audience from its home base in Chicago, all of which served as an antidote to the solid white press and radio. But television was too expensive; there was not sufficient Black money to finance a separate TV outlet.

It was 22 years ago that the Supreme Court decreed that separate education was unlawful. And 20 years ago that Rosa Parks refused to move to the back of the bus. And in the intervening years, these two dramatic events led to a change in television. More and more Blacks began to appear on the screen, though at first only on news programs as victims, victims of cattle prods, water hoses, and all the other devices used by white citizens and police to deter them from seeking their civil rights, though no doubt some people saw them not as victims but as aggressors, demanding privileges rather than rights. We also watched on television Black children and their parents and Black college students having rocks hurled at them, invectives screamed at them, and even the governor of a southern state block their entrance to a school door as they attempted to enter previously all-white schools, though the violence of early efforts to desegregate schools was mild by comparison with that of more recent years.

By 1968, the news on television regularly featured some civil rights events and then, in that year, all other news was overshadowed by the assassination of Martin Luther King, Jr., and the news of the fierce reaction across the country to his death, the burning of white property in Black sections of major cities.

84

Following these events, a very dramatic change began to occur in television programming. Television executives apparently took seriously for the first time their public mandate. As Blacks demanded integrated housing, schools, unions, political parties, and job opportunities, television seemed to lead the way. All-white programs were gradually integrated. Black actors and actresses began to join Sammy Davis, Jr., and Bill Cosby in a variety of shows, even to have their own shows, even to gain top Nielsen ratings. Black faces began to appear in commercials. And in the news programs, considerable attention was given to Blacks winning elections, being named to the Supreme Court, being a part of the mainstream, it appeared, of American life. In most recent years, even the greater impact of the recession on Blacks has been well reported by the networks. Television viewers have been regularly reminded that the 12 percent of its population that is Black is a real part of the nation, no longer the "invisible" part that Ralph Ellison described in 1953, only one year before *Brown* v. *The Board of Education of Topeka.*

For which the networks are to be commended. They had, in their early years, followed meekly the lead of the American press, ignoring Blacks, but the events of 1968 moved them rather quickly to the forefront when they opened to Blacks the greatest source of visibility the nation offers. That they were not leaders in the days when real courage would have been required—southern stations would not have bought shows featuring Blacks nor could the networks be sure that any local affiliate would have bought such shows—is simply to say that they are ordinary men and women, lacking great courage. Certainly, the record of the network people in the McCarthy era is not a testimony to their courage or even much good sense. The accusation against them that they are liberals, anti-establishment, is ludicrous in the light of the McCarthy era. But people change and personnel are replaced.

By 1968, Edward Epstein found that "the overwhelming majority of the correspondents at NBC thought of themselves as liberals or held positions on public issues which Epstein regarded as liberal."[2] However, Michael Robinson points out that, though they hold liberal positions, their reporting of the news reflects the organizational constraints on them far more than their political attitudes (1975).

It is possible, though, that the charge of leftwing bias made against the network folk can be accounted for in part by their opening of the

FLORENCE HAMLISH LEVINSOHN is managing editor of *School Review.* Her column of television criticism appears regularly in the journal.

doors to Blacks. There is no evidence that those who make such charges are pleased to see their television screens regularly reminding them that 12 percent of Americans are Black and that their demands for equal rights will continue to play a role in elections.

That the opening of the television casting and newsrooms to Blacks has had a distinctly positive effect on their general condition in America cannot be denied. Those few to whom television has paid enormous salaries and given wide publicity are exquisite new models of success for Black kids. And the very presence of people of their own race finally playing as legitimate players in the most visible game in America cannot be of small psychological importance. For their day-to-day relationships with whites, this visibility cannot but be of great importance. "Sanford and Son" has surely provided a common language for Blacks and whites who did not easily chat at work or in other places they were together. The Jeffersons cannot but help ease the process of Blacks moving into white neighborhoods.

Despite these undeniable benefits to be gained from television's having finally begun to include Blacks in mainstream programming, we need to ask whether TV's news coverage of school desegregation over the years has not had quite the opposite effect, whether it may not have incited some of the violence that appears to be increasing against desegregation. These deleterious effects result not from intent, though, but rather from television's mode of reporting news.

In the *New Yorker* last year, Michael Arlen discussed the disservice to the American public performed by network television's reporting of the news of the war in Vietnam. "I think it is wrong or foolish to imagine that television news in some idealized form could have somehow solved the problem of Vietnam for us. But I think it is evasive and disingenuous to suppose that, in its unwillingness over a space of ten years to assign a true information-gathering function to its news operations in Washington and Vietnam, American network news . . . [did not] contribute to the unreality, and thus the dysfunction, of American life" (Arlen 1975, p. 132).

Arlen points out how television news reported the war in terms of battles—" 'sweeps' and 'missions' and 'patrols' and 'reconnoiters' and 'air patrol' "—of head counts, wins and losses, official government reports, never revealing the true nature of that war, its impact upon the people of Vietnam, or its impact on our own servicemen fighting there. This was not, however, a reflection of bias. Robinson reports, "On one major political issue—American involvement in Vietnam —the [liberal] bias was imperceptible at first. Only toward the end of the war did the networks begin to exhibit an unambiguous point of view" (p. 118).[3] Even when their liberal biases began to be revealed, the content they reported did not change much; it remained a report of the violence being waged, though toward the end of the war, there was disapproval expressed of that violence.

What is crucial here is that television news has gone for the violent, as it does in so much of its programming. It is quick and easy to report the news. It is the sensational that sells the news. This is not to say that there should be no violence reported in the news. Or that the incredible violence that marked the war in Vietnam should not have been shown to the American people. Far from it. But there were many types of violence in that war. There was the slaughter of innocent villagers and, even more so, the forced removal of Vietnamese from their homes, the burning of villages, the My Lai massacre, the iron cages and other means of torture of political prisoners by the Vietnamese with the help of the Americans. More important, however, there was decision making about the war which was reported simply as, for example, the president's decision to send another 50,000 troops abroad.

That the television people had a great deal of information about how decisions were being made and who was making them and who was not making them, for instance, the Congress, seems evident from the regular gossip that comes out of Washington that newspeople and politicians spend a great deal of time in each other's company, that what David Gelman in *Newsweek* (1975) calls "social journalism" tremendously augments the press conference. *Newsweek* quotes one TV journalist as saying, "When you see someone like Joe Kraft talking in a corner with Henry [Kissinger], Joe's gonna get a story and Henry's gonna get a point across. A lot gets accomplished" (Gelman 1975, p. 89).

It is also possible that this "social journalism" prevents newspeople from reporting all the facts. *Newsweek* quotes another TV reporter as saying, "Elliot Richardson caved in to Nixon on everything until the Saturday Night Massacre. But he was an unalloyed hero to the press in this town because he played the dinner circuit and charmed a lot of people. Most of the Watergate crowd were looked on as loathsome, partly because they stayed home and showed each other goddam home movies and sneered at the press parties" (p. 90). Whatever the television newspeople reveal or don't, however, it is clear that there was a liberal bias reflected in the news coverage of the last years of the war in Vietnam and the Watergate events. But this bias did not provide any better reporting of the news, for the temptation to go for the quick and easy is not touched by the political views of television newspeople. They rely on the drama of the film to sell their shows, and they view as most dramatic the most violent, whether the violence is on the battlefield or simply among arguing congressmen.

The lesson of television coverage of the Vietnam war, it seems to me, applies equally to TV's coverage of the civil rights movement, especially to school desegregation. Unwittingly, I believe, for I do not think it has represented a conscious policy or even an awareness of what was being done; the 20 years' effort by the courts, the federal government (until the Nixon-Ford years), and the liberal community to attain integration of the schools has been treated as a war against desegregation. Battles and head counts have been reported. Since 1954, when Eisenhower sent federal troops into Little Rock to enforce the law, we have watched white officials and white parents disrupt the orderly lawful process of desegregating the schools. Overturned or burning buses, rocks and sticks, angry mobs screaming outside schoolhouses, and bewildered, frightened children. It seems that there is an angry mob of white parents in the doorway of every school in the nation, either anticipating or reacting to a court order to desegregate.

But there has been much more peaceful school desegregation than violent. When, as in Denver and other cities, the busing of children to achieve desegregation is accomplished peacefully, it is briefly commented on by newscasters who close with what has now become a rather classic television comment, "There were no incidents reported," as if "incidents" are natural accompaniments and their absence must be duly noted. This line, by itself, is a mark of the view television newspeople take of the war against desegregation, though they would surely claim that they report the peaceful integration of a school system. Missing from these reports are films of integrated classrooms, school corridors, and lunchrooms, comments by school people, parents, or kids to match the films of bus burnings, rock throwing, angry pickets, screaming parents, which are so dramatically shown when there are "incidents."

The television war against desegregation is a bloody one, one that cannot but instill fear in the minds of parents and children and in the minds of public officials. There is no doubt that there has been and will continue to be some bloody opposition to desegregation. But there is a good deal more to the story, which requires the "true newsgathering function" that Arlen referred to. The public is entitled to know all of what is occurring in the courtrooms, the offices of school administrators, the offices of planners, teachers' lounges, union offices, city halls, and on the buses and in the classrooms where desegregation is taking place. The public is entitled to know more about the process of achieving school desegregation than the protests of some angry whites and an occasional two-second report of a court decision or a peaceful action. More important, it is possible that if the public were provided with the whole story it might have a different view of the issues.

That this "dramatic" coverage is endemic to television news gathering is further evidenced by the history of its coverage of the civil rights movement. Only after Martin Luther King's death did the networks reveal the miles of film that had been made of him in events other than "incidents." The three-hour documentary of King's life, shown several times since his death, usually on his birthday, shows him preaching, talking, in meetings, doing all the things that comprised the activities of those who led the demonstrations across the South and later in the North. Before his death, it was only the demonstrations and, for the most part, only those moments of the demonstrations when violence occurred. True, most of the violence portrayed was of brutal police against peaceful marchers, violence that stirred the sympathy of many Americans who had been indifferent. But it is also probably true that the police violence portrayed on television news for so long offered some incentive and some legitimacy to those whose indifference was replaced by hostility, not because television commentators ever endowed the violence with legitimacy by their words but because their regular selection of film to be shown so endowed it.

Michael Robinson offers a theory, in "American Political Legitimacy in an Era of Electronic Journalism: Reflections on the Evening News," that a sense of the legitimacy of the law has declined in America in direct relationship to the expansion of television news. "I have begun to envision," he states, "a two-stage process in which television journalism, with its constant emphasis on social and political conflict, its high credibility, its powerful audio-visual capabilities and its epidemicity, has caused the more vulnerable viewers first to doubt their own understanding of their political system. . . . But once these individuals have passed this initial stage they enter a second phase in which personal denigration continues and in which a new hostility toward politics and government also emerges" (Robinson 1975, p. 99). This occurs, Robinson suggests, because those who are most likely to rely entirely on television for their news are receiving a limited view of the news. "Themes must be simple and interesting; venality, social discord, bureaucratic bungling, and especially the good old days. . . . The theme of social discord is extraordinarily well-suited to television. It is a hook from which one can hang a good deal of sensational film footage. . . . When there is planned violence, or violence that takes place through an extended period of time, the networks can be expected to move enormous amounts of equipment to the staging area" (p. 113). And those who rely entirely on TV for their news, who do not read any other media (Robinson estimates this group at 10 percent, but estimates that a "clear majority," 56 percent, get their news "principally" from TV [p. 105]), are also the least educated, the ones who are least likely to be able to resist the notion that "they are being *informed* by following television news" (my emphasis) who cannot recognize that television is "narcoticizing viewers and unwittingly justifying their reliance upon one medium. . . . The networks have, in the last ten years, undermined the tendency to supplement one medium with another. For much of the population—a growing percentage—the only supplementation of information is among networks, not between media" (p. 109).

Certainly it is true that the lawlessness that has characterized the opposition to school desegregation has increased as television coverage of that opposition has expanded. Since the brief John Cameron Swayze program in television's early days to the brief Huntley-Brinkley report that began in 1956 to the two or so hours of news on every network today, a regularly reported news event has been the violence associated with the civil rights movement and the effort to desegregate schools. The massive peaceful desegregation of southern rural schools has received hardly a word by TV commentators while the struggles in Pontiac, Michigan, in Prince Edward County, Virginia, and other places where it has been violently opposed have been relentlessly covered. Television cameras actually go everywhere. The networks have miles of film shot of every event that possesses even a small potential for big news. But what is shown is only the "big" news, and, of that big news, the largest portion is about the violence, or at least the discord, of American life, the disorder, the law breaking.

Anyone who has participated in any public action that was filmed by a television crew is aware of this fact. How many civil rights and antiwar demonstrations I participated in and then hurried home to watch the evening news, watching narcissistically for my own face and those of my friends whom I knew had been in several shots, and watching to see what the news editors had considered the news worth broadcasting, perhaps something I had missed in a very large demonstration in which I might have been blocks away from where the "big" news was being made. In the same way, I've watched the specials on the antiwar movement and the civil rights movement to see what footage was considered of historical import. One learns, after a while, that television newspeople consider peaceful demonstrations quite uninteresting. Thousands of people, marching for several hours across a city, with a full complement of police in attendance, with a permit to stop traffic at every intersection for miles, merit a brief clip. But if the marchers should be ambushed along the way by a group of antagonists, if there should be rocks thrown and some physical abuse, this entire sequence will be shown, though it may have accounted for only a few minutes of the entire demonstration, without any footage shown of the rest of the march, enough to insure that the ordinary television watcher can safely assume that the march was another one fraught with violence, though they may not be sure who was fighting who or who initiated the violence.

Assuming that most people, almost everyone, never participate in any public demonstration, this distortion of events must lead people to view such events as scenes of violence. Is it unreasonable to suggest that those white citizens who pelted Senator Kennedy with tomatoes in Boston were simply acting out learned responses? Would the whites who oppose school desegregation in Boston have been so violent in their demonstrations if they had, for years, been watching scenes of the actual peaceful demonstrations that occurred in the sixties?

More important, would they have been so inclined to oppose the law had they not been watching nightly the opposition to the law expressed elsewhere? Let's examine how this might occur. If Robinson's estimate is correct that "the networks speak to an audience which contains an enormous pool of politically unskilled individuals—those who rely on an eighth grade civics curriculum to comprehend national politics," and if he is further correct that the perceptions of these people are naive and that these are the people who "shifted first toward political cynicism and frustration" (p. 131), we have to examine what it is these people see on the television news. What they have been seeing is what newspeople view as "big" or sensational news, what newspeople believe is the only news that sells, and, after all, television is in the sales business, selling the products of the advertisers who pay the bills.

Consider for a moment that the newspaper with the largest circulation in the world publishes practically no news. Soviet citizens pay three kopecks daily for *Pravda* to read government propaganda and a few bits of inconsequential news published only in the bottom corners. Sensational news, the thing that Americans believe is all that sells—plane crashes, murders, the deaths of public figures, the jailing of dissidents—is not reported in *Pravda*, or any other Soviet paper, or on the evening television news. Russians are kept completely in the dark about any events that can be conceived even vaguely to reflect badly on the regime. Yet they buy more newspapers than any other people (Smith 1975). What this tells us is that newspapers—and the electronic newspaper—are crucially desired by most people. Sensational news sells better than less sensational when there is competition. But people hunger for news of their world. And they are vitally influenced by that news and the way it is presented. The Soviet leaders understand this and use their "news" organs as propaganda instruments. American newspeople make a strenuous effort to maintain a free press, an instrument of information rather than propaganda, and resist every effort by the government to attempt to use their media for propaganda purposes, despite regular complaints to the contrary from the left and the right. With almost no exceptions, newspeople do not express their biases in their words. But in the selection of what part of the story they present, a selection made not out of bias but out of a failure to recognize that a news story can have drama beyond the facts of violence and disorder, they express unwittingly a bias that legitimizes violence and discord, that legitimizes opposition to the government and to the law. But it is the constraints on TV newspeople to sell their time (CBS, the most profitable of the networks, showed a profit after taxes for 1974 of $108.5 million. Its income for that year before taxes was $135.7 million. NBC and ABC showed smaller, though quite sizable, profits also, but what is most important is that the rise in profits in the past few years for all the networks has been spectacular [Halberstam 1975]) and to conform to a variety of regulations beyond the news-gathering function that leads to this selection, not any conscious effort to achieve these legitimizing ends. It is the constraints on the broadcasters that prevent them from using their imagination in the service of reporting the news. More than Hearst ever yielded to the sensational to sell newspapers, the TV newspeople yield to what they find easiest in the face of these constraints.[4]

Now, if what many Americans receive as their only news coverage is what they see on television and if what they see there tends to be the violent and discordant in American life, and if they are influenced by what they see, they might come to view violence and discord as characteristic of American life, which would dismay and disturb them. If, further, the violence they see is most often the flaunting of the law, they might come to believe that flaunting the law is at least not unacceptable. For children, this view from the television news is surely a more effective lesson than the opposite view of the law they are taught at school. Finally, if flaunting the law is at least acceptable, then those who disagree with the law will have less hesitation to flaunt

Florence H. Levinsohn

it. And if they feel strongly about their disagreement with the law, they would be less hesitant about using violence to make their disagreement known.

Since 1954, there has been more peaceful integration of schools than violent. These successful and peaceful efforts have not been brought dramatically to the attention of the American public. Television newspeople have not learned how, have not made the effort, to dramatically convey these peaceful transactions. They have failed to assume the responsibility for "true news-gathering."

The question is, if TV newspeople were to assume a true news-gathering function, were to assume responsibility for regularly reporting the continuing story, across the country, of school systems and individuals who obey the law of the land, would their stories and films have a beneficial effect on desegregation? Has the manner in which they have so far told the story actually had the deleterious effects I have described? If the answer to the second question is yes, is the answer to the first necessarily also yes? We can't know. But we can guess. We can speculate that many people are very much influenced by what they see on television. We can speculate that the growth of the antiwar movement at the turn of the decade resulted at least in part from the decision by newscasters to begin bringing more news of the war to the people. Those of us who followed the events of that war closely from the beginning were astonished to find the TV newscasters finally revealing what we had been reading in a variety of sources not normally read by the ordinary TV watcher. We would not be saddened to be astonished again to see TV newscasters giving more detailed accounts of the events of school desegregation. We would be willing to take our chances that the larger story might not bring more people to the support of desegregation just as we were willing to take our chances earlier that the larger story would not bring more people to oppose the war. It may be that the opposition to school desegregation springs from sources so strong that the use of violence results not from the example of television news but from intense racism and anger at the changes being imposed on some people. Lillian Rubin's poignant description of those most inclined to resist school desegregation forces us to consider that possibility.[5]

But if the assumption is correct that the account provided by TV so far, which has stressed the flaunting of the law, has incited people to oppose it, we can make a counterassumption that coverage that stresses the upholding of the law would encourage people to follow suit, certainly an assumption worth testing. It would be "wrong or foolish," as Arlen said, "to imagine that television news in some idealized form could somehow 'solve' the problem" of the resistance to school desegregation, but it is not wrong or foolish to hope, even to expect, that a different result would accrue from a different kind of coverage of this process.

Notes

1. Friends have reminded me that there were, in fact, a few Black personalities making regular appearances on TV prior to 1968—Rochester, Amos and Andy, Sammy Davis, Jr., Bill Cosby, Sidney Poitier, and in addition, a few actors and actresses played domestic servant roles. My favorite TV historian, Lester Fishhaut, even suggests that "Studio One" and other such shows that pushed the frontiers forward a bit occasionally featured a Black. But if one considers the number of times one might have seen all these people over one season's schedule, it is, I think, not a great exaggeration to say that "one searched nearly in vain" for a Black face in those years.

2. Quoted from Robinson (1975). I am indebted to Paul Hirsch for bringing this article to my attention.

3. Ibid.

4. For a further discussion of these constraints, see Robinson (1975).

5. See Rubin's article in this volume and her more exhaustive treatment of the subject in *Busing and Backlash* (1972).

References

Arlen, Michael. "The Road from Highway 1." *New Yorker* (May 5, 1975), pp. 122–33.

Gelman, David. "Social Journalism." *Newsweek* (December 1, 1975), pp. 89–90.

Halberstam, David. "CBS: The Power and the Profits." *Atlantic Monthly* (January 1976), pp. 33–71.

Robinson, Michael. "American Political Legitimacy in an Era of Electronic Journalism: Reflections on the Evening News." In *Television as a Social Force: New Approaches to TV Criticism.* Aspen, Colo.: Aspen Institute, 1975.

Rubin, Lillian. *Busing and Backlash: White against White in an Urban School District.* Berkeley: University of California Press, 1972.

Smith, Hedrick. "In Moscow, the Bigger the News, the Smaller the Story." *New York Times Magazine* (November 23, 1975), pp. 32 ff.

The Courts, the Legislature, the Presidency, and School Desegregation Policy

BETTY SHOWELL
University of Chicago

One need only recall the long and tortuous racial history of America to realize the depth of the racist legacy that has so thoroughly shaped American institutions and perpetuated the subjugation and isolation of its racial minorities (Pettigrew 1975; Weinberg 1975; Gittell and Hevesi 1969). This is not to argue that racism, individual or institutional, is inevitable or that it cannot be effectively combated and eradicated. But the attitudes, arrangements, policies, and practices which underlie the increased separation of Blacks and whites in this country are deeply embedded in the American subconscious and just as deeply engrained in its institutions.

Generally, studies of racial isolation are concerned with its doctrinal aspects (separate but equal, etc.), the extent of racial mixing, attitudes toward desegregation, technical solutions for accomplishing desegregation, official compliance, or the effects of desegregation (on achievement, discipline, residential patterns).

Since very little research has been devoted to school desegregation as a result of institutional policies (Crain and Street 1973), my inquiry will focus on this area. I view segregation as the result of institutional arrangements at the federal, state, and municipal levels that not only structure relationships between Blacks and whites but also govern their differential access to public services (housing, education, etc.). More specifically, I see school segregation resting on a set of understandings about exclusion from (or within) specific schools and involving apportioning schoolchildren differentially according to a discriminatory criterion. Whatever that criterion, the apportionment is either to a specific building, *away from* a specific building, or a combination of both (Weinberg 1966).

Racial segregation, in both northern and southern cities, is not the

95

result of fortuitous circumstances unrelated to the activities of the government and its agencies but is the result of direct and indirect governmental policies and activities designed to foster racial exclusion and subjugation (Weinberg 1975; Gittell and Hevesi 1969; Jones 1975). Finally, I view desegregation as the elimination of exclusionary political and legal structures and agreements and the inclusion of all statuses, classes, and races in the power groups and institutional arrangements which govern the distribution of symbolic, cultural, and material advantages.

The Legislature, Desegregation, and Public Policy

Although not a federal responsibility (education is not mentioned in the Constitution of the United States but is by tradition reserved to the states under the tenth amendment), educational policy and governmental actions have been inextricably entwined for years, and there is no indication that the trend will be reversed. The most significant piece of civil rights legislation since the Civil War has been Title VI of the Civil Rights Act of 1964. In what has been regarded as one of the most sweeping and important sentences in federal statutory law, the act, in forbidding discrimination in the use of federal funds, provided that no person in the United States shall, on the grounds of race, color, or national origin, be excluded from participation in, be denied the benefits of, or be subjected to discrimination under any program or activity receiving federal financial assistance. While Congress did not intend that this legislation be used to enact a positive program of integration (to insure that it was not used for this purpose, the act stipulated that "nothing shall empower any official or

---

BETTY SHOWELL is a doctoral candidate in the Department of Education at the University of Chicago, on leave from the Baltimore city school system, where she was director of the Model Early Childhood Learning Program, which won the Pacesetter's Award for Innovative Education given by the President's National Advisory Committee on Education. She played a significant role in assisting in the analysis of new administrative functions in the system-wide reorganization of the district and developed and implemented the training program for its top-level administrators. Prior to that responsibility, she was the first woman to participate in the Rockefeller Foundation's program to train minority-group administrators at the superintendent's level and served as a superintendent-intern in Berkeley and in Gary, Indiana.

court of the United States to issue any order seeking to achieve racial balance in any school by requiring the transportation of pupils or students from one school to another or one school district to another in order to achieve racial balance"), the act did seem to herald a period of revolutionary change in American race relations, a change that appeared to be supported by a broad spectrum of political forces. The 1964 act, like the Supreme Court *Brown* decision of a decade earlier, seemed certain to end the policies and practices emanating from the more than 100 years of lawful racial subjugation and exclusion.

Basic social and political arrangements that had seemed impossible for decades began to take shape. Other changes also began to occur. But as the enforcement of desegregation efforts began to extend beyond tokenism and beyond southern "freedom-of-choice" plans to the vigorous use of legislative and judicial authority to support change, the underlying political consensus (which had been responsible for the bill's passage) began to erode. In retrospect, it appears that from the beginning the consensus was fragile. However, what was clear was that, once actual changes in century-old traditions and biases began to take place, the nation's policymakers began to resist, and a new consensus was soon reached. This consensus, it seems, extended only to action limiting the legality of the most vicious, openly fostered forms of racism. It did not include attacking the more invidious forms of racism that reached beyond surface equity. When the Department of Health, Education, and Welfare (HEW) began attempting to enforce the act's provisions outside the South (in Chicago, Detroit, Indianapolis, Pontiac), massive confrontations began that further eroded congressional support. These clashes in northern districts not only sealed the fate of HEW action in the North for years to come but also aroused the suspicion and hostility of a number of northern urban congressmen who later joined the southern conservatives to support legislation that would hamstring HEW's enforcement efforts in the future (Orfield 1975).

De Facto Segregation and Public Nonpolicy

In the controversy, it became obvious that a substantial number of legislators believed desegregation to be a special "southern" case and that only southern desegregation should be subjected to federal regulation. While the legislators and courts seemed to recognize the segregation of southern Black pupils and teachers as a product of past and present political actions and thus subject to legislative direction,

97

they often contended that racial isolation in northern communities was unrelated to public policies and institutional arrangements and hence not subject to federal regulation (to substantiate this position, they excluded de facto segregation from the provisions set forth in the Civil Rights Act). Northern segregation, they reasoned, was the result of unintentional and uncontrollable housing patterns and not the consequence of specially mandated public policy. The nation's policymakers seemed to lose sight of several important facts. First, public policy can reasonably be defined to include nondecisions as well as decisions; therefore, segregation measures may reflect public nonpolicies or nondecisions. Second, in most northern and western states, segregated housing and education facilities and prejudicial zoning and districting laws were socially acceptable and legal until well into the present century. Not until the 1940s was residential segregation made illegal. Even in states where it was technically illegal, one could show that residential segregation was the result of deliberate racial districting and zoning policies.

There are those who view the attempts to assign differential descriptions to segregation (de facto vs. de jure) as a smoke screen designed to confuse the issue, deny its pervasiveness, absolve society of any responsibility for its persistence, and prevent a national commitment to its elimination (Jones 1975; Weinberg 1975). They argue that the courts and the legislature, in order to maintain the status quo or camouflage their own inability to grapple with the everyday realities of this society, have espoused the theory that there are various types of segregation, over some forms of which government has no control. Meyer Weinberg (1975) argues persuasively that de facto segregation is regarded by many as one such variety: accidental, unintentional, and utterly beyond the control of human agency. De facto segregation, unlike the de jure variety, it is asserted, is caused by neutral and impersonal social forces, not by governmental or school agencies.

But abundant and persuasive evidence exists that segregation, whether de jure or de facto, is in fact sustained by official policies contrary to the fourteenth amendment. Historical analysis and numerous court actions provide evidence that this distinction is artificial. Such a distinction, Weinberg notes, has neither theoretical nor practical cogency, especially with regard to urban areas where the influence of elected and appointed officials is everywhere in evidence. Further, the economic and political salience of the urban school system makes it highly unlikely that it can be politically or economically autonomous. Thus, the idea of its being unaffected by the ideology and actions of officialdom is highly unrealistic. Similarly, the growing interdependence of all aspects of urban living and the increased probability that any single decision or act will have extensive repercussions throughout the community greatly increase the likelihood that governmental agencies will continue to influence and/or control essential areas of educational policy, especially those affecting the distribution of and accessibility to economic, social, and political resources.

Neither the political realities of urban/suburban living nor governmental precedents have kept Congress or the Supreme Court from ruling that de facto segregation is not within their purview. Their refusal to resolve the issue of de facto segregation (in the face of lower-court decisions sanctioning this type of segregation) has led to a national policy that supports de facto segregation in northern and western schools, since without federal regulation these states and their political subdivisions are free to preserve their own separatist arrangements. What seemed a nonpolicy regarding de facto segregation was tantamount to a policy designed to preserve segregation by superimposing a policy of geographical zoning on the existing pattern of residential segregation. By so doing, the government insured the perpetuation of public-school segregation. Recent figures demonstrate that, while substantial progress has been made in eliminating the dual system of public schooling in the South, racial segregation in the North (and West) has generally continued unchallenged (Gittell and Hevesi 1969; Kirby, Harris, and Crain 1973). Congress and the Supreme Court, through nondecision on the issue, have given sanction to a pattern of segregation which, though not greatly unlike "southern-style" segregation, nevertheless seems to have been regarded as inviolate.

Slowing the Desegregation Movement

Like many state legislatures of the 1950s, Congress in the late 1960s and early 1970s expended great effort in formulating rhetorically effective but unconstitutional legislation. Each year since 1966, it has managed to pass at least one amendment to the 1964 Civil Rights Act designed to restrain school integration. Among the amendments which indicate the legislature's antidesegregation policy are the following. Congress

> Voted to limit the powers of the federal government in school desegregation matters;

Forbade the spending of federal funds for voluntary as well as court-ordered desegregation;

Forbade federal officials to encourage integration or even suggest that local governments comply with the clear requirement of the Constitution as interpreted by a unanimous Supreme Court;

Engineered a partial repeal of the 1964 Civil Rights Act by limiting and decentralizing HEW enforcement and deferral powers;

Enacted bills which infringed upon the autonomy of the federal courts;

Sought to delay court-ordered school desegregation orders;

Forbade HEW to require the "assignment of students to public schools in order to overcome racial imbalance" (this amendment was intended to prohibit desegregation action in the South beyond "free-choice" plans which offered Black children a chance to transfer to white schools);

Tightened the original draft of the Civil Rights Act so as to exclude enforcement activity in the North;

Amended the act to forbid the Justice Department to file litigation supporting busing children for the purpose of creating racial balance;

Drafted an amendment to the Civil Rights Act to force HEW to accept token integration plans (free choice, etc.) as being in full compliance with the act;

Amended the act (in direct opposition to a recent Supreme Court decision) to require that transportation of students to achieve racial balance must not take effect until either the school system concerned had appealed the case all the way to the Supreme Court or the time permitted for filing the appeals had elapsed (the Supreme Court had ruled earlier that desegregation orders must be implemented immediately, even while appellate courts were considering the appeals from lower courts);

Passed the Federal Elementary and Secondary Education Act of 1974 which requires, among other things, that children cannot be bused farther than the next closest school;

Forbade legal-service offices to use federal or private funds for school desegregation cases, thus cutting off public resources for enforcing constitutional requirements.

It seems apparent that, in a period which was widely viewed as a time of revolutionary change in American race relations, Congress was enacting legislation devoid of any pretense of moving the nation toward a unitary system of education. Thus the legislative struggles of the two decades since the *Brown* decision have produced little substantive legislation supporting school desegregation (Orfield 1975). The basic impulse of the legislation has been to prohibit judicial efforts to enforce the desegregation requirements of the Constitution itself and to repeal the school desegregation requirements of the 1964 Civil Rights Act.

Although sufficient power and authority reside in Congress to establish as national policy the goal of eliminating minority-group isolation in public education, this body has made few attempts to use its public powers in that area. Instead, it has used its authority to support negative legislation and to pursue a policy of nondecision with regard to substantive desegregation issues. To the detriment of prodesegregation forces, it helped shape the isolationist rhetoric of the White House and of Capitol Hill opponents. The idea of integration has been replaced with such terms as "forced busing," and generally law-abiding citizens have come to believe that court orders are illegitimate and subject to change by politicians. All the while, little support has been offered to those educational institutions attempting to comply with the constitutional mandates of the thirteenth and fourteenth amendments.

In short, through the use of public authority and influence, the country's highest legislative bodies have succeeded in slowing the momentum of the desegregation process and have embedded more firmly in the fabric of our society and its institutions old segregationist notions and practices that early Americans fought a civil war to abolish.

The Executive Branch and School Segregation Policy

On the heels of President Johnson's "great society" programs and the passage of the Civil Rights Act, Richard Nixon came into office as the first president since Woodrow Wilson openly and publicly committed to slowing the momentum of racial change. With his administration came what has been interpreted as the escalation of a national antidesegregation mood and the beginning of a strategy to limit the civil liberties of Black Americans (Jones 1975; Ribicoff 1975).

Early in his campaign for the election, Nixon clearly implied that he viewed integrating urban schools as a visionary scheme designed to divert the nation's attention and energies away from its more urgent problems. In an address before the southern caucus at the GOP national convention, he attacked HEW and the federal courts for pressing too hard for desegregation and reiterated his belief that judges were unqualified to make local school decisions. As a remedy for the "illegal" judicial decisions that had been handed down, he vowed to provide a more conservative Supreme Court, endorsed "freedom-of-choice plans" (which had proven to give no choice at all to most Black

101

students), and further eroded official and public confidence in integration efforts by asserting that both the courts and HEW had made decisions which should be rescinded (Orfield 1975).

Upon election, Nixon pressed virtually to end enforcement of the Civil Rights Act; this not only contributed to the public's ambivalence about the correctness of earlier decisions and enforcement efforts but also emboldened other federal, state, and local officials, whose actions in turn led to an avalanche of anti-*Brown* statutes and court decisions (Motley 1975).

1. For the first time since 1954, the Justice Department began to go to the Supreme Court as an opponent of civil rights and desegregation proponents.

2. The lack of enforcement of existing law by HEW was so blatant that, in an extraordinary decision (*Adams* v. *Richardson*), a unanimous court of appeals found HEW guilty of intentionally subverting the 1964 Civil Rights Act.

3. The entire process of desegregation enforcement became so politicized that HEW regional offices were bypassed, with negotiations taking place instead between congressional offices in Washington and local officials.

The power of the White House was firmly hedged against desegregation enforcement (Jones 1975). The now infamous Buchanan memorandum counseling the Nixon administration to abandon racial integration as a goal suggests that the rash of antidesegregation policies was no mere accident but the result of well thought out, carefully orchestrated political leadership. Perhaps the most striking occurrence was early in 1972, when President Nixon publicly stated that he might well support a constitutional amendment unless Congress, through legislation, could end busing. This most extreme proposal called for amending the Constitution to forbid any requirement of positive local action to desegregate urban schools. The proposed amendment would have prohibited any desegregation plan that was based on segregated school patterns caused by housing segregation, selection of segregated school sites, or other causes. It would have prohibited not only busing but also pairing, minority-to-majority transfer plans, and numerous other techniques used to achieve urban school desegregation. This proposed amendment, which enjoyed considerable congressional backing, would have been the most manifest and blatant example of anti-Black sentiment to emerge from Congress since the Civil War and would have sounded the death knell of integration (Orfield 1975). It was the first serious discussion of a constitutional provision intended to limit the rights of Black Americans in over a century.

Gerald Ford, then House GOP minority leader, strongly endorsed the idea of a constitutional amendment limiting desegregation. President Nixon, however, later rejected going the amendment route, not on theoretical but on practical grounds; the ratification process was too long and too beset by numerous technical and political difficulties. Instead, the president, in concert with Congress, initiated a series of equally destructive antidesegregation bills which were designed to give more immediate relief. The president's bill (the Emergency School Assistance Act, ESAA-1972) included the following restrictive conditions:

1. It prohibited the use of the new ESAA aid to establish or maintain the transportation of students to overcome racial imbalance (in spite of strong and continuing requests from local school officials for permission to use the money for court-ordered busing).
2. It put a moratorium on court desegregation orders.
3. It prohibited the courts from ordering the transfer of any elementary school student farther than to the next closest school to his neighborhood or from substantially increasing the total busing in a school district.
4. It attempted to tell the courts what kind of desegregation plans they could approve.
5. It attempted to outline the priority the courts must give to various desegregation remedies.
6. It authorized school boards to reopen existing court orders which went beyond the standards the administration set.

If there were any doubts about the executive branch's position on desegregation, Senator Abraham Ribicoff observed, one need only note the prohibition in ESAA against the expenditure of any funds appropriated under that act for the purpose of busing. Furthermore, the administration did little to help crack the housing barriers which separate the races, hamper urban desegregation efforts, and threaten to make of our metropolitan areas two distinct enclaves consisting of affluent white suburban areas and poor nonwhite central cities.

The Courts and School Segregation as Public Policy

By far the bulk of the deliberation over the desegregation of schools has taken place in the courts. While in recent years Congress and the executive branch have assumed larger roles in the controversy, it is still true that the federal courts are where the cause of desegregation has been fought more actively. Even so, it has taken the Supreme Court more than half a century to reach its present position regarding the disestablishment of dual systems of public education and the development of a unitary, nonracial system of public education. Only now is the judicial mandate beginning to be articulated as to the duties and responsibilities of school authorities to remove the vestiges of unconstitutional educational arrangements.

From Separate and Unequal . . .

From one perspective, it can be argued that the American system of jurisprudence, which ideally should have guaranteed equal educational opportunity for all children, actually has aided the cause of segregation by its hesitation (it is just now beginning to address itself to northern desegregation), its lack of clarity (what does "with all deliberate speed" mean—20 years later?), and its equivocation on many of the vital issues regarding the implementation of urban desegregation plans (neighborhood schools, de facto segregation, metropolitanism). On these and other equally critical issues, the courts may have been the chief perpetuator of the exclusionary policies affecting the nation's educational systems, since it was the courts that permitted unjust, discriminatory laws to remain on the books. What we are faced with is dismantling a legal and extralegal system of deliberate segregation and planned deprivation, many aspects of which originated in the North before the Civil War and enjoyed the protection of the United States Supreme Court.

In *Plessy* v. *Ferguson* in 1896, the Supreme Court granted constitutional protection to deliberate segregation by its "separate-but-equal" ruling regarding transportation. The Court noted further that a race can be politically and civilly free even though legislation authorizes discrimination against it in all fields of social and economic endeavor. Judicial support for this separatist ideology was reaffirmed three years later in *Cummings* v. *County Board of Education,* a dispute arising out of a white school board's decision to close down a Black school in order to use the money for a white school. As a result of this litigation, the Supreme Court established a state's right to withhold public funds from Black schools if a school board preferred to spend the money on a white school. Justice Harlan's decision in *Cummings,* that the fourteenth amendment did not apply, gave school boards the go-ahead to deliberately and systematically exclude Black children and provided additional legal support for government and school-district policies fostering racial isolation and subjugation. The philosophy emerging from *Plessy* v. *Ferguson* and *Cummings* was one of racial inferiority. These two decisions reduced Blacks to the condition of a subject race and exempted them from the rights and privileges enjoyed by other Americans.

For the next half century, the courts labored under the separate-but-equal doctrine. Findings suggested that, with reference to buildings, curricula, teacher qualifications, and other "tangible" factors, the Black and white schools involved had been equalized. Even in the numerous cases where inequalities were found (e.g., *Cummings* v. *County Board of Education; Gong Lum* v. *Rice*), the validity of the separate-but-equal doctrine itself was never challenged.

Though still not coming to grips with the full implications of the separate-but-equal doctrine, the courts did find, in *Sweatt* v. *Pointer*, that inequality existed between Black and white law schools not in terms of the "tangible" qualities cited in earlier decisions but in terms of "those qualities which are incapable of objective measurement but which make for greatness in a law school."

. . . To Separate Still

It was not until 1954—just 22 years ago and almost 100 years after the adoption of the thirteenth, fourteenth, and fifteenth amendments —that the Supreme Court, in the landmark *Brown* case (*Brown I*), was willing to accord full constitutional recognition and significance to the reality that "separate" could never be "equal," because its very genesis and its only purpose for being was discriminatory. In *Brown I,* the Court declared that the separate-but-equal doctrine had no place in the field of public education, and therefore dual school systems must be ended with all deliberate speed. Although *Brown I* called attention to the pervasiveness of segregation ("Segregation has long been a national problem, not merely a sectional concern"), it confined its regulatory power to school districts which operated judicially mandated, racially exclusive schools. While it made illegal the outright segregation which characterized such systems, it made no mention of making illegal the material effects and inequalities of segregated education resulting from urban/suburban inequities, gerrymandered school districts, and tracking and redistricting (the courts, like the legislature, ruled that the resolution of these issues did not fall within its purview). The Court compounded the difficulties inherent in making operational an edict containing so many deliberate omissions by agreeing one year later (*Brown II*, 1955) to apply the 1954 antisegregation decree on a gradual basis. This interpretation of the 1954 decision is regarded by some (Motley 1975; Wright 1975; Robison 1975) as a "disaster," a "promise of indefiniteness." "We cannot really know what would have happened if the court had said, 'Do it now,' " observed jurist Constance B. Motley. Gradualism gave southern governments a chance to recognize and gird themselves to forestall any change. It was a very serious mistake (Robison 1975), a mistake that allowed school districts to institute so-called freedom-of-choice plans, to devise new school-zoning schemes, and to make a few token transfers, but to do very little that would have necessitated substantial redistribution of student and staff populations. Subsequent research and litigation have supported the position of those who argue that the Court's order to desegregate gradually was a mistake and was among the principal reasons that *Brown I* and *II* failed to disturb the nation's system of segregation or to effect an overhaul of its methods of allocating social and educational resources.

For more than a decade following the unanimous *Brown* decision, the Supreme Court stood by while lower federal courts reviewed on a district-by-district basis such issues as pupil-assignment laws, transfer policies, and state administrative remedies. Yet another decade was to pass before the Court would consent to review the issue of northern desegregation, despite the fact that de facto segregation had been approved in four circuit courts and rulings in numerous other suits were pending. Their refusal to grant a review of the issue was interpreted as tacit approval of the lower court's decision that the Constitution does not require a school system to eliminate racially imbalanced schools in the absence of proof that a board is at least in part responsible for their segregated condition.

In a series of decisions leading to the 1973 northern segregation suit and the later 1975 metropolitan busing suit, the Supreme Court reaffirmed through various court renderings its support of neighborhood schools, de facto segregation, urban/suburban inequalities, and racially imbalanced schools. It has refused consistently to interfere with school board practices that create neighborhood schools for white neighborhoods, while Black children have been turned away repeatedly when they attempted to enroll in the nearest so-called neighborhood school. It has approached de facto segregation with the same lack of perception and reluctance that characterized legislative decisions and has (in spite of its own statements suggesting otherwise) refused to view segregation in its national context—the result of deliberate actions by various levels and branches of government.

In housing as well as in education, the courts have tended to condone the segregation of metropolitan landscapes along racial and ethnic lines and the methodical division of the cities and isolation of the nation's minorities (Wright 1975). Under the guise of neutral laws designed to facilitate local control over community decisions, the courts have enacted some decisions which from all appearances are steps backward, away from the presumed goal of achieving a unitary, nonracial system of education. In the 1965 *Bell* v. *School City of Gary* litigation, the Supreme Court, like several circuit courts, held that the equal-protection clause of the fourteenth amendment does not create an affirmative duty for school districts to correct racial imbalance resulting from a neighborhood-school plan that was not consciously constructed to segregate the races. In the later (1967) *Deal* v. *Cincinnati Board of Education* decision, a lower court held that "there is no constitutional duty on the part of the School Board to bus Negro or white children out of their neighborhoods or to transfer classes for the sole purpose of alleviating racial imbalance that it did not cause."

Similarly, a 1970 Supreme Court decision related to racial isolation due to housing patterns (*James* v. *Valtierra*) held that the equal-protection clause is not violated by a state constitutional provision requiring a referendum and approval of a majority of the electors before low-rent public housing—but not other types of publicly assisted housing or other forms of public subsidies—may be constructed in a community. Judicial decisions such as the foregoing, which uphold the maintenance of racially imbalanced schools in cities with specially zoned or racially restrictive housing patterns, amount to establishing a public policy reflecting a tolerance of racial isolation, inasmuch as there are no technological or physical reasons why housing patterns should not be considered in determining alternative desegregation plans or why children must be assigned to neighborhood schools. By upholding the authority of communities to erect broad restrictions on housing, the Supreme Court has provided approval again of one of the most frequently used barriers to desegregating the nation's schools.

The Court's myopic view of school desegregation is equally evident in other rulings that pose as solutions to the problem. A three-judge court in *Spencer* v. *Keigler* (1971) concluded that it could not order desegregation of New Jersey school systems based on a suit alleging de facto segregation, holding that the "continuing trend toward racial imbalance caused by housing patterns is not susceptible to federal judicial intervention." That same year, in another landmark ruling (*Swann* v. *Charlotte-Mecklenburg Board of Education*, 1971), the Court on the one hand set forth standards instructing school administrators and lower-court judges about the means of accomplishing the termination of dual school systems and at the same time declared that there was no constitutional duty to make year-by-year adjustments in the racial composition of student bodies once the original desegregation plan had been implemented.

Judicial retreat from providing protection of the rights of urban minorities, facilitating equal educational opportunity or the elimination of differential systems of resource allocation, is even more evident in *San Antonio Independent School District* v. *Rodriquez,* in which the Supreme Court upheld the common system of financing public education and reversed the district court's decision. Among the Court's most notable pronouncements were that education is not a fundamental interest and that a state need not provide equal education to all its children.

The results of the *Rodriquez* doctrine have been even harsher than the doctrines which characterized the pre-*Brown* era. For, although *Plessy* v. *Ferguson* required separate schools in 1896, it required that those schools be equal. However, *Rodriquez* (1973) permits separate schools in cities and suburbs in the same state to offer a staggering disparity in educational opportunity. As a matter of policy, educational opportunities in central-city schools, says *Rodriquez,* need only be "adequate"; there is no compelling reason why they must be equal to suburban opportunities. Here again the Court legitimated the doctrine of separate and unequal schools.

A year later the Court, in *Milliken* v. *Bradley* (1974), retreated even farther. Justice Thurgood Marshall, filing a dissenting opinion in the Detroit case, noted that, "after many years of small, often difficult steps toward the great end, the Court today takes a giant step backward." *Milliken* focused the Court's attention on the basic reality of the relationship between school segregation and residential segregation. The evidence before the Court indicated that Black children had been confined intentionally to an expanding core of virtually all-Black schools immediately surrounded by a receding core of all-white schools. Despite this evidence, the Court, in denying the plaintiffs relief, decreed that minority populations in the central city may be limited to the level of education pertaining there, even in the face of overt discrimination within a city. If the plaintiffs had won in *Milliken,* the case would have represented a breakthrough of unprecedented proportions, measured by the practical standards of results that could be achieved. *Milliken,* unlike many other important school desegregation decisions of the past, could have sparked massive school desegregation, and on a metropolitan scale (Sloane 1975).

Justice William O. Douglas, another of the dissenters in *Milliken,* suggested that the Court, having ruled a year earlier in *Rodriquez* that poor schools must pay their own way, had now succeeded in reversing racial problems to the period antedating the "separate-but-equal" regimes of *Plessy* v. *Ferguson.*

Except for the seminal decisions in *Brown* and the later decision in *Cooper* v. *Aaron* (1958), Judge J. S. Wright notes, the Supreme Court has taken very few initiatives during the past two decades in moving the nation toward racial justice. Instead, it has been repeatedly the vehicle by which the growth of residential and thus educational apartheid has been encouraged and legalized. That the judiciary cannot itself restructure our metropolitan areas and educational systems goes without saying. But the judiciary must play an interstitial role and must guarantee that the political process, which is designed to implement majority rule, does not tread on the rights of minorities to equal opportunity and full enjoyment of their constitutional rights. It is from this role that the Supreme Court appears to have retreated, and it is this retreat which is so dangerous.

Summary

I have focused here on the legal and extralegal policies that generated and perpetuated racial segregation in public education. After an examination of selected judicial decisions, legislative actions, and executive decrees, I have concluded that public policies pertaining to segregation resulted from deliberate, persistent, and oftentimes direct governmental activity.

While there is no denying that the last 20 years have produced several landmark pieces of legislation and one or two historic court decisions, there is nevertheless strong evidence that these legislative and judicial decisions have been hamstrung by restrictive amendments and punctured by ambiguities that rendered the decisions ineffective in promoting equal access to the nation's educational resources. There is also no denying that the poor and the minorities lost ground in absolute as well as relative terms under federal and local policies contrary to their best interests.

Indications to date point to a retrogression in race relations, sanctioned and perpetuated by governmental agencies that, by the use of economic, social, and legal barriers, have accelerated the trend toward residential, political, and educational apartheid. Indications are that the courts, Congress, and the president are prepared to believe that whatever should have been done with regard to racial isolation has been done already. But, if school desegregation policies are not to further separate Blacks and whites in American society, far greater coordinated efforts on the part of different branches and levels of government are necessary than have been made until now. The correction of racial injustices that have existed since the foundation of this country is a moral and constitutional obligation of transcendent importance. Its realization will require a redefinition of the roles and policies of our political and judicial authorities and a reaffirmation of our basic belief in equality under the law.

References

Crain, R. L. and Street, C. "School Desegregation and School Decision-Making." In *The School in Society: Studies in the Sociology of Education,* edited by S. D. Sieber and D. E. Wilder. New York: Free Press, 1973.

Gittell, M., and Hevesi, A. S., eds. *The Politics of Urban Education.* New York: Praeger Publishers, 1969.

Jones, N. R. "An Anti-Black Strategy and the Supreme Court." *Journal of Law and Education* 4, no. 1 (January 1975): 203–8.

Kirby, D., Harris, R. T., and Crain, R. L. *Political Strategies in Northern Desegregation.* Lexington, Mass.: Lexington Books, 1973.

Motley, C. B. "Twenty Years Later." In *Continuing Challenge: The Past and the Future of Brown* v. *Board of Education,* edited by the University of Notre Dame Center for Civil Rights. Evanston, Ill.: Integrated Education Associates, 1975.

Orfield, G. "Congress, the President, and Anti-busing Legislation." *Journal of Law and Education* 4, no. 1 (January 1975): 81–139.

Pettigrew, T. F. "Exploring the Future: Race Relations in the Twenty-first Century." *Journal of Law and Education* 4, no. 1 (January 1975): 39–41.

Ribicoff, A. "The Future of School Integration in the United States." *Journal of Law and Education* 4, no. 1 (January 1975): 1–21.

Robison, C. B. "Speeding Reforms." In *Continuing Challenge: The Past and the Future of Brown* v. *Board of Education,* edited by the University of Notre Dame Center for Civil Rights. Evanston, Ill.: Integrated Education Associates, 1975.

Sloane, M. E. "Milliken v. Bradley in Perspective." *Journal of Law and Education* 4, no. 1 (January 1975): 209–18.

Weinberg, M. *Race and Place: A Legal History of the Neighborhood School.* Office of Education, Department of Health, Education, and Welfare. Washington, D.C.: Government Printing Office, 1966.

Weinberg, M. "School Desegregation and Planned Deprivation." *Integrated Education* 13, no. 3 (May–June 1975): 112–15.

Wright, J. S. "Are the Courts Abandoning the Cities?" *Journal of Law and Education* 4, no. 1 (January 1975): 218–26.

School Integration: Ideology, Methodology, and National Policy

RAY C. RIST
National Institute of Education

In a world that is so full of complexities, paradoxes, and absurdities, it is foolhardy to make unequivocal statements. Thus to say that one is absolutely for or against school integration (or busing, or cultural pluralism) is ultimately to utter nonsense. Very quickly, one's stance on school integration becomes enmeshed in political, pedagogical, and ideological crosscurrents. Facile political and rhetorical statements on this topic obscure basic dilemmas that are matters of state as well as of culture. Furthermore, an added complexity in discussions of this type is that the national discourse on school integration exists on many levels and with many sets of untested and unexplicated assumptions. School integration has multiple realities. Thus any attempt at a reflection on one's personal values and beliefs as well as prescriptions for action are necessarily limited. No single value system or perspective can be so catholic as to encompass all the divergences inherent in the phenomenon.

With these disclaimers and qualifications aside, I shall answer in the affirmative the question of whether school integration is still a good and desirable goal. I do so for four reasons, each of which is briefly elaborated upon below. But beyond the question of whether, at the level of values, one believes in school integration, there is a need to discuss avenues and methods to achieve in the specific what remains for many children, minority and white alike, only an abstraction. These opportunities for praxis are also treated here in some greater detail than the articulation of my particular value position.

School Integration: Issues of Ideology

In suggesting reasons for the desirability of an integrated public school system in the United States, I do not assume that, as such, these reasons are all necessarily internally consistent with one another. Nor do I assume that taken in toto they constitute my "world view" or gestalt so far as race relations are concerned. But these views do constitute the underpinnings of my own continuing efforts from within the federal government to achieve viable and humane integrated educational settings.

First and foremost, there will be no justice and no equal protection under the law for minority students so long as they are contained in minority enclave schools. I do not accept the conventional distinctions between school segregation that result from de jure or de facto causes. The mechanisms that have been operant in this society to generate racial separation and isolation are so intertwined that it is meaningless to assume that there are clear distinctions in reality, regardless of attempts in legal theory. At all levels of government there have been official practices designed to achieve racial segregation; there have not been comparable practices aimed at achieving racial integration.

Though it has been politically expedient of late to refer to "quality education" as if it were in juxtaposition to "integrated education," I reject these overtures for our returning to the status quo ante of separate but equal. Quality education in this society does not appear likely for minority children when they are kept isolated from integrated settings. And to deny minority children (or any children for that matter) the opportunity for a quality education is against the law.

Which leads to point two. If all groups of children were relatively equally distributed throughout the various components of the education system, and if all participated in an educational system where resources made available at public expense were equitably distributed, issues of school integration would be moot. But in this society children are not so distributed. Likewise, resources are not so distrib-

---

RAY C. RIST is currently head of the Desegregation Studies Division at the National Institute of Education, Washington, D.C. He previously was associate professor of sociology at Portland State University. He is author of more than 40 articles and also four books, including a forthcoming study of the processes of desegregation in a formerly all-white elementary school.

uted. Consequently, the resources available as students move through the education system are distributed unequally and thus unequally utilized (Rist 1970, 1973). And it does not take statistical tables or charts to confirm what is self-evident—that the resource distribution is not skewed in favor of minority students. Thus the mandate for school integration is strengthened if one believes that such inequalities are offensive. In a multiracial society where one race has most all the power and control over resources, integrated education becomes perhaps the single most critical instance where minority students are able to experience and utilize resources originally directed toward the benefit of white students.

We have witnessed in these past few years the stoning, blockading, and even burning of buses. Most if not all such instances have involved whites as the aggressors. The visceral hatred displayed by many white persons against Black children defies a rational explanation. And yet, morning after morning, Black parents continue to put their children on the buses. Their affirmation of integrated education, for any number of reasons, suggests that to withdraw the opportunities and options for such an education for their children would be viewed as detrimental. When so many people have risked so much to have their children participate in integrated settings, it is simply intolerable to say that integration is now irrelevant. To argue for a separate but equal practice in public education thwarts the aspirations and expectations of many Black people. Education has been viewed as a key means of achieving entrée in order to participate in the American Feast. It would be catastrophic to assume that we are in an age where it could again be possible to hang out the "white only" signs.

There is a final basic reason why I affirm the desirability of integrated education in this country, and it is at the same time the least empirical but the most foreboding. I ask, what are the consequences if we do not pursue this goal?

During the 1960s, much of the inherent conflict and systematic inhumanity of our society was exposed. In reflecting on the Black-white cleavage, the National Advisory Commission on Civil Disorders (Kerner Commission) noted: "This is our basic conclusion: Our nation is moving towards two societies, one black, one white—separate and unequal, reaction to last summer's disorders has quickened the movement and deepened the division. Discrimination and segregation have long permeated much of American life; they now threaten the future of every American" (National Advisory Commission on Civil Disorders 1968, p. 1).

I have no reason to believe that these trends have been reversed. Granted, there has been some improvement in the lot of Black people in education and health, but these are more than offset by the losses in income and employment. So long as this society passively (sometimes actively) condones such disparities and caste-like conditions, and pursues no alternatives, the quality of life and the inherent satisfaction of participating in American society will steadily decrease. If the final accommodation is to the reformulization of a "separate and unequal" status, regardless of public pronouncements to the contrary, everyone (Black and white) will experience a loss of personal discretion as well as an increase in overt mechanisms of social control.

I should like to think we are capable of deciding otherwise. School integration is not the "cure-all" or "quick and dirty" solution to the ills of this society. But so long as it is pursued, it represents a vision and goal for this society which is infinitely better than retreating to the racism of *Plessy* v. *Ferguson.* The tragedy is that it is increasingly difficult to convince people of the correctness of this view when efforts are made to translate the sentiments into action.

"We shall overcome." The question remains, what happens if we do not?

School Integration: Issues of Methodology

Whether Americans are committed to the goal of racial togetherness is open to question. But there is no doubt that if it is to be achieved, the schools and the processes operant within them will be one key institutional setting central to its success. Given my personal preference for the desirability of integrated education in this society, the following are offered as possible mechanisms to create viable and humane integrated settings for children. And given that education, least of all integrated education, does not occur in a social and political vacuum, what follows is an effort to address the need for an "inside-outside" approach. In short, while there are efforts needed within the school, there are also a variety of activities necessary in the community if integration is ever to move beyond that generated by the rolling of the buses. What follow first are comments on what I perceive as a key internal strategy of the school and·second on the relation of housing and education, a crucial link in the long-term prognosis for school integration.

Service/Status Equalization Strategies

In the writings on implementing school integration, it has become a part of the conventional wisdom that remedial services are a necessary component to any viable program. Academicians (Pettigrew 1974; Mercer 1973; Willie and Reker 1973; St. John 1975), practitioners (Smith et al. 1973; Foster 1973), and various branches of the federal government, including the U.S. Commission on Civil Rights, the Congress, and the Department of Health, Education, and Welfare, have all noted the importance of providing remedial services. The most general rationale for such services is that in bringing minority students into classes with white students, the minority students will need additional assistance in order to compensate for the past inadequacies of the segregated schooling process. Further, if such services are not provided, the minority students will almost inevitably find themselves lumped at the bottom of their class in terms of academic achievement, and, with few if any resources to change their position, they will simply remain there. This resultant situation is seen as negative for a variety of reasons.

If the issue is really that, in desegregating schools, many minority students come into the new situation hindered in their ability to successfully compete with white students in a context that accentuates white norms, then programs that only sporadically and marginally attack this issue are inadequate to the task. To assume that one can remedy past educational neglect through 20 or 30 minutes a day of "peer tutoring" or "team teaching" is tenuous at best. What makes the whole discussion of remedial services so important is that there is a significant body of research literature that suggests that minority students will face severe obstacles to achieving more than the most minimal acceptance by white students so long as their achievement levels remain far behind (see Katz 1964; McPartland 1968; St. John 1972). And further, this lack of acceptance and sense of rejection that minority students frequently experience loops back to further inhibit their academic performance—a classic example of the vicious cycle. And to carry this still further, it becomes difficult to argue for the benefits of desegregation to the Black students if their acceptance and popularity is at least in part dependent upon their academic achievement and if no serious or comprehensive efforts are made to substantially alter their achievement patterns so that they can come to compete on a par with new classmates. What benefits then can possibly accrue from being left down and out? As Cohen (1975) has noted in this regard:

> If it is indeed the case that popularity is simply a by-product of achievement in many majority white classrooms, [Black students who] cannot compete for grades will not be benefited by desegregation. Even more important, if the underlying reason for this correlation is the fact that majority white classrooms are achievement-oriented while some majority black classrooms are not because

they have too many students who have no hope of success on a traditional middle-class curriculum, then, one can just as easily reason that changing the curriculum in these all black classrooms so as to encourage success and achievement norms will produce improved achievement as one can argue for desegregation to produce equality of educational output.

Though it is an open question if, in all-minority schools, there are reasonable opportunities for "achievement norms" operationalized, the issue here is how to integrate classrooms where both white and minority students can flourish and develop. What appears necessary is to develop means of making it so. And such an approach does not hinge its validity on whether one can scientifically "prove" the benefits of integration as opposed to segregation. Indeed, if the moral, political, and ethical commitment is made to creating multiracial educational settings for children, the task is to make those settings as humane, lively, and supportive as possible. It is in this context that a new and much expanded notion of school "service" is warranted.

The belief I have seen operant in majority-white schools that a bit of remedial tutoring and perhaps a few pictures of Black people on the classroom walls will be sufficient to overcome both the unequal academic skills many Black children bring to the school and the subsequent unequal status that lack of skill affords them is naive at best and malicious at worst (Rist 1974). What must be addressed, instead, are the interrelations of racial, social, and academic status. It is my view that all three are inextricably interwoven in the context of an integrated school and its classrooms. Thus any attempt to deal with one as though it were in isolation from the others is thwarted by the realities of its interdependence. It was this refusal I observed firsthand in a formerly all-white school integrated with the voluntary transfer of 25 Black children. The failure of the teachers and principals to recognize the centrality of this triad of racial, social, and academic status both created and perpetuated a situation in which the Black children were all situated in the lowest reading groups in their respective rooms. They concomitantly experienced low acceptance and frequent rejection from their peers. At this particular elementary school it was as though there had been a collective and implicit agreement that race did not exist, and the social status ramifications of an intensely competitive academic setting were nil.

In trying to posit methods of modifying and transforming school practices so as to minimize as much as possible the distresses and hazards of school integration, little assistance is forthcoming from the research literature. While there are measures upon measures of self-esteem, myriad reports of academic achievement, and while scale

116

after scale assesses racial tolerance, there is little to tell us how to increase any of them. Yet we are not completely without guideposts. It is my estimation that the most promising avenues of investigation are those that are associated with and intersect the following topics: teacher expectations, production of equal status behavior in students, and classroom instructional processes. Consider, for example, the following comments by Cohen (1975). I consider them reflective of one significant line of research that appears to recognize the independence of the various processes at work in an integrated setting.

> Continuing theoretical and laboratory work had made us realize that bringing together groups of children separated by a wide social gulf in a school setting where there is competition of scarce rewards and where there are typically large achievement differentials on conventional academic skills, makes the problem of producing "equal status experience" just about *twice* as difficult. In the first place, even if the children were all of the same race but entered schools with differential skills and aptitude for the conventional curriculum, a status order based on classroom achievement would emerge which would be just as effective in triggering self-fulfilling prophecies as race. In other words, the achievement status which emerges in competitively structured classrooms is capable of infecting new situations so that those who have low achievement status will expect to do less well on any new task when combined with those students who have a higher achievement status in the classroom. . . . In addition, from another laboratory study, we had grounds for believing that competition aggravates the effect of diffuse status characteristics such as age or race. . . . We now realize there are still several other factors which make the desegregated school a very difficult place in which to produce equal status interaction. Of prime importance is the narrowness of the conventional curriculum. . . . This means that if students enter the desegregated situation with a lower level of skills they are fated to be perceived as having little academic ability in almost every class they attend—there is no escape from this fate. This will occur even if there is no tracking or ability grouping. . . . Still another factor may have been of vital importance: success of the cooperative treatment in the field experiment has led to the hypothesis that a key factor may well have been the presence of interracial classroom teams of teachers and a school administrative structure which was carefully balanced between black and white throughout its ranks (starting with black and white co-directors). Not only were the students shown a rare organization where power and authority were shared between blacks and whites, but classroom teams modeled "equal status behavior" every day of the summer school.

Building on these past seven years of research, Cohen and her associates now plan "to experiment with a non-competitive small group curriculum featuring multiple human abilities, combined with a strictly non-competitive, but individualized program in the basic skills area. We would hypothesize that if the academic and racial status problems are effectively treated, we should not only see equal status behavior, but improvement in black achievement."

I have quoted from Cohen at some length to demonstrate the multifaceted approach that I believe so necessary if prevailing patterns of academic and status inequalities are to be confronted. Attempts with paper and pencil tests or sporadic interventions to fundamentally alter the dynamics of the classroom situation are illusory. Instead, there is an urgent need for a variety of well-planned and well-executed experiments into ways of dealing with classroom heterogeneity so as to neither demean the minority student nor create antagonisms and stereotypes for the majority student. St. John (1975) writes of the need for new patterns of "social engineering" in integrated classrooms. She is correct. The participants in such settings are in need of new processes for relating to one another. In their absence, present situations will perpetuate themselves.

Integration: A Metropolitan or Neighborhood Solution?

Though it would have been more accurate in the quote from the Kerner Commission noted earlier to say that the United States already does exist as two separate societies, there is, nonetheless, a profound implication for any discussion of school integration —namely, to integrate schools in American society necessitates the crossing of boundaries between distinctive social (caste?) groups in the system. And perhaps the most visible indication of such boundaries is the overwhelming racial segregation in housing patterns. The cities of this society have been transformed within a period of three decades from a situation of being almost exclusively white to one where now seven of the 10 largest have Black populations of at least 30 percent. And in the suburban rings around the central cities, the population remains overwhelmingly white. By 1970, six-tenths of all Black people were central city residents, while only 5 percent were living in suburbs.

It is only belaboring the obvious to say that cities like Racine, Wisconsin; Portland, Oregon; or Des Moines, Iowa, with a Black population of 5 or 6 percent face quite different issues in discussing school desegregation than do, for example, cities like Washington, D.C. or

Detroit, Michigan where the Black populations are above 70 percent. Yet all have something in common—residential segregation. If one opted for neighborhood schools in these cities, white children would overwhelmingly go to school only with other whites and Black children would attend only with other Blacks. Des Moines, Portland, or Racine could successfully desegregate their schools within the boundaries of the city, but such could not be possible in cities like Newark, Washington, Detroit, New Orleans Parish, or Saint Louis. All have more than a 65 percent Black enrollment. Here the only apparent solution to the racial separation is metropolitan consolidation. And it is here that the Supreme Count said "no" with its Detroit *Milliken* v. *Bradley* decision in 1974.

By refusing to decide in favor of litigation directing the metropolitan approach to the desegregation of the Detroit public schools, the Court reaffirmed its stance of supporting desegregation only so far as it could be accomplished within school districts. It was faced with one of two alternatives—to support the constitutional right of children to an education not encumbered by segregationist practices or to support the widely acknowledged right within a federal system of local communities to manage their own affairs. In the end, the Court opted for local autonomy by saying, "No single tradition in public education is more deeply rooted than local autonomy over the operation of schools; local autonomy has long been thought essential both to the maintenance of community concern and support for public schools and to the quality of the educational process" (*Milliken* v. *Bradley*, S.Ct. 73-434, 1974).

In the aftermath of this decision, some attention has been paid to the seeming loophole for future metropolitian remedies found in the comments of Justice Stewart. Being the "swing" justice, voting in this instance with four Nixon appointments to the Court, does give import to his comments. He noted in his remarks, "This is not to say, however, that an inter-district remedy of the sort approved by the Court of Appeals would not be proper, or even necessary, in other factual situations. Were it to be shown, for example, that state officials had contributed to the separation of the races by drawing or redrawing school district lines . . . ; purposeful, racially discriminatory use of state housing or zoning laws, then a decree calling for transfer of pupils across district line or for restructuring of district line might well be appropriate."

In the instance of Detroit, the justice indicated he found no such evidence suggesting that school officials either in or outside Detroit were involved in any of the activities listed above. Rather, the justice invoked his own notion of the dynamics of urban growth as an explanation for the separation of the races between city and suburbs. "It is this essential fact of a predominantly Negro school population in Detroit—caused by unknown and perhaps unknowable factors such as in-migration, birth rates, economic changes, or cumulative acts of private racial fears—that accounts for the 'growing core of Negro schools,' a 'core' that has grown to include virtually the entire city."

The implication in these remarks appears to be that if the justice could be shown that the causes of racial separation were not "unknown and perhaps unknowable," he would be willing to switch his vote and move to favoring metropolitan solutions. Yet the question remains as to what level of inference and proof the justice would require, for though much in human societies may be "unknown and perhaps unknowable," it is surely the case that "the tight, unremitting containment of urban blacks over the past half-century within the bowels of American cities is not one of them" (Pettigrew 1974).

If there is one area in the study of American race relations where extensive research has led to the fruitful understanding of social processes, it is in the area of housing segregation. In fact, it is now so well understood that there have been developed mathematical models that can explain and predict with high degrees of accuracy the trends and outcomes resulting from current patterns (Hermalin and Farley 1973; Farley and Taeuber 1974; Farley 1975; Pettigrew 1975). It remains uncertain, however, to what degree the justice would base a reversal in his position on social science data alone. He appears to have constructed a personal "social theory" of urban race relations based on a belief that the key factors are "unknown and perhaps unknowable." In this context, one "theory" becomes as good as another in trying to explain what is occurring in the cities of America.

Is there an alternative to simply waiting for Justice Stewart to change his mind? I believe there is, and I believe it is applicable not only to cities like Detroit, Washington, or Saint Louis, where there are large Black central city populations, but to other cities like Minneapolis, Portland, Los Angeles, Harrisburg, and Charlotte, where the Black population is considerably smaller. What appears both feasible and desirable is to develop a concerted effort to residentially desegregate our metropolitian areas. To encourage the desegregation of the suburbs in particular is to encourage housing to share with schools the task and responsibility of reversing present trends and moving toward new goals in our society.

The following things make this alternative attractive: (1) Economic factors no longer adequately account for the concentration of Black people in the central city and their absence in the suburbs, (2) with metropolitan desegregation there would be an increase in integrated neighborhood schools, and (3) the burden of integrating our society does not fall exclusively on the schools. Each of these factors bears brief mention.

A conventional wisdom sometimes used to explain why Black people are under-represented in suburban communities suggests that they have been unable to afford the housing found there. It has not been racism or blatant discrimination that has kept them out, but economic factors. Though there may well be some historical validity to this claim, it no longer holds true. Hermalin and Farley (1973) found that on the basis of data collected from the 1970 census, economic factors can no longer account for the disproportional concentration of Blacks in the central city. Pettigrew (1974, p. 14) has worked from the same data and tabulated the following: "In metropolitan Chicago, 54 percent of the whites live in the suburbs compared with only 8 percent of the Blacks though 46 percent of the area's Blacks would be expected to do so on economic grounds alone; in metropolitan Detroit, the comparable figures are 73 percent, 12 percent and 67 percent; in metropolitan Washington, D.C., 91 percent, 20 percent and 90 percent; in metropolitan Minneapolis, 58 percent, 7 percent and 49 percent; and in metropolitan Baltimore, 58 percent, 5 percent and 51 percent."

These data indicate a substantial potential market of Black people for suburban housing. Tying to this the results from various opinion polls, which indicate that a majority of whites now favor integrated neighborhoods and favor sending their own children to integrated schools so long as busing is not involved, suggests that residential integration can create a situation where there would emerge schools both integrated and neighborhood based. But it must be emphasized that what is entailed are all suburban communities, not simply those on the fringe of the Black central city, such as East Cleveland, Ohio, or University City, Missouri. As St. John (1975, p. 131) has noted, "The type of neighborhood that would contribute to the achievement of integrated schools and society would not be the familiar, racially changing, lower class neighborhoods on the edge of the black ghetto . . . the benefits of desegregation have rarely been realized in such neighborhoods. Not a single sector but the whole suburban ring—stable working-class and middle-class areas alike—would have to be opened to racially mixed housing."

A second benefit seen deriving from residential integration would be the growth in number of integrated neighborhood schools—an emphasis on "neighborhood." This is suggested, though I remain somewhat skeptical of the importance of "neighborhood" schools for at least two reasons—that millions of students each day travel long

121

distances to schools, distances beyond any conceivable definition of neighborhood, with no demonstrable negative effects on either them or the endeavors of schooling, and second, that with one of every four families moving each year, the notion of "neighborhood" as a long-term place where one puts down roots and establishes "community" seems spurious in the present context of our society.

But even with these reservations, there is much that appears beneficial in having integrated schools which have been created voluntarily and naturally as the consequences of residential integration. The desire to have educational institutions that one believes are responsive and of a scale that one does not feel lost in a mass may only be possible in schools derived from residentially integrated neighborhoods. For the alternative, in their absence, is the aggregation and centralization of school systems so as to be able to effect school integration through large-scale transportation programs that negate any notion of neighborhood or neighborhood schooling.

Residential integration minimizes the need for court orders which seek to overcome residential segregation in order to create integrated schools. It appears that a decision in the white suburbs will soon have to be made—either open up housing to Black and other minority people and thus keep neighborhood schools, or else keep the housing market closed and confront court orders for the rolling of the buses. For many years, the suburbs have been able to have the best of both. How much longer they will be able to maintain this situation is a matter for speculation, but that it will last indefinitely is a tenuous assumption at best. Again, the more neighborhoods do integrate, the greater the likelihood that neighborhood schools can flourish.

Finally, there is the issue of how seriously this society wishes to create and sustain integrated milieus for children. To date, the responsibility has fallen almost exclusively on the schools, with all the limitations that this implies for the variety and duration of such settings. By moving to create integrated residential areas, the number of situations, both formal and informal, in which such interaction could occur would be greatly expanded. To inhibit and thwart interracial interaction through the perpetuation of residential segregation means that the school becomes, for many children, the sole source of such cross-racial contact. And unless we want another generation of children to grow up into the violent and fearful atmosphere of a Boston, or experience the smug racism of white superiority, we need to change our ways. It is not a state of pure unity and brotherhood that we must seriously try to create by integrating our society, but rather a degree of social cohesion that allows for Blacks and whites to work together, to listen to one another, and to come to trust one another. To do so would be no mean achievement.

Note

The views expressed here are solely those of the author and no support or endorsement by the National Institute of Education or the Department of Health, Education, and Welfare is intended or should be inferred.

References

Cohen, E. "The Effects of Desegregation on Race Relations: Facts or Hypothesis." *Law and Contemporary Problems,* vol. 39 (1975).

Farley, R. "Racial Integration in the Public Schools, 1967–1972: Assessing the Effect of Governmental Policy." *Sociological Focus* 8, no. 1 (1975): 3–26.

Farley, R., and Taeuber, A. "Racial Segregation in the Public Schools." *American Journal of Sociology,* vol. 79 (1974).

Foster, G. "Desegregating Urban Schools: Review of Techniques." *Harvard Educational Review,* vol. 43 (1973).

Hermalin, A. I., and Farley, R. "The Potential for Residential Integration in Cities and Suburbs: Implications for the Busing Controversy." *American Sociological Review,* vol. 38 (1973).

Katz, I. "Review of Evidence Relating to Effects of Desegregation on the Intellectual Performance of Negroes." *American Psychologist,* vol. 19 (1964).

McPartland, J. *The Segregated Student in Desegregated Schools: Sources of Influence on Negro Secondary Students.* Baltimore: Center for the Study of Social Organizations of Schools, Johns Hopkins University, 1968.

Mercer, J. "Racial/Ethnic Segregation and Desegregation in American Public Education." University of California at Riverside, Program Research in Integrated Multi-Ethnic Education, 1973.

National Advisory Commission on Civil Disorders. *Report of the National Advisory Commission on Civil Disorders.* Washington, D.C.: Government Printing Office, 1968.

Pettigrew, T. "A Sociological View of the Post Milliken Era." Paper presented to the U.S. Commission on Civil Rights in Hearings, Washington, D.C., 1974.

Pettigrew, T., ed. *Racial Discrimination in the United States.* New York: Harper & Row, 1975.

Rist, R. C. "Student Social Class and Teacher Expectations: The Self-fulfilling Prophecy in Ghetto Education." *Harvard Educational Review,* vol. 40 (1970).

Rist, R. C. *The Urban School: A Factory for Failure.* Cambridge, Mass.: M.I.T. Press, 1973.

Rist, R. C. "Race, Policy and Schooling." *Trans-Action/Society,* vol. 12 (1974).

St. John, N. H. "Social Psychological Aspects of School Desegregation." In *Rethinking Urban Education,* edited by H. Walberg and A. Kopan. San Francisco: Jossey-Bass, Inc., 1972.

St. John, N. H. *School Desegregation: Outcomes for Children.* New York: Wiley-Interscience, 1975.

Smith, A.; Downs, A.; and Lachman, M. L. *Achieving Effective Desegregation.* Lexington, Mass.: Lexington Books, 1973.

Willie, C. V., and Reker, J. *Race Mixing in the Public Schools.* New York: Praeger Publishers, 1973.

Desegregating Urban Areas: Is It Worth It? Can It Be Done?

CHARLES S. BULLOCK III
University of Houston

Since the 1950s, school desegregation has been a matter of concern to more than the South, though it seemed to many, in 1954, that it was largely a southern problem: the law in the North did not require racial isolation. In fact, by 1970 the schools of the South were less segregated than were those of the North. The better overall record of the South is, however, due largely to the great progress in rural districts. Urban districts in the South, while certainly less segregated today than in the past, often continue to have high levels of racial isolation. Consequently, greater differences in amounts of school segregation are now found between urban and rural districts than between South and North. Southern rural systems have carried out pairing and zoning so as to achieve almost perfect racial balance within their schools.[1] Urban districts generally have great disparities; often within a city some schools are almost all white, some almost all Black, and others with various ratios in between.

The Question

Whether something approaching the degree of desegregation that has been achieved in the rural South is to be required in metropolitan areas nationwide remains questionable. Resolution of this question depends on a number of factors. A first item is the ability of the government to gain compliance with policy decisions requiring desegregation. If citizens will not obey court orders or administrative decisions requiring massive desegregation, then further consideration is pointless. The experiences in the South, however, suggest that a firm federal commitment to desegregation can succeed. Despite defiant

125

threats, prolonged protestations, and predictions of dire consequences, communities throughout the South retreated from generations of segregation, once it became clear that dual schools were not a viable alternative. The sanctions necessary to breach the bulwark of white supremacy varied among communities. Districts which most adamantly refused to change could generally be brought into line by court orders threatening to impound the state education funds which comprised a large component of their budgets (Bullock and Rodgers 1975*a*). Except for a handful of overwhelmingly Black districts in which the few whites fled to private, segregated academies, desegregation has been accepted in the South. Frederick Wirt, commenting on the relative lack of violence which accompanied initial desegregation, observed that, "measured against the Everest of diatribe predicting an avalanche if law sought to change this way of life, the resulting violence was only a sand dune" (Wirt 1970, p. 304).

A second consideration is whether the benefits derived from school desegregation justify the effort.[2] Although all the evidence is not yet in, an affirmative answer seems warranted. In addressing this topic, four dimensions are relevant: academic achievement, racial attitudes, life opportunities, and preparation for functioning in a desegregated society. Despite unevenness in the method used, in the environmental conditions, and in the measures applied, there is little evidence that desegregation is academically deleterious to either race. A general conclusion seems to be that desegregation, at worst, has no independent effect on achievement and, at best, helps Blacks.

Even, however, if it cannot be shown that desegregation makes a statistically independent contribution to achievement, factors associated with desegregation may be linked to academic performance. For example, the socioeconomic status of a student's peers has been found to be associated with achievement. In most American communities, middle- and upper-class Blacks are relatively few, meaning that if the benefits which accompany exposure to higher socioeconomic peers are to be reaped by poor Blacks, racial desegregation will be necessary.

In addition to bringing about contact across racial and socioeconomic lines, desegregation has often resulted in Blacks being

---

CHARLES S. BULLOCK III is professor of political science at the University of Houston. He is coauthor of *Law and Social Change: Civil Rights Laws and Their Consequences* (1972) and *Racial Equality in America: In Search of an Unfulfilled Goal* (1975), and coeditor of *The New Politics* (1970) and *Black Political Attitudes* (1972).

educated in better facilities and by better-trained teachers. Desegregation has given Blacks access to the same facilities, curricula, and teachers as whites have. Moreover, some districts have taken advantage of the fluid situation produced by the turmoil of desegregation to adopt new instructional techniques, upgrade conditions and procedures, and expand or reassign staff.

Some Georgia educators see in the aftermath of desegregation improvements in the quality of education offered the poor of both races. They explain that the success in achieving desegregation has given some Black parents a relatively high sense of political efficacy. Blacks are increasingly bringing grievances before the boards of education and demanding that the educational needs of their children be met. As one educator candidly acknowledged:

> There were always problems, but we did not face up to them. Now, because we've got Blacks and whites in the same classrooms, we have to look at the fundamental issue of how to deal with wide ranges of ability. In the past, when we had white schools, the people who were really running the schools—who attended PTA meetings, who were on the board of education, and who were the friends of the principal—were those whose children had the kind of IQ that the schools meant success for. White students who did not achieve were from uninfluential families. We thought we were meeting the needs of the children because those who did poorly and their parents didn't have enough clout to do anything about it. Because of the race issue we have people in the schools who, even though they might not have money and they might have low achievement levels, are not willing to be quiet and are forcing themselves to be heard. This forces the school people to reassess their approach to the whole problem of how to deal with a wide range of people in the classroom.[3]

As with studies of the consequences of desegregation for achievement, the evidence on the impact of desegregation on racial attitudes is mixed. St. John (1975, pp. 64–81) reports that studies showing attitudinal improvements and declines are about evenly divided for both races. Scholars have not blithely assumed that all forms of interracial contact reduce tensions. Instead they have postulated that, if desegregation is to lead to improved racial attitudes, the races should be of equal social status, not be in competition with one another, be mutually interdependent, and the contact should be supported by the authorities (Allport 1954; Pettigrew 1971). Frequently one or more of these conditions is absent in desegregated schools; therefore, it is not surprising that some research has found interracial contact to be associated with greater prejudice.

On the positive side, one longitudinal study reports that, although only 8 percent of the white sample wanted to desegregate, a year after dual schools were eliminated 27 percent of the whites believed desegregation was beneficial although only 3 percent saw it as improving the quality of education (Bullock and Braxton 1973). Most of the benefits perceived by whites resulted from a better understanding of Blacks. A second study which involved almost 900 newly desegregated southern districts reported that 41 percent of the students believed that there were improvements produced by going to school with members of the other race (United States Senate 1972, p. 229).

A third dimension for evaluating school desegregation is the potential effect on lifetime economic opportunities. Although little research has been conducted on this proposition, tentative conclusions are that Blacks who were educated with whites do obtain better jobs as adults. Robert Crain (1970) explains this finding by noting that many job leads are obtained from one's friends; whites generally have better jobs than Blacks; and Blacks who were in school with whites have more white friends than do other Blacks.

The last criterion for appraising the consequences of school desegregation is whether it better prepares a person to function in the world he or she is likely to inhabit as an adult. While advances toward a nonracist society have not come as rapidly as one might wish, clearly we have left the Jim Crow past. Our society now has both races represented among salespeople, secretaries, mechanics, etc. Chances are that most of today's youth will work in desegregated environments. Moreover, there are some slight increases in the racial heterogeneity of residential developments (Sørensen, Taeuber, and Hollingsworth 1974). Evidence indicates that the earlier one comes into close contact with dissimilar groups, the less the hostility and the greater the ease with which subsequent interaction occurs (St. John 1975, p. 81). Also Blacks who attended desegregated schools are more likely to prefer biracial environments as adults (United States Commission on Civil Rights 1967, pp. 111–13). Therefore, to mitigate racial tensions for future generations, biracial contact should be provided for today's youth at as early an age as possible.

Problems in Urban Desegregation

The foregoing suggests that school desegregation has frequently positive and rarely negative consequences. It would seem to follow, therefore, that its benefits should be spread throughout urban areas which remain segregated. Many people, however, both Black and white, have concluded that the costs accompanying dismantlement of dual schools in urban centers outweigh the benefits. There are obvious logistical problems in producing racial balance in an urban system with largely homogeneous racial residential developments served by neighborhood schools. Some parents of both races object to plans which transfer young children to schools in other sections of the city.

A second problem emerges in big-city systems which are becoming predominantly Black in enrollment. In 1972, Black enrollments were 96 percent in Washington, D.C., 77 percent in Atlanta, and more than 50 percent in 15 of the other 100 largest systems. In a growing number of cities there are too few whites to create biracial learning environments throughout the system. Leaders of the local NAACP chapter in Atlanta recognized this several years ago. They withdrew from a suit sponsored by the national NAACP which sought greater racial balance in the system and negotiated their own bargain with the school board. The scarcity of whites and their concentration on the fringes of the district meant that a racial balance plan that would require extensive busing would probably fail to create stable biracial enrollments. The local NAACP, therefore, worked out an agreement with the board of education providing that a Black would be chosen to replace the white superintendent and that half of the higher administrative positions would go to Blacks.

A third problem in desegregating urban districts is that any major reallocation of pupils may stampede white families into the suburbs. This is particularly likely to occur if whites are to be transferred to inner-city schools or if their children will attend a majority Black school.[4] In metropolitan areas, white suburban schools offer the escape provided by segregationist academies in parts of the rural South. The exodus of middle-class whites will further contribute to urban districts' problems by reducing their tax bases. Moreover, whites who remain in urban districts but send their children to private schools will become less willing to support school bond referenda.

When busing seems the only means to achieve racial balance, some Black leaders prefer to see the money spent on improving ghetto schools. They view money spent on busing as wasted, especially if whites will probably leave the desegregated schools. In sum, then, plans to desegregate urban districts, particularly if they call for much busing, will generally be unpopular and may lead whites to forsake public education, at least for a period long enough to test the possibilities.

Because of the seeming futility in trying to achieve racial balance throughout urban districts with large Black enrollments, a number of desegregation proponents have urged that central city districts and their suburbs be merged. Litigation seeking this end is designed to counter some of the obstacles to urban desegregation. By consolidating white suburban districts with city systems having large minority enrollments, there should be enough white and minority pupils so that there would be sizable enrollments of both groups. Also, by consolidating the schools of a metropolitan area, it is hoped that enrollments will stabilize. It is expected that, once whites recognize that the schools throughout a metropolitan area all have approximately the same ratio of Black to white pupils, they will see no advantage to moving to the suburbs. If whites stayed in the central city, then racial balance could be achieved with less busing and disruption.

The utility of metropolitan suits is questionable. Some Black leaders oppose the concept for political reasons. In cities with large Black populations, Blacks see the potentiality of controlling the schools if they become largely Black. Such an achievement would provide a power base for the ambitious as well as facilitate changes in the cirriculum and operation of the schools to make them more relevant to Black needs and interests. Educators and politicians who see an advantage in Black control of a city school system will fight moves to dilute their influence by expanding the white clientele. Moreover, Black politicians may oppose consolidation of city and suburban schools, fearing that this would create a precedent for metropolitan consolidation of other services, thereby curbing their influence which rests on large concentrations of Black voters.

A second obstacle is that the remedy of a metropolitan suit may not even be viable. The only decision rendered by the Supreme Court in a metropolitan consolidation case held that it was not constitutionally necessary to consolidate 53 school systems in the Detroit area.[5] This decision was probably not the final word on this matter since Justice Stewart, whose vote was decisive in the 5–4 ruling, sketched out conditions under which he believed metropolitan consolidation might be necessary. In a concurring opinion he wrote that, "Were it to be shown, for example, that state officials had contributed to the separation of the races by drawing or redrawing school district lines . . .then a decree calling for transfer of students across district lines or for restructuring of district lines might well be appropriate."[6]

Some lower courts have already distinguished cases from the Supreme Court's ruling. In St. Louis, the federal district court has ordered consolidation of three suburban school districts—one of which was all Black, one 35 percent Black, and the other 3 percent Black.[7] This decision hinged on a showing that (1) the 35 percent Black district and the all-Black district had once been united but were separated in an effort to promote segregation; (2) the two white majority districts had refused consolidation with the Black district for racial reasons; and (3) to maintain segregation, the 35 percent Black system used to send its Black students to the Black system.

In a second case, the Sixth Circuit Court of Appeals ruled that two systems in the Louisville, Kentucky, area must be treated as a single unit for achieving racial balance.[8] In 1972 the central city district was 51 percent Black while the suburban one was 96 percent white. The Circuit Court differentiated the Louisville situation from Detroit's on several grounds: (1) the suburban Kentucky district formerly had a de jure system; (2) a single county with two systems was involved (rather than the 53 systems in three counties in Detroit), therefore desegregation should be easier to achieve; (3) district lines had been breached in Louisville when doing so promoted separation; and (4) Kentucky law facilitates county-wide school district consolidation.

Fuller explanation of whether cross-district desegregation plans are required by the Constitution, and if so the conditions under which they are necessary will come in future Supreme Court decisions.

To anticipate the Supreme Court—often a risky enterprise—it would seem that metropolitan plans would certainly be required under conditions like those in the St. Louis suit where students were once bused across district lines to maintain segregation. In a 1973 case involving Denver schools, the Supreme Court ruled that *within* a system it was necessary to correct racial imbalance if the system, through official action, had ever acted to cause or maintain segregation.[9] The Denver decision, when combined with Stewart's opinion in the Detroit case, suggests that the idea that schools have a duty to achieve racial balance if they contributed to the imbalance extends to situations in which students were bused across district lines to maintain segregation. Stewart's opinion hints that his vote might shift to the side of those believing that metropolitan plans are necessary if the plaintiffs demonstrate that school systems engaged in behavior which they knew, or reasonably should have known, would promote racial separation.

More questionable and certainly more difficult to define will be the distinction based on size made by the Circuit Court in the Louisville case. It is clear that less disruption would be occasioned in achieving racial balance in two systems having a total enrollment of 122,000 than in 53 systems with a total enrollment of more than 300,000. It remains unclear, however, at what point the number of systems or size of enrollment would create so many problems that the difficulties would more than offset the benefits of desegregation.

Adherence to the criterion in the Detroit suit, which states that all districts in a metropolitan suit must be guilty of discrimination before they can be included in a cross-district plan, would, of course, limit the applicability of this approach. In many urban areas, particularly in the South and border states, some suburbs once bused their Black pupils into the central city and therefore would be subject to a multidistrict remedy. It may be impossible, however, to show that areas which have suburbanized recently, say since 1960, have done anything to contribute to the racial imbalance which now exists. Under such conditions, metropolitan plans, like single-district plans, might often be counterproductive. To explain: if only the central city and the older suburban districts were included in a metropolitan plan, then white parents who wanted to avoid desegregation could simply move to a newer suburb which was not included in the suit.

Even situations like that in Louisville, where most of the metropolitan area is encompassed in two districts, may not be fully amenable to a cross-district remedy. Given the antipathy shown by many white parents for extensive transfer programs, it is possible that a sizable number of them would move to districts not covered by a metropolitan desegregation plan. Other whites who did not move might enroll their children in private schools, thereby thwarting the intent of the plan. Both relocation and transfer to private schools would reduce the number of white students, contributing to the fears of the remaining whites and inducing more of them to remove their children from the desegregation program.[10]

For example, in the Atlanta area, whites are leaving some of the closer-in suburbs in the face of Black in-migration, forsaking what are generally considered to be some of the best schools in the state. New developments are springing up in counties which are one step removed from the city and are outside the area covered in the metropolitan desegregation suit pending in federal district court.

This sort of behavior suggests that the approach which succeeded in the rural South may fail in urban areas. Forcing districts to implement racial balance plans succeeded in rural areas partially because families could not physically leave the community. Farmers could not sell their land and buy elsewhere, nor could merchants and professionals easily relocate to a new community. Roots often generations deep combined with financial considerations to keep whites from leaving their homes.

Another consideration—and one which may be subject to some debate—is that rural whites may have been, on the whole, less fearful of the consequences of desegregation. The fact that relatively few whites left the public schools even in most districts served by private, white academies suggests that whites were less fearful of desegregation than they have been in many urban areas, North and South.[11]

Rural whites in districts not overwhelmingly Black may have been willing to accept even majority Black schools because they could anticipate a stable racial composition in the future. Unlike urban whites who may fear that a plan to achieve racial balance is but a prelude to an almost all-Black school or school system, rural whites know the ratio of Blacks to whites in the district. Moreover, rural whites know that unless whites forsake public education en masse these ratios will not shift significantly. Consequently, in a number of the rural Georgia districts, many leading citizens remained committed to public education and used their influence to dampen private school movements.

Alternatives

Because of district size, white fears, and the ability of whites to move from desegregating schools, it appears unlikely that techniques which succeeded in desegregating the rural South will enjoy the same degree of success in urban areas. While threats to impound education funds or, alternatively, inducements of additional federal aid may succeed in urban districts having a small minority enrollment and covering a relatively small geographic area, extension of the coercive approach seems inauspicious for larger districts with greater minority concentrations. Programs requiring more than token busing appear to be increasingly unpopular among both races and have triggered violent reactions in several cities and precipitous declines in white enrollments in many others. Elaborate plans to produce racial balance may succeed only in the short run, leaving increasingly minority systems as whites escape the geographic confines of the plan. Consequently, if widespread school desegregation is to be more than a transitional phenomenon in urban areas, new techniques must be tried.

So far the burden of promoting school desegregation has been laid exclusively on the school system. Although appropriate and necessary that schools not discriminate, acting alone they cannot rid society of the racism which makes school desegregation unacceptable to many. Focusing exclusively on schools' responsibilities produces a situation in which they are asked to create biracial islands in a sea of racial polarization. Some schools have complained that their struggle to desegregate is impeded by policies of other federal agencies which facilitate segregation.[12]

I would like to offer several proposals for using federal aid as an inducement to promote desegregation. Most of these offer incentives to communities to diversify the economic range of housing available.

Policies which permit low-income families to move to suburbia will promote school desegregation since such programs will increase the housing options of a larger share of Blacks than whites. The last proposal will suggest an incentive for district consolidation. All these suggestions have the advantage over busing of being voluntary. Districts which do take steps to promote desegregation will be rewarded; others can remain segregated, but they pay a price for doing so. Another common feature shared by these proposals is that they are designed to desegregate metropolitan areas rather than being limited to individual districts.

Housing and Urban Development

An important change which would expedite school desegregation would be to design federal housing programs to promote biracial residential developments. To date, federal housing programs have done little to foster biracial living on anything more than a token basis. For example, open-housing legislation helps Blacks move to white neighborhoods, but it does nothing to increase the supply of moderately priced homes. Thus, open-housing laws enable middle-income Blacks to move to middle-income white neighborhoods; they do not help poor Blacks who are left behind in the ghetto.

There are two aspects of federal policy which may facilitate residential desegregation. One, which seems not to have become fully operational is the requirement that before a federal agency constructs or acquires new quarters there must be a study to determine the availability of inexpensive existing housing in the vicinity and its accessibility to minorities. If deficiencies are found, the community in which the proposed facility would be located must agree on a plan of corrective action. There is little evidence of the effectiveness of these plans or of federal enforcement of the agreements made. Of course, even if this program succeeds, it will affect only a small proportion of the suburban housing market.

A recent innovation in federal housing efforts has been to grant cash subsidies to the poor for housing. Operating currently on an experimental basis, this program enlarges the range of housing within the financial capabilities of the poor. The degree to which this advances residential desegregation, however, is unclear.

Subsidies, while permitting some greater latitude in housing selection, will do nothing to facilitate lower-income penetration of the more expensive suburbs. What is needed is dispersal of less expensive housing so that more minorities can live in the more affluent school districts. Dispersal might be achieved by making *receipt of funds under the Better Communities Act of 1974 (the umbrella legislation for large sums distributed by the Department of Housing and Urban Development for housing, water and sewer mains, planning, and other urban programs) contingent upon the recipient community's agreement to zone a certain amount of land for low-cost housing.* This inexpensive housing could take the form of cluster housing, public housing, or units privately constructed under federal subsidy. The housing could be apartments, townhouses, or single-family residences. To promote an equitable distribution of less expensive housing in a metropolitan area, standards could be set specifying the number of units for which a community must zone to be eligible for federal funds. The number of inexpensive units might be determined by the total number of residential units in the community and the number of inexpensive residences extant. Each town, city, or county in an urban area would be expected to have approximately the same proportion of inexpensive housing units. Such standards would mean that communities which already have large low-income populations would immediately qualify for federal aid. Suburban areas developed with middle- and upper-income housing would have to prepare to accept some less expensive units or forgo federal money. Since the proportion of inexpensive homes needed to qualify for federal aid would be small (because the goal would be to distribute low-income housing proportionally throughout a metropolitan area), communities could accept their quotas without fear of being inundated and having the character of the community altered.

This program could be administered so that, as new suburbs develop, they would have to accept their proportionate share of low-income housing units in order to qualify for federal funds. Thus whites could not escape to all-white communities by moving farther out, except by paying the price of doing without federal aid. This would overcome the weakness of metropolitan school plans in which whites can avoid desegregation by moving to newly developed areas beyond the confines of the plan.

Dispersal of economic and racial groups throughout a metropolitan area would greatly reduce the need for busing. While neighborhood school zones might have some imbalance, particularly in the elementary grades, a small amount of busing for short distances should be able to correct it.

There are, of course, some suburbs which are so affluent that they would opt to forfeit federal funds rather than accept a more heterogeneous population. This they could do but at a cost to their taxpayers.

Zoning requirements would be inappropriate for communities

135

which are fully developed. These areas would be exempted, although should redevelopment programs be undertaken within them, the re-developers' plans would have to make provisions for low-income housing or federal aid would be lost. Some fully developed suburbs will, of course, acquire minority residents in time through processes of natural change. The fully developed suburbs are often older and closer to the central city. These factors may result in their houses and apartments costing less, and they would therefore be in the price range of a larger share of the Black population than would newer units built farther out.

Transportation

Residential development, as well as the placement of commercial and industrial facilities, is largely determined by the transportation net-work. The development of metropolitan areas depends heavily on the location of major thoroughfares. Thus farmland produces a crop of houses or apartments once it is made accessible to places of work by the opening of new roads or improving existing ones. Industrial parks and office complexes spread out from the urban core, drawing sustenance from limited access highways. These facilities, by decen-tralizing employment opportunities, permit workers to live farther from the central city but within a reasonable commute to work.

As is readily apparent, an important ingredient in the far-flung highway network which facilitates urban sprawl is the interstate high-way system. The federal government pays up to 90.5 percent of the cost of these ribbons of concrete and asphalt. It also contributes 50 percent of the expenses for many other primary highways which are increasingly being widened to accommodate more traffic in urban areas. More recently, extensive federal aid had been pledged to de-velop urban rapid transit. In short, the federal government has played and will continue to play a sizable role in expediting urban decentral-ization. In the absence of federal transportation programs, the costs of roads and rapid transit would fall on state or local governments, and therefore many might go unbuilt. This would make decentralization and white flight less viable options.

Federal highway and rapid transit funds could be made contingent on a plan to disperse economic and racial groups. Standards akin to those I suggested for housing could be formulated. There is a distinc-tion, however, in that housing and urban development grants confer a selective benefit while transportation grants confer something of a collective benefit.[13] To explain, sewers or water mains, urban renewal, or funds for planning benefit almost exclusively the community to which they are given. In contrast, construction of a new thoroughfare or rapid transit line may contribute to the development and expand the tax base not only of communities through which they run but also of adjacent communities. Therefore, it would be neither fair nor sufficient to require pledges only from the communities through which a proposed highway or transit line would pass. Instead, in smaller metropolitan areas it might be necessary for all counties and cities to agree to a regional plan for the distribution of inexpensive housing. In larger metropolitan areas it might suffice to obtain agreement to plans from the communities to be affected, using a zone of specific width on either side of the proposed transportation artery to determine the localities likely to benefit.

In both cases, federal transportation assistance could be held up until agreements were reached to set aside some undeveloped land to house proportionate shares of the area's low-income families. The location of access ramps to federally assisted expressways and of rapid transit stations could also be used to encourage acceptance of low-income residents.

General Revenue Sharing

Distribution of general revenue sharing funds could also be made contingent on the promotion of racial and economic residential heterogeneity. Indeed, since all governments receive some money under this program, requiring cities and counties to take steps to increase housing options for low- and moderate-income families would potentially have more widespread impact than would attaching conditions to urban development and transportation funding.

Education Aid

In addition to proposals for desegregating metropolitan areas, federal aid to education could be structured to encourage cross-district racial balance. Attaching conditions to federal education money is less desirable as a long-term solution than are the previous proposals since it is not related to producing residential desegregation. However, since residential desegregation will take time, manipulation of federal education funds might encourage some districts to consolidate their schools so as to produce additional desegregation.

Indeed, use of federal education funds to promote desegregation might be even more successful now than were the fund cutoffs invoked in the late 1960s in the South.[14] Many southern schools at that time received most of their funding from the states and got relatively few federal dollars. Federal contributions have increased, and non-southern districts rely primarily on locally raised revenue. Consequently, in the North and West, a loss of federal aid would have to be made up—if at all—through higher local school levies. Bleak economic conditions and taxpayer outrage at current assessments suggest that withdrawal of federal funds would create hardships in many districts which could not be ignored.

To further racial balance across district lines, federal aid to education could be made contingent on development of plans to achieve racial balance among neighboring districts having varying racial compositions. In developing guidelines for such a program, consideration would probably be accorded to things such as proximity, transportation networks, racial dispersals, and size. The overriding consideration, however, should be to maximize interracial contact. Therefore, it would be inadequate for a group of white suburbs to band together. Instead, insofar as is possible, white suburbs would have to include districts with large minority enrollments in their plans. Working within the limitations set by geographic and traffic patterns, suburban districts might work out agreements with the central city district to combine with adjacent city schools. Such liaisons would break large central city districts into manageable parts. It might be possible to develop wedge-shaped superdistricts radiating from the center of the city and embracing a number of suburban systems.[15] Within each superdistrict, pairing or educational parks might be used to bring suburban whites into contact with inner-city minority children.

Districts with less than a certain proportion minority enrollment and within a specified distance of districts having larger minority student bodies would have to seek to establish a cross-district educational program to qualify for funding. If their overtures were rejected, they would be eligible for funding. Districts with minority enrollments above a specified level would automatically qualify for aid. They would lose eligibility only if they refused to enter into agreements with nearby districts having small minority enrollments.

To make multidistrict desegregation even more attractive, this could be made a prerequisite for the additional funding offered under the Emergency School Aid Act. Currently a number of urban systems receive ESAA money even though they have not achieved racial balance among their schools. Continuing to restrict ESAA eligibility to districts with minority enrollments above a prescribed level while calling for cross-district programs would, in essence, create a dowry for central city districts, encouraging suburban suitors.

The Need For Leadership

The proposals offered for using federal money to induce suburban communities to accept some low- and moderate-income residents and thereby promote school desegregation would doubtless meet opposition. The proposal to set prerequisites on general revenue sharing and on funding under the Better Communities Act contradicts the concept of these programs which were envisioned as "no strings attached" grants. Certainly each of the suggestions would draw criticism that it led to federal intervention in matters traditionally left to states and localities.

More accurately, the suggestions do not presage new federal involvement, but only new conditions. Literally, for generations, federal money has gone to programs which tacitly, if not overtly, contributed to the racial and economic separatism which now exists. Federal housing programs have operated in such a biased manner that the United States Commission on Civil Rights (1970, p. 469) has concluded that "FHA [Federal Housing Administration] was a major factor in the development of segregated housing patterns that exist today." There is no legal reason why federal programs should not now help correct the conditions they helped spawn.

Since all the proposals made here call for voluntary participation, communities can avoid the requirements; they simply pay a price for doing so. Tying federal funds to steps toward desegregation might create public pressures for corrective actions in communities which do not qualify for funding. At least they should provoke less violence than has erupted in the wake of some major busing efforts.

Nonetheless, only the naive would expect that new conditions will be eagerly imposed for funding, especially when the result would be dilution of residential homogeneity. Changes proposed in this paper to facilitate residential desegregation would be unpopular with many whites. Consequently, their adoption is unlikely in the absence of strong presidential leadership.

Without presidential leadership, bureaucrats, even if they have the authority, are unlikely to incorporate proposals such as those suggested here on funding guidelines. The perspective of program administrators is often that their job is to advance realization of department policy goals—roads built, houses constructed, money distributed—and this often leads federal officials to help grant applicants qualify. Therefore, program administrators may suffer role conflict if called on to apply criteria which impede funding or otherwise hinder advancement of agency programs. Orfield (1969, pp. 48–61), however, reports that in the mid-1960s Office of Education officials, when called on to shift from being mere providers, were able to become enforcers of desegregation laws.

To the extent that changes offered here would require congressional action, this is likely to come about, if at all, only with strong urging from the White House. As the consequences of civil rights legislation have spread northward, a number of congressmen who once supported such laws have bowed to pressures from their constituents. Therefore, it is unlikely that Congress would act to advance civil rights in the absence of aggressive presidential direction.

Julian Bond is quoted as having said that "Black people are no longer chic."[16] Without a widespread feeling among whites that something should be done and a president committed to promoting desegregation, it is unlikely that much progress will come in larger metropolitan areas. Many employees of HEW's Office for Civil Rights acknowledge that the tools currently available under Title VI of the 1964 Civil Rights Act and under the Emergency School Aid Act are insufficient. While some smaller urban areas may be desegregated through more consistent application of the techniques available, short-term change appears to be all that is presently possible in larger areas. Often the progress which is made in reducing racial isolation may erode as whites leave desegregated schools for private institutions or for the suburbs. Only major policy changes which will desegregate schools by desegregating attendance zones hold out hope for countering these trends.

Notes

Preparation of this paper was aided by the experiences gained in conducting research projects funded by National Institute of Education grant number NE-G-00-3-0182 and National Science Foundation grant number GS-38157. Professors Roger Durand and Harrell Rodgers made helpful comments on an earlier draft. Of course, I alone am responsible for the content of the paper.

1. See, e.g., Rodgers and Bullock (forthcoming).
2. For reviews of the relevant literature, see St. John (1975); Bullock and Rodgers (1975c, pp. 115–40); Carithers (1970, pp. 25–47).
3. This off-the-record interview was one of many conducted in the course of research funded by National Science Foundation grant GS-38157.

4. Polls have shown that many more white parents will tolerate some desegregation than will accept a majority Black school (Wirt 1970, p. 236).

5. Milliken v. Bradley (1974).

6. Ibid., p. 3132.

7. United States v. State of Missouri (1975).

8. Newburg Area Council v. Board of Education (1974).

9. Keyes v. School District No. 1 of Denver (1973).

10. District consolidation and busing to achieve desegregation are probably responsible for the drop in enrollment from 145,000 to 122,000 between 1972 and 1975 in the Louisville area.

11. For several years approximately 10 percent of the South's white pupils have been in private schools (Houston *Chronicle,* September 22, 1975, sec. 4, p. 24).

12. The school board of Decatur, Georgia, when ordered to desegregate its last all-Black neighborhood school, complained that "We feel that our problem is caused by the fact that two federal agencies, HEW and Housing and Urban Development (HUD), do not operate under the same interpretation of the Civil Rights Laws and are not responsive in the same way to the Supreme Court's interpretation of those laws. The existence of our school system is being threatened because HUD uses freedom of choice and 'first come, first served' to fill 400 units of federal housing located in the center of Decatur with black families while HEW and the Justice Department contend that white children must come out of these apartments or the schools be charged with discrimination. Beacon Elementary School is surrounded by 400 units of federal housing and it is HUD's present intention to see that 95 percent of these apartments are filled with black people, while HEW and the Justice Department demand that 40–50 percent of the Beacon Elementary children must be white. . . . If HEW *and* HUD were forced by the Justice Department to work toward a common goal, the Decatur schools would have no problem to solve. As matters now stand, HEW is working for integration and HUD is working for segregation" (Exhibit 4 on file with the District Court of the Northern District of Georgia, United States v. Georgia, Civil no. 12972, file III).

13. For a discussion of the differences in selective and collective benefits, see Olson (1968).

14. Weaknesses in the fund cutoff approach to southern segregation are discussed in Bullock and Rodgers (1975*b*).

15. Cf. Pettigrew (1971, pp. 70–80).

16. Quoted in Goldman (1973, p. 29).

References

Allport, Gordon W. *The Nature of Prejudice.* Cambridge, Mass.: Addison-Wesley Publishing Co., 1954.

Bullock, Charles S., III, and Braxton, Mary Victoria. "The Coming of School Desegregation: A Before and After Study of Black and White Student Perceptions." *Social Science Quarterly* 54 (1973): 132–38.

Bullock, Charles S., III, and Rodgers, Harrell R., Jr. "Coercion and Southern School Desegregation: Implications for the North." *School Review* 83 (1975): 645–62. (*a*)

Bullock, Charles S., III, and Rodgers, Harrell R., Jr. "Perceptual Distortion and Policy Implementation: Evaluations of the Effectiveness of School Desegregation Techniques." Paper presented at the annual meeting of the Southwest Political Science Association, Palacio del Rio Hotel, San Antonio, Texas, 1975. (*b*)

Bullock, Charles S., III, and Rodgers, Harrell R., Jr. *Racial Equality in America: In Search of an Unfulfilled Dream.* Pacific Palisades, Calif.: Goodyear Publishing Co., 1975. (*c*)

Carithers, Martha W. "School Desegregation and Racial Cleavage, 1954–1970." *Journal of Social Issues* 26 (1970): 25–47.

Crain, Robert L. "School Integration and Occupational Achievement of Negroes." *American Journal of Sociology* 75 (1970): 593–606.

Goldman, Peter. "Black America Now." *Newsweek* (February 19, 1973).

"Many Southern 'Academies' Are Going Permanent." Houston *Chronicle* (September 22, 1975), sec. 4, p. 24.

Olson, Mancur. *The Logic of Collective Action.* New York: Schocken Books, 1968.

Orfield, Gary. *The Reconstruction of Southern Education.* New York: Wiley-Interscience, 1969.

Pettigrew, Thomas F. *Racially Separate or Together.* New York: McGraw-Hill Book Co., 1971.

Rodgers, Harrell R., Jr., and Bullock, Charles S., III. *Coercion to Compliance: The Role of Law in Effectuating Social Change,* forthcoming.

St. John, Nancy H. *School Desegregation: Outcomes for Children.* New York: Wiley-Interscience, 1975.

Sørensen, Annemette; Taeuber, Karl E.; and Hollingsworth, Leslie J., Jr. *Indexes of Racial Residential Segregation for 109 Cities in the United States, 1940–1970.* Madison, Wis.: Institute for Research on Poverty, 1974.

U.S. Commission on Civil Rights. *Racial Isolation in the Public Schools.* Washington, D.C.: Government Printing Office, 1967.

U.S. Commission on Civil Rights, *Federal Civil Rights Enforcement Effort.* Washington, D.C.: Government Printing Office, 1970.

U.S. Senate. *Toward Equal Educational Opportunity.* Report of the Select Committee on Equal Educational Opportunity. Washington, D.C.: Government Printing Office, 1972.

Wirt, Frederick M. *Politics of Southern Equality.* Chicago: Aldine Publishing Co., 1970.

Open Enrollment and Fiscal Incentives

GEORGE RICHARD MEADOWS
University of Wisconsin—Milwaukee

In the 1960s many large-city school systems adopted policies permitting students to transfer from their neighborhood schools to others they found more desirable, if the second school was not overcrowded. The adoption of these open-enrollment plans was motivated in part by the desire to eliminate racial segregation in the schools resulting from residential segregation and in part to allow students with special educational needs and interests to take advantage of specialized curricula offered only in certain schools.[1] While these programs did accomplish the second goal, they did not much alter patterns of segregation. Apparently, an effort that relies on voluntary integration has little hope of success. In a 1973 survey of desegregation techniques used by urban schools, G. Foster concluded that open enrollment "has never accounted for a significant amount of desegregation" (1973). There has been general skepticism among policymakers about the potential for accomplishing desegregation by voluntary means. Before there was even much evidence to indicate what its impact might be and before any efforts were made to significantly influence voluntary actions, the U.S. Commission on Civil Rights expressed its skepticism in a delineation of six major limitations of such plans (U.S. Commission on Civil Rights 1967).

Yet the policy of open enrollment as a means to desegregate the schools still offers a handsome alternative to mandatory busing, which has stirred such intense controversy and perhaps even increased racial tension; and its potential needs to be explored further. What mainly needs to be explored is whether some incentive program that heightens the attractiveness of a transfer plan can accomplish what has not been accomplished by simply offering the option to transfer. In particular, it seems urgent to examine how selected fiscal incentives for open enrollment might help to achieve greater racial and socioeconomic integration.

143

In the vast literature on desegregation, one often encounters the view that desegregation is not a racial issue—that it is, instead, an issue concerning educationally *advantaged* and *disadvantaged* children. That is, truly integrated schools will contain representative mixtures of students from all ethnic *and* socioeconomic backgrounds and not just meet some predetermined criteria of racial balance alone.[2] While this view of desegregation is much more complex because it demands some generally accepted objective criteria to distinguish between advantaged and disadvantaged students, it seems to me in the long run to be a much more realistic and useful one.

I begin with three premises: that experience with district-wide, unrestricted (color-blind) open-enrollment plans have not generally increased integration in individual schools, although significant proportions of students voluntarily transferred out of neighborhood schools; that, if school integration can be achieved through a voluntary program, this is preferable to a nonvoluntary program which accomplishes the same objectives at a similar cost; and, finally, that the integration of our public schools is a necessary condition for the achievement of an integrated society.

Open Enrollment in Theory and Practice

John McAdams argues in the *Public Interest* (1974) that open enrollment has been successful in several instances and could be made viable in many others. He suggests that two types of open-enrollment plans must be distinguished: color-blind programs, in which transfers are permitted without regard to the racial composition of the sending or receiving school; and non-color-blind programs, in which transfer approval is contingent upon the racial composition of both the sending and receiving schools. In every case in which open enrollment has resulted in significant gains in school integration, the program was not color-blind and had specific desegregation objectives. Conversely, in those communities where open enrollment was administered with-

---

GEORGE RICHARD MEADOWS is assistant professor of economics at the University of Wisconsin—Milwaukee. He is currently completing a detailed econometric analysis of system-wide transfers for the eighth and tenth grades and is constructing a model that can predict rapidly expanding expenditure needs that result from technical and social factors in the Milwaukee public schools.

out specific objectives with respect to improving racial balance, little, if any, progress was made.

Milwaukee, which has had a color-blind program since 1964, provides an example of this plan. Students are allowed to transfer to any underutilized school in the system. Although parents must provide for the child's transportation to the nonneighborhood school and must secure a personal interview with the principals of both the sending and receiving schools, no justification for the transfer is required, nor does the race of the applicant make any difference.[3] In January 1972, the superintendent of Milwaukee Public Schools released a study of the effect of open enrollment upon (among other things) school population and racial proportions, concluding that most schools had some transfers in and out; the Black student population was more dispersed, but significant changes in racial balance were limited to a few schools; many whites previously in predominantly Black schools transferred to other schools; overcrowding in several schools was alleviated; and, in the elementary schools, the effect of transfers upon racial balance has been insignificant, except in a few instances (1972, p. 14).[4] These results seem to support McAdams's generalization concerning color-blind programs—that they tend to reproduce the initial degree of segregation because of the general unwillingness of people to voluntarily integrate (1974, p. 69).[5] But, even if we accept these conclusions, there are still grounds to support the principle of voluntary choice of educational outcomes that underlies open enrollment. For example, the fact that approximately 15 percent of the total population of the Milwaukee public schools utilize the transfer option leads us to believe that many families use the option to secure better education for their children, quite apart from the racial mix of the school. If this is true, it seems possible that some means could be found to build techniques for desegregating schools into such a largely volunteer program.

Economic Model of School Transfers

All families with school-age children must decide where their children will attend school. Choices are usually restricted to the neighborhood public school or a nonpublic school, but under open enrollment the choice is enlarged to include nonneighborhood public schools.[6] This choice may be viewed as an economic decision. Conceptually, the choice is no different from deciding which grocery store or doctor to patronize. Every school in the choice set is viewed by the family in two major dimensions: the price of attending that particular school and

145

the quality of educational services offered. The price of schooling to a family includes property taxes for school purposes; transportation expenses, if they are not publicly provided; and, in a case in which transfers are permitted, any information and application costs which must be incurred to make an informed decision and to actually secure the transfer.

The outcome of any educational process is usually described in terms of the amount of learning that has occurred—the more learning that results, the greater the quantity of education received. Learning, however, is usually subdivided into cognitive learning (acquiring the ability to read, write, and calculate) and socialization (learning values; acquiring interests, attitudes, and motivations). Family perceptions of educational quality will thus be regarded as having both cognitive and noncognitive dimensions.

The "rational" consumer of educational services, then, will compare schools and select the one that maximizes net educational benefits. Consider, for instance, a school district divided into two attendance areas (*A* and *B*). Assume further that attending a non-neighborhood school is more costly simply because of increased transportation costs. Under these circumstances, "rational" residents of attendance area *A* would enroll their children in attendance area *B* only if the assessed value of the additional educational services offered in *B* equaled or exceeded the additional cost of attending that school. If, as is normally the case, attending a nonneighborhood school is more costly to the family, it then follows that the decision to transfer would be made only to a school perceived as clearly superior to the neighborhood one. It also follows that, in any school district with an unrestricted open-enrollment policy, the transfer traffic would be one way—from those of poor quality to the better ones. Further, if perceptions of school quality are importantly influenced by the ethnic composition of the school, transfers by members of one group may be followed by transfers by others of that group. Again, one would expect these transfers to be predominantly unidirectional (receiving schools having smaller minority populations than sending schools), so that the resulting ethnic balance, after all transfers are completed, would not differ appreciably from the initial distribution. According to the literature cited earlier, this is a fair summary of how unrestricted open-enrollment plans have actually worked thus far.

It can also be argued that this kind of transfer activity can be expected to have effects which extend beyond the school doors to the neighborhood at large. To see this, we have to expand the focus of our consumer-choice model to include the choice of real property. Although most of the following discussion will be limited to the choice of a residence, the analysis is easily extended to urban properties of all types.

Economic Model of Residential Choice

When a family purchases a residential dwelling unit, it acquires, in addition to a given quantity of shelter, an economic[7] and social location, the right to receive local public services (schools, parks, police and fire protection, etc.), and the obligation to pay local taxes on the property. Thus we can say that housing, as a commodity, is a multidimensional "bundle" of attributes, including many things other than the physical characteristics of the dwelling. If housing is viewed this way by most families, it would be reasonable then to expect actual market prices of specific dwelling units to reflect variations in *all* these characteristics. For example, suppose that there are two identical houses in the same community, and each is located in a different school-attendance area (again *A* and *B*). Assume that transfers between attendance areas are *not* allowed. Assume further that the immediate neighborhoods surrounding the dwellings are similar, that nonschool local services are identical, and that both locations are equally accessible to major shopping and employment centers. Finally, let us suppose that, although the property-tax levy is the same on both dwellings, the schools in the two attendance areas are *not* commonly perceived to be of equal quality—rather, that schools in *A* are somehow thought to be significantly better than schools in *B*.[8] Under this set of circumstances, the model described above would predict that the market sale price of the dwelling in attendance area *A* would tend to exceed that of the one in *B*. This differential would exist because potential buyers would be willing to pay a premium to live in *A* or, conversely, would be willing to live in *B* only if the sale price (relative to *A*) were discounted to compensate for the inferior quality of schooling available. Thus we could say that the superior quality of the schools in attendance area *A* are *capitalized* into the sale price of the dwellings in *A*, as a result of the competitive bidding of potential buyers in this market. If this example were restated, so that the only difference between the two dwellings was the property-tax bill for school purposes, the same result would obtain. That is, the model would predict that competitive bidding would establish a sale-price differential in favor of the dwelling with the lower tax bill—this being the case of capitalization of a tax differential.[9]

This model does not predict the magnitude of these sales-price differentials; it only suggests the presence of the differentials and their directions. The magnitude of the differentials will depend upon, among other things, the similarity and intensity of preference for education among potential buyers. Of course, whether such a differential actually exists is an empirical question. Although much empirical work remains to be done in this area, recent research tends to confirm the presence of both tax- and service-level capitalization and the idea that it can account for significant variations in the market values of otherwise similar parcels of real property.[10]

Neighborhood Tipping—an Application of the Residential Choice Model

In a recent paper on the changing racial makeup of selected schools and neighborhoods in Milwaukee under open enrollment, Robert Wegmann (1974) described the interaction of minority transfers and the racial composition of neighborhoods. The racial mix of the schools almost always leads that of the neighborhood; once the tipping point (usually thought of as in the range of 30–50 percent minority students) is reached in the schools, the neighborhood begins a rapid and ultimately drastic change as whites flee and nonwhites move into the newly available housing. Wegmann concludes, "Unless the school system is willing to intervene in order to hold the percentage back below the tipping point, the school will not only *not* be 'naturally' integrated, it will not be integrated at all; and neither will neighborhood integration have much chance of survival" (p. 13).[11]

Although it would be naive to ignore the reality that some of this white flight is rooted in racial prejudice and the attendant desire to reestablish social distance between themselves and those perceived to be inferior, families who might otherwise want to remain in an integrated neighborhood are faced with a powerful incentive to join the flight. As Anthony Downs (1970) put it, there is a "widely-held belief by American homeowners that any sizable entry of low-income households into their neighborhoods will depress the value of their homes." The strength of this incentive is illustrated by the recent estimate by the Internal Revenue Service that real estate comprised 58 percent of the net worth of the poorest class of wealth holders included in the sample in 1969.[12] For all wealth holders included in the sample, real estate accounted for 23.6 percent of total net worth in 1969 (U.S. Internal Revenue Service 1972). The process of racial change tends, of course, to occur in neighborhoods where real estate constitutes the largest part of a family's wealth. That these people would experience fear and even panic at what they perceived as a threat to their most precious financial resource is not surprising. The fact that little is known of the actual impact on property values of changing neighborhoods seems, unfortunately, not to have influenced people's beliefs.[13]

The belief that property values will fall then becomes a self-fulfilling prophecy, as frightened homeowners offer their homes for sale and accept low prices in an effort to get out before the situation "deteriorates even further." This process is often hastened by blockbusting and red lining, so that after a short period of time an integrated neighborhood becomes segregated again (Kain and Quigley 1975, p. 73). Although there is some evidence that this process does not always occur (Molotch 1969), it is likely that, in the absence of specific intervention at the school level, the rising minority enrollments in schools may overwhelm the possibility that white flight will not occur.

Non-color-blind Open Enrollment

McAdams and Wegmann hold that, for open enrollment to help achieve integration, it must be modified. The question is: what form should the modification take? The most obvious policy modification is to adopt specific goals and/or standards with respect to ethnicity. This could be done either by designating specific sending and receiving schools or by disallowing any transfers that worsen the racial balance (relative to the standard adopted) in any school. Wegmann and McAdams and others favor this approach or some variant of it. But such plans fail to satisfy several critical criteria; namely, they offer no positive incentives for *any* family to seek an integrated school. Furthermore, families who would send their children to nonneighborhood schools for purely educational reasons would be prevented from doing so if this did not serve to improve racial balance. The potential for success of any policy that fails to meet these tests is surely questionable.

Color-blind Open Enrollment with Fiscal Incentives

To the extent that families view education for their children in terms of the costs and the quantity of educational services, they select schools on the basis of the magnitude of the net benefit received. How would these choices be affected if families were offered fiscal incentives to choose one school over another? Consider a hypothetical family that can choose among five schools: the neighborhood school (N), three nonneighborhood public schools (*A, B,* and *C*), and a private school (*P*). Table 1 contains illustrative benefits and costs of these schools to such a family, assuming that the family must provide transportation to the nonneighborhood schools. The dollar value of educational "benefits" produced by any school can be interpreted as the maximum dollar bid the family would be willing to make for a place in that school if those places were let at auction.[14] Given a community that is not changing racially or otherwise, it seems clear that, from a purely economic standpoint, a family would choose the neighborhood school (*N*), where net benefits are maximized at $400.

Suppose, however, that the racial composition of the neighborhood school changes, and the family revises downward its estimate of the value of education received. If the value of benefits received at *N* are reduced by more than $200, the family would now maximize its net benefit by transferring the child to school *A*. To the extent that parents' perceptions of school quality are influenced by the racial and socioeconomic composition of a school, transfers out will be induced by the transferring in of youngsters who appear to negatively affect this composition. But, in view of the model of educational choice above, this tendency is *not* inevitable. Suppose, for example, that costs were made to vary so that the integrated school was cheaper to attend than the segregated school. Had the total cost of attending the now integrated neighborhood school *N* in table 1 declined by, say, $250, the value of benefits received at *N* would have to fall by at least $450 before a transfer became attractive.

Although total direct costs of education to the family could be changed by varying any component (property taxes and/or transportation expenses), perhaps the easiest way to accomplish this would be to adopt a system of transfer fees and bonuses. Such a scheme might

TABLE 1
Hypothetical Dollar Benefits and Costs of Educational Opportunities

| | EDUCA-TIONAL | COSTS | | | | |
SCHOOL	BENEFITS	School Property Taxes	Trans-portation Expense	Tuition	Total Costs	NET BENEFIT
N	900	500	...	...	500	400
A	800	500	100	...	600	200
B	500	500	150	...	650	−150
C	850	500	200	...	700	150
P	1,100	500	100	500	1,100	...

work as follows: the total proportion of minority and nonminority residents of the school district are used as the "standard" (reference point) for each school. Transfers to any underutilized school are permitted, with the proviso that a family requesting a transfer that negatively alters the receiving school's ethnic composition must pay a transfer fee (of, say, $250), while those requesting a transfer that improves ethnic balance in the receiving school are awarded bonuses in the same amount. For example, consider a school with 50 percent minority enrollment and a "standard" of 40 percent minority. In this school, integration is encouraged by requiring minority students wishing to transfer in to pay the transfer fee, while the school is made more attractive to nonminority families because they would receive a transfer bonus if they elected it. This plan has the additional appeal that those who elect to pay the transfer fee and who thus do not contribute directly to achieving racial balance do contribute indirectly, because their transfer fees help pay the transportation expenses of those who elect transfers to racially balanced schools. The plan could be further enhanced by offering transportation subsidies to those students whose transfers move the receiving school closer toward the ethnic "standard."

Although it might be more complicated, there is no reason why a similar plan of differential pricing could not be worked out to promote the integration of high- and low-achieving youngsters. In this case, the transfer "standard" (percentage reading below grade level) would probably have to be applied to each grade separately. A recent study of educational settings and learning in the Philadelphia public schools suggests that some important learning gains for *all* students result (especially in the elementary schools) in classrooms which are integrated with respect to both race and educational achievement (Summers and Wolfe 1975).

One immediate question emerges: how large would these transfer fees and bonuses have to be in order to have a significant impact upon transfer behavior and thus on racial and socioeconomic balance? Research that James Moody and I are now engaged in on actual open-enrollment transfer activity in Milwaukee public schools may provide some estimates of at least the minimum value of such a fiscal incentive.[15]

The Impact of Property Owners

The omission of families without school-age children from a discussion of educational policy can have serious consequences, especially for a consideration of open enrollment. There is no reason to believe that the only people (or even the first) to flee racially changing neighborhoods are those with children in the public schools. The incentive to leave the neighborhood is the same for all property owners if, as Downs suggests, they fear for their property values. It will never be possible, or indeed desirable, to prevent property owners from selling and moving elsewhere if they choose to do so. But a plan like the one I've just proposed can have no real chance to achieve integration if no effort is made to allay this legitimate fear that property values (for all parcels) will plummet as integration proceeds.

Although there is some question about what actually happens to property values as a neighborhood approaches and then passes the tipping point, it seems that the mere expectation that they will fall causes some to flee. The changing ethnic composition of the neighborhood is capitalized into lower property values. But this capitalization could be offset by lowered property-tax rates for residents in a changing neighborhood. Thus, in principle, the adjustment of property-tax rates could support the adjustment of transfer fees to assist open education to achieve desegregation.

Actually implementing such a system of appropriately varying property-tax rates would of course be a complex procedure. To begin with, more detailed research is needed on the sensivitity of property values to changes in racial and socioeconomic characteristics of schools and their surrounding neighborhoods. Such research would provide estimates of the required tax adjustment, if the capitalization effects assumed above are in fact observable. It is comforting to note that, if differential school pricing actually resulted in a fairly uniform integration of schools, the need for a tax adjustment to offset potentially falling property values would disappear. The property-tax scheme is required only to the extent that the school-pricing scheme fails to accomplish its objective.

The obvious public authority to assume responsibility for making such tax adjustments is the state. All states engage in some form of aid to public education. The most common form of aid is the provision of matching grants to insure that some predetermined level of expenditure per pupil is met. In the last few years, there have been countless court suits requiring that the role of the state as a wealth equalizer (with respect to school finance) be expanded. Two famous cases are *Serrano* v. *Priest* in California and *Rodriguez* v. *San Antonio* in Texas. As a result of these legal actions, there has been a distinct movement in certain states toward an expanded role in wealth (tax-base) equalization. Wisconsin has recently adopted a formula for equalization of district wealth as a proposed step in this direction. The scheme of property-tax subsidy for changing neighborhoods could be included in this kind of plan. As wealth equalizing works now in Wisconsin, state aid received by any district is determined by property valuation (property wealth) per pupil and the cost of schooling inputs. To this plan could simply be added those racial and socioeconomic factors, if any, that are also found to be significantly related to changes in property values.

Apart from the technicalities of such an approach, there is one major obstacle in any big-city school district that must be overcome. The induced changes in property values that we have been discussing are usually localized geographically, within the limited number of city blocks which comprise a neighborhood. This means that any reduction in school property-tax costs must and should be focused on the properties within this neighborhood. It will do no good to have a tax reduction (increase in state aid) dissipated throughout the whole community. This means that some way would have to be found to subdivide, at least for tax purposes, large school districts into smaller neighborhood districts.

Furthermore, there is the question of whether such a system of fiscal incentives can facilitate open enrollment if the district in which the policy is being implemented is just one of several school districts in a single metropolitan area. The answer in general, I think, must be no. Some families faced with paying several transfer fees would simply move to a suburb. Thus, if limited to the central city school district, the effect of this plan could be that the responsibility for maintaining racially balanced schools would fall on those families unable to choose either to move out or to pay transfers out and who, further, would benefit from receiving transfer bonuses. The political problems that would result resemble those we have today in Boston and other such cities. Whether states and school districts will form metropolitan districts or, failing that, would be willing and able to pay bonuses and lower property taxes enough to provide incentive for those who are not the poorest is a political question. A related problem in many big-city school districts is that the racial mix of the district student population is such that, if every school in the district were in perfect racial balance, every school would be beyond the tipping point. Surely, if our experience to date with voluntary programs like open enrollment tells us anything, it is that schools must be prevented from exceeding these tipping points. In these circumstances, the only available alternative is plans which are metropolitan in scope.

Conclusion

Can our public schools be integrated voluntarily? Apparently, the hope that they could motivated many school systems to adopt open-transfer policies in the past decade. Thus far, the results have not been encouraging to those favoring integration. Although many pupils utilized the option to transfer, marked improvements in integration have been rare. Nevertheless, interest continues in voluntary approaches because of the political upheaval associated with mandatory programs.

Proposed modifications of voluntary-transfer policies have generally centered on adopting greater restrictions on the option to transfer and/or enlarging the set of participating schools to include the suburbs. James Coleman's (1975) recent suggestion that every child in a metropolitan area be given the right to transfer (subject to capacity limitations) to any other school with a smaller proportion of his own race than his neighborhood school combines both features. Nevertheless, strong reservations concerning the probable efficacy of this and similar reforms are suggested by the economic model of educational choice presented. Not only do these proposals generally lack direct positive incentives for participating families, but they also pay inadequate attention to the interaction between open transfers and neighborhood tipping. Generally, it is shown that voluntary-transfer programs have little chance for success unless direct positive incentives are provided for participants, fears of declining property values in integrating neighborhoods are stilled, school tipping is prevented, and suburban school districts are included. A proposal combining monetary transfer fees and bonuses and property-tax reductions in integrating neighborhoods is shown to meet these criteria.

Is school desegregation still a good idea? If the collective decision of our society is *yes* (as I hope it will be), the next task is the determination of how best to achieve it. This paper has begun the investigation of voluntary approaches. In their entirety, the proposals presented are complicated; nevertheless, they fulfill what I believe is a minimum set of necessary conditions for widespread acceptance and eventual success. Whether these proposals also satisfy sufficient conditions must be left to the judgment of the reader. In any case, it is hoped that this analysis facilitates the search for a viable policy.

Notes

An earlier draft of this paper was presented at the American Educational Research Association Convention, April 1975, Washington, D.C., (ERIC Clearinghouse on Urban Education, ED 104-988). The author wishes to thank Florence Levinsohn for several clarifying and substantive contributions.

1. Open enrollment is only one of several plans with similar objectives. For a discussion of open enrollment and five other related plans, see Heller (1970).

2. Recent examples of this argument are found in Strickman (1972) and Rodgers and Bullock (1974).

3. There have been a few recent exceptions to this general rule. In several schools with a 40-60 percent proportion of minority students, student bodies have been "frozen" to prevent the school from "tipping" and becoming increasingly minority populated.

4. This study was made at the directive of the Milwaukee Board of School Directors, September 7, 1971.

5. This conclusion should *not* be interpreted as a criticism of the Milwaukee school system for adopting an unrestricted open-enrollment policy. A fair criticism of this policy decision would have to be made within the context of an explicit statement by the school board regarding the goals of its open-enrollment policy. The author is unaware of any such statement.

6. At this point, we will ignore those families who choose nonpublic schools.

7. That is, proximity to employment, shopping, and recreational centers.

8. This general perception might stem from a variety of relative comparisons regarding such things as average class size, average test scores on standardized tests, proportion of graduates going on to college, racial and socioeconomic composition of student bodies, extent of curriculum diversity, and age and state of repair of physical facilities.

9. In more technical language, we would say that the market-value differential equals the property-tax or the time-discounted, expected stream of service differential. A more complete discussion of tax and benefit capitalization may be found in Musgrave and Musgrave (1973, pp. 413–17).

10. A well-known example of this research is Oates (1969).

11. Wegmann is a former member of the Milwaukee Board of School Directors.

12. The Internal Revenue Service study of wealth holdings is limited to those with a gross wealth of at least $60,000. The "poorest" class of these wealth holders noted above are those with a *net* wealth of less than $60,000.

13. The actual impact upon property values as a result of changing racial and socioeconomic composition is a subject about which we know very little. For an excellent summary of the existing research on the impact of race, see Kain and Quigley (1975, pp. 72–82). A recent study of three inner suburbs in St. Louis is found in Sutker and Sutker (1974, pp. 105–35).

14. It causes no difficulty that school places are not actually awarded in this fashion. We will also assume that the valuation a family places on a particular school is independent of the other alternatives available.

15. A preliminary report on this research is contained in Moody (1975).

References

Coleman, James S. "Racial Segregation in the Schools: New Research with New Policy Implications." *Phi Delta Kappan* 57 (1975): 75–78.
Downs, Anthony. "Residential Segregation: Its Effects on Education." *Civil Rights Digest* 3 (1970): 2–8.

Foster, G. "Desegregating Urban Schools: A Review of Techniques." *Harvard Educational Review* 43 (1973): 5–36.

Heller, Robert W. "Desegregation, Integration, and Urban Schools," In *Toward Improved Urban Education,* edited by Frank W. Lutz. Worthington, Ohio: Charles A. Jones Publishing Co., 1970.

Kain, John F., and Quigley, John M. *Housing Markets and Racial Discrimination: A Microeconomic Analysis.* New York: National Bureau of Economic Research, 1975.

McAdams, John. "Can Open Enrollment Work?" *Public Interest* 37 (1974): 69–88.

Milwaukee Public Schools. "Open Enrollment Study." Mimeographed. Milwaukee, Wisc., 1972.

Molotch, H. "Racial Change in a Stable Community." *American Journal of Sociology* 75 (1969): 226–38.

Moody, James. "Open Enrollment: A Study in Revealed Preferences for Educational Outcomes in a Big City School System." Paper presented at the American Educational Research Association Convention, April 1975, Washington, D.C.

Musgrave, Richard A., and Musgrave, Peggy B. *Public Finance in Theory and Practice.* New York: McGraw-Hill, Inc., 1973.

Oates, Wallace E. "The Effects of Property Taxes and Local Public Spending on Property Values: An Empirical Study of Tax Capitalization and the Tiebout Hypothesis." *Journal of Political Economy* 77 (1969): 957–71.

Rodgers, Harrell R., Jr., and Bullock, Charles S., III. "School Desegregation: Successes and Failures." *Journal of Negro Education* 43 (1974): 139–55.

Strickman, Leonard P. "Desegregation: The Metropolitan Concept." *Urban Review* 6 (1972): 18–23.

Summers, Anita A., and Wolfe, Barbara A. "Which School Resources Help Learning? Efficiency and Equity in Philadelphia Public Schools." Federal Reserve Bank of Philadelphia, *Business Review* (February 1975).

Sutker, Solomon, and Sutker, Sara Smith, eds. *Racial Transition in the Inner Suburb.* New York: Praeger Publishers, 1974.

U.S. Commission on Civil Rights. *Racial Isolation in the Public Schools.* Washington, D.C.: Government Printing Office, 1967.

U.S. Internal Revenue Service. *Statistics of Income, 1969: Estate Tax Returns.* Washington, D.C.: Government Printing Office, 1972.

Wegmann, Robert G. "Neighborhoods and Schools in Racial Transition." Paper presented at the American Educational Research Association Convention, April 1974, Washington, D.C.

The Ultimate Solution: Desegregated Housing

HARRY N. GOTTLIEB
Leadership Council for Metropolitan Open Communities

De facto school segregation is the result of racially segregated housing and residential patterns. Therefore, the extent to which there is progress, or lack of it, in achieving racial desegregation in housing is of major importance in considering the potentiality for desegregation of the schools.

Since the heart of the matter is in our metropolitan areas, I will explore here patterns and progress toward achievement of racial housing integration in metropolitan communities—both central city and suburban. Much of the material will be drawn from the Chicago metropolitan area, a fitting example since this city has ranked at or near the top in measurements of racial segregation in the schools (Kirby, Harris, and Crain 1973). It is no coincidence that it is also considered one of the most residentially segregated areas as well.

Meaningful desegregation is potentially most feasible in both education and housing if it can be dealt with in a metropolitan-wide context. *Milliken* v. *Bradley,* the U.S. Supreme Court decision which rejected a metropolitan school integration plan for Detroit, was certainly a setback, but comparable litigation in the field of housing is now in the judicial works.

Another important metropolitan development is the dramatic growth of jobs in the suburbs. Through the 1960s, millions of new jobs were created in the suburbs, and there is little indication of a change in this trend. (Chicago gained about 500,000 suburban jobs in the sixties while the level of employment in the city remained static.)

At the same time, there has been very little suburban housing developed for people earning under $12,000 annually, thus creating an imbalance in the location of jobs and housing which is particularly onerous to minorities who disproportionately are in the lower-income brackets. High unemployment among inner city Blacks is caused, to some extent, by the increasing remoteness of job growth, the costli-

157

ness of reverse commuting which usually must be by automobile, and the overall disadvantage of competing for jobs which are far away.

Thus it is logical that recent efforts toward achieving desegregation in housing have increasingly emphasized the need to produce more low- and moderate-income housing opportunities in the suburbs. What's more, the need for such housing in the suburbs has begun to make some political sense to elected local leaders who recognize the need to find relief from the increasing housing distress of many of their present constituents. While it is recognized that more suburban low- and moderate-income housing must open new opportunities for Blacks and other minorities, *numerically*, the benefits will primarily accrue to whites, most of whom already live there.

In 1974 the median price of a new home in the United States was $41,300, with a monthly housing expense of $486. Only 15 percent of the nation's families receive the annual income of $23,330, which is the minimum income necessary to afford such housing costs. Even the median sale price of an existing home in 1974, $35,600, can be afforded only by the 20 percent of the population which earns $21,170 or above (U.S. Congress 1975). It is well known that Black and Spanish-speaking populations have been increasing in central cities while white populations have declined. Along with this racial dichotomy there is an increasing economic disparity, with concentrations of poverty in the cities and growing affluence in the suburbs. The consequences of these patterns and trends in housing have had tremendous implications for efforts to achieve socioeconomic desegregation in schools, particularly in the central cities. In growing numbers of cities there are not only too few whites to achieve meaningful racial desegregation; often there are also not enough economically advantaged people to achieve meaningful economic desegregation.

Exacerbating these trends has been the very low priority accorded to housing on this nation's agenda during recent years. The two-year Nixon-imposed moratorium on federal housing subsidy programs represented a "benign neglect" of housing which has almost been matched by the neglect of housing as an issue among the citizenry, civil rights organizations not excepted. Such issues as Watergate,

---

HARRY N. GOTTLIEB was formerly vice-president and director of Draper and Kramer, Incorporated, a leading Chicago real estate and mortgage banking firm. Since 1972 he has been associated with a Chicago-based fair-housing organization, the Leadership Council for Metropolitan Open Communities.

Vietnam, inflation, the energy shortage, recession, and unemployment and crime have occupied center stage.[1]

But jobs, education, and housing are a tightly linked triumvirate, and the effect of neglect of any one of the three must have major consequences on the others. It is therefore inevitable that public consciousness of our housing deficiencies will increase, accompanied by a clamor for remedial action.

This paper can only skim some of the aspects of housing issues which bear heavily on racial and economic segregation in our metropolitan areas:

1. Legislation. The Housing and Community Development Act of 1974 adds some new tools for attacking housing segregation.

2. The courts. Federal and state courts are breaking some new ground on housing and zoning questions.

3. Mixed-income housing. Led by state housing finance agencies, many new housing developments are now designed to accommodate people of various income levels—a relatively new tool to promote both economic and racial integration.

4. To what extent progress? There have been some significant inroads made against racial and economic housing segregation. There are instances where this has had a notable effect on school desegregation. But we have only scratched the surface of the problem.

5. A housing agenda. A Chicago metropolitan area fair housing organization has launched a comprehensive attack on segregated housing.

6. Outlook. Those primarily concerned with desegregated education cannot expect major changes in housing patterns in the near future. But for the long term there is much potential for housing desegregation—its pace depending in large measure on the priority of resources and effort devoted to it.

Legislation

During the 1960s and the early 1970s, the federal government maintained an active posture toward housing for low- and moderate-income families. The public housing program, which began during the 1930s, continued to produce thousands of housing units each year for people in the lowest income brackets. Private housing developers, with the assistance of deep interest rate subsidies sometimes combined with rent supplements, were able to produce housing units for people in both low- and moderate-income categories. The Housing

Act of 1968 created programs which permitted subsidies benefiting both home owners and renters. In the years 1970–73 more than 1.5 million dwelling units were produced by new construction or rehabilitation under various federal subsidy programs.

Despite the fact that these programs produced sound housing for many hundreds of thousands of people, there were some serious problems. The programs came under increasing attack from many quarters. The plight of the Pruitt-Igoe high-rise development in St. Louis represented to many people a symbol of the failure of public housing. The 1968 housing act programs were also experiencing various difficulties, including high mortgage-default rates.

As a result of this mounting criticism, President Nixon declared a moratorium of indefinite duration on all federal housing subsidy programs in January 1973. Even though President Ford in one of his first official acts signed the Housing and Community Development Act of 1974, the moratorium was in effect for more than two years because of the time necessary to tool up for implementation of the new legislation.

The Housing and Community Development Act of 1974 is the first major piece of federal housing legislation since 1968. In several respects, this is landmark legislation because it breaks some significant new ground in federal housing policy: (1) For the first time, congressional findings have been directed to the problem of economic as well as racial segregation; (2) communities and counties throughout the nation, in order to be eligible for a broad range of federal community development block grants, must prepare and implement housing assistance plans related to the needs of people in low- and moderate-income brackets; (3) for the first time in federal housing legislation, housing needs are related to the location of employment opportunities. Housing needs must be met not only for those already residing in a community but also for those "planning or expected to reside in the community as a result of planned or existing employment facilities"; and (4) strong encouragement is given to development of mixed-income housing.

The legislation expresses concern for "the concentration of persons of lower income in central cities" and sets out to achieve "the spatial deconcentration of housing opportunities for persons of lower income."

A new housing subsidy program was created, entitled (rather unfortunately) Section 8, that provides for eligible tenants to pay 15–25 percent of their income for rent, while the balance of the rent is paid, with government funds, directly to the owner of the housing. Section 8 serves low- (those whose income is 80 percent or less of the median income for the area) and very low-income families (whose income is 50 percent or less of the median income for the area). At least 30 percent of those served must be in the very low-income bracket.²

This program is designed for use in connection with dwelling units provided by new construction, substantial rehabilitation of existing housing, or sound existing units not requiring major rehabilitation. The eligible family is expected to find its own housing, thereby presumably providing a wide range of choice regarding type and location.

The degree to which Section 8 will in fact provide a wide range of housing choice for minority families will depend primarily on the vigor with which the U.S. Department of Housing and Urban Development (HUD), state housing finance agencies, and local housing authorities enforce equal opportunity and affirmative marketing requirements. It will also depend on the effectiveness of fair housing organizations in reaching and counseling eligible applicants regarding their rights and opportunities under the program.

The Courts

The Civil Rights Act of 1968, plus the U.S. Supreme Court ruling that year in *Jones* v. *Mayer,* which reaffirmed and upheld the 1866 Civil Rights Act, have outlawed racial discrimination in the sale, rental, and financing of all housing.

What has been much less clear is the legal status of *economic* discrimination, particularly as it is demonstrated by suburban exclusion of low- and moderate-income housing. Civil rights advocates have pointed out the racially discriminatory effect of such exclusion because of the disproportionate number of Blacks and other minorities who are in low- and moderate-income brackets. This exclusion becomes particularly damaging to minorities in an era when jobs are increasingly located in the suburbs, many of which have been virtually all-white communities.

There have been some recent judicial decisions which indicate that courts are beginning to give legal recognition to the relationship between economic and racial discrimination. Following are brief summaries of a few of the more significant recent decisions on this subject:

1. *Gautreaux* v. *Chicago Housing Authority, James T. Lynn et al.* Whereas the U.S. Supreme Court opinion in *Milliken* v. *Bradley* declined to permit metropolitan desegregation relief in the Detroit area public schools, the *Gautreaux* opinion rendered by the U.S. Court

of Appeals for the seventh circuit in August 1974 found that a metropolitan area plan is "necessary and equitable" to remedy the segregated public housing in the City of Chicago. Justice Tom C. Clark noted that the problems of logistics, finance, administration, and political legitimacy which might attend such relief for public education do not apply to such relief in housing.

The *Gautreaux* opinion states: "Our task therefore, and that of the District Judge, is to determine how great a degree of public housing desegregation is practical. *Milliken* v. *Bradley* dealt only with schools. Public housing may be quite different. . . . Any remedial plan to be effective must be on a suburban or metropolitan area basis. . . . The parties are in agreement that the metropolitan area is a single relevant locality for low rent housing purposes and that a city-only remedy will not work." Despite the statement of agreement by the court, HUD promptly appealed this decision to the U.S. Supreme Court. Clearly the outcome of this litigation will be most important in determining the extent to which low-income housing will be realistically treated as a metropolitan-wide rather than a city-only problem.

2. *Metropolitan Housing Development Corporation* v. *The Village of Arlington Heights et al.* The United States Court of Appeals ruled on June 10, 1975, that the failure of the Village of Arlington Heights (Illinois) to grant zoning for Lincoln Green, a proposed moderate-income rental development to be financed under FHA Section 236, "has racially discriminatory effects"; and "since no compelling justification for the decision exists, the refusal to grant the requested zoning change is a violation of the Equal Protection Clause of the Fourteenth Amendment." In addition, the court found that "the instant case reflects the unfortunate fact that the Chicago metropolitan area has been segregated in terms of housing." In the light of the 1970 census figures showing only 27 Blacks in a total Arlington Heights population of 64,884, the court further stated that "the rejection of Lincoln Green has the effect of perpetuating both the residential segregation and Arlington Heights' failure to accept any responsibility for helping to solve this problem . . . indeed, it has been exploiting the problem by allowing itself to become an almost one hundred per cent white community."

One important aspect of this decision is that it was not necessary to prove the *intent* of racial discrimination. "Merely because Arlington Heights did not directly create the problem does not necessarily mean that it can ignore it," the court said. "Historical context and ultimate effect" are the crucial elements.

The decision also took considerable note of the absence of other action within the village to produce low- and moderate-income housing, thus magnifying the impact of refusal to grant zoning for Lincoln Green. The U.S. Supreme Court agreed to review this case in December 1975.

3. *Southern Burlington County NAACP* v. *Township of Mount Laurel.* The Supreme Court of the State of New Jersey rendered its decision on this case March 24, 1975, striking down local zoning ordinances that exclude poor persons or families with low or moderate incomes and ruling that every community in the state must share in meeting the housing needs of its surrounding region. "We conclude that every municipality must, by its land use regulations, presumptively make realistically possible an appropriate variety and choice of housing. More specifically, presumptively it cannot foreclose the opportunity of the classes of people mentioned for low and moderate income housing and in its regulations must affirmatively afford that opportunity, *at least to the extent of the municipality's fair share of the present and prospective regional need therefore,*" the court said (emphasis added).

The court found that regional considerations were mandatory because of the importance of shelter and the seriousness of housing problems in the state as evidenced by legislative findings and enactments:

> The universal and constant need for such housing is important and of such broad public interest that the general welfare which developing municipalities like Mount Laurel must consider extends beyond their boundaries and cannot be parochially confined to the claimed good of that particular municipality. It has to follow that, broadly speaking, the presumptive obligation arises for each such municipality to plan and provide, by its land use regulations, the reasonable opportunity for an appropriate variety and choice of housing, including, of course, low and moderate cost housing, to meet the needs, desires and resources of all categories of people who may desire to live within its boundaries. Negatively, it may not adopt regulations or policies which thwart or preclude that opportunity.

In a concurring opinion, one judge stated that the decision begins to cope with "municipal land use regulation—the use of the zoning power to advance the parochial interest of the municipality at the expense of the surrounding region and to establish and perpetuate social and economic segregation." Although this opinion was issued by a state rather than a federal court, it is expected that courts throughout the country will give it consideration in future land use and zoning cases.

Mixed-Income Housing

I have already noted that the Housing and Community Development Act of 1974 gives strong encouragement to development of mixed-income housing. A very small proportion of federal housing funds is made available for the conventional public housing program which, while it has fulfilled desperate housing needs of many thousands of lower-income families and senior citizens, often concentrates and tends to separate lower-income people.

The legislation's new Section 8 Rental Assistance Program gives certain priorities to new and substantially rehabilitated housing developments in which 20 percent or less of the occupants may receive subsidies.

Of at least equal importance is the use of Section 8 subsidies in connection with sound existing housing. Under this phase of the program, a family receives a certificate of family participation from the local housing authority and then finds its own dwelling unit in the open market. In most cases, such housing units will be in rental developments which are not otherwise subsidized, and no one except the recipient of the subsidy and the housing owner or manager need be aware of it.

As an illustration of how this program can work, the Housing Authority of Cook County (Illinois) has been allocated funds by HUD to subsidize 602 tenants in existing housing throughout the county (with the exception of the City of Chicago and one or two suburbs which have their own housing authorities).

The program is guided by several principles set forth in the housing assistance plan adopted by the Cook County Board of Commissioners which include (1) housing appropriately priced for lower-paid workers should be developed as well as made available in existing units, near centers of employment in all parts of Cook County; (2) a primary objective of this plan is to achieve spatial deconcentration of housing opportunities for persons of lower income; (3) the housing market throughout the county must function without discrimination due to national origin, race, religion, sex, age, or physical handicap.

While the housing authority gives priority to residents of suburban Cook County, in keeping with the spirit of the Housing and Community Act of 1974 which defines "resident" to include those "expected to reside" in suburban Cook County by reason of employment opportunities, inner-city residents are supposed to receive parity of consideration if they indicate that housing is sought to be near present or prospective employment.

The primary factor in the recent trend toward mixed-income housing developments has been the creation of state housing finance agencies. Most of these state agencies are charged by their legislatures to serve low- and moderate-income families as well as those in somewhat higher income brackets. The state agencies are authorized to issue tax-exempt revenue bonds and therefore have been able to make loans to housing developers at below market interest rates. These interest savings are passed along in the form of lower rents.

But to meet the needs of lower-income people, the use of federal subsidies has been necessary. An example of the use of federal subsidies by state housing finance agencies is provided by the Illinois Housing Development Authority (IHDA). During 1975, IHDA financed 17 developments in 13 Illinois cities containing a total of 3,274 dwelling units. Of these units, 1,374 received federal subsidies under Section 236, thus bringing IHDA-financed housing within the range of people earning under $12,000.

Through 1975, IHDA total financing produced more than 11,800 units. Henceforth, IHDA will be using the Section 8 program to bring many of its housing units within the range of very low income families because of the federal requirement that at least 30 percent of all Section 8 subsidies must serve this group.

Since large-scale mixed-income housing is a relatively new phenomenon, there is as yet no widespread evidence of its workability. The Massachusetts Housing Finance Agency, however, that has typically used a mix involving middle, moderate, and low income groups, reports that a study of tenant attitudes found a high level of satisfaction with its mixed-income housing developments among all income groups involved (1974).

Also uncertain at this writing is the degree to which state-financed mixed-income housing developments will serve minority families in virtually all-white areas. The Illinois Housing Development Authority has a strong affirmative marketing policy which reportedly has resulted in Black occupancy of up to 20 percent in the developments it finances.

To What Extent Progress?

Despite Chicago's reputation as a segregated city, there are some examples in both city and suburbs of desegregated housing patterns which have shown evidence of enduring beyond the brief interval between the time the first Black moves into a neighborhood and the moment the last white departs.

One of these is the Hyde Park–Kenwood community on the city's

South Side lake front, anchored by the University of Chicago, and bounded on three sides by virtually all-Black communities. When Blacks began to find housing in Hyde Park–Kenwood shortly after restrictive covenants were outlawed about 25 years ago, there was some doubt that whites would continue to be attracted in sufficient numbers to maintain stabilized desegregation.

But a vigorous stance by the university, a consistent commitment to stable racial integration by community groups (including both Blacks and whites), and an urban renewal program which attacked both residential and commercial blight have combined to keep the community attractive to people of all races, and thus a relatively even racial balance has been maintained.

This does not mean that there is a thorough mixture of races throughout Hyde Park–Kenwood, because there are some heavy residential concentrations of both whites and Blacks along with some areas of racially mixed housing. But the pattern of life—the organizations, churches, shopping facilities, art fairs, bridge tournaments, and many other activities, are notably interracial.

But what about the public schools? Whites are in the minority in public school attendance, largely because so many of them attend one of the several private schools, along with a number of upper-income Black children.

In the autumn of 1974 there were only 1,210 white students in Hyde Park–Kenwood public grade and high schools, 25.1 percent of the total Hyde Park–Kenwood public school population. Although one of the schools has more than 99 percent Black attendance, the other six contain a mixture ranging from 8.5 to 52 percent white. All of the white students attend desegregated schools, as do 2,740 of the 3,401 Blacks.

But Hyde Park–Kenwood is only one part of a much larger South Side area comprising School District 14. Of the 16,687 Black students in the district, only the above noted 2,740 Black students attend schools having less than 99 percent Black enrollments. So, despite Hyde Park–Kenwood, five out of six Black students in District 14 attend fully segregated schools. It could hardly be otherwise when whites comprise only 6.7 percent of the students in the district, unless there were a citywide or metropolitan-wide school desegregation program.

There is no such program. So even though a residentially integrated Hyde Park–Kenwood makes a contribution to integrated education, it is a small island in a sea of residential segregation.

Thirty miles south of downtown Chicago, the Village of Park Forest, population about 30,000, has a desegregated school system.

Its largest grade and junior high school district includes a subdivision outside of the village limits occupied almost entirely by Blacks, most of whom are at a lower socioeconomic level than Park Forest's white and Black citizens. From that subdivision come more than 70 percent of the Blacks enrolled in School District 163.

Park Forest's Blacks, according to the 1970 census, were 2.3 percent of the total population. Current estimates range between 5 and 10 percent. In the 1974–75 school year, 7.5 percent of the students in District 163 were Park Forest Blacks and 19.5 percent were Blacks from the neighboring subdivision, bringing the total Black enrollment to 27 percent.

The school board of district 163 decided voluntarily to achieve school desegregation by busing, and it was supported by the village government of Park Forest, even though the decision brought the large number of Blacks to Park Forest schools from outside the community. With the exception of one school where 46 percent of the students are Black, the 11 schools had Black enrollments between 21 and 30 percent, all very close to the 27 percent of the total. Thus all 3,590 students, including 969 Blacks, attend desegregated schools.

The Park Forest experience illustrates clearly that, as Blacks find increasing housing opportunities in the suburbs, there will be pockets of racial and economic resegregation, so that even in these cases busing will be necessary to achieve racial and economic desegregation.

There are not many racially mixed housing situations in the Chicago metropolitan area comparable with Hyde Park–Kenwood and Park Forest. When we consider that, in these two areas, there are only about 3,700 Black students in desegregated schools out of total Black population which had passed 1,230,000 for the Chicago metropolitan area in 1970, it is obvious how small an impact has been made numerically.

Nevertheless, the Park Forest program illustrates the real possibility of putting 100 percent of minority children who move to the suburbs into desegregated schools.

What progress, then, is being made in opening housing opportunities in the suburbs to minorities, and to what extent are they taking advantage of such opportunities?

The 1970 census indicated a total population of 6,979,000 in the six-county Chicago metropolitan area. Of the total, 5,673,000 (81.3 percent) were white, 1,231,000 (17.6 percent) Black, and 75,000 (1.1 percent) of other races. Of the Black population, 1,103,000 (89.6 percent) lived in the central city, 128,000 (10.4 percent) in the suburbs. Black suburban residents were but 3.6 percent of the suburban total of 3,609,000.

We do not have precise figures to show how much the Black population in the suburbs has grown since the 1970 census, but merely for illustrative purposes let us use one recent estimate that the increase has been 40 percent. This would have increased the Black suburban population from 128,000 to 179,000 in about five years. Even without any total suburban population growth, that would increase the proportion of Blacks in the suburbs only from 3.6 percent of the total in 1970 to 4.9 percent.

But in the five years 1970–74, about 190,000 housing units were built in Chicago's suburbs. Assuming that 90 percent of these units (to allow for losses due to demolitions, etc.) increased the total suburban population by 3.5 persons per dwelling unit, the total suburban population would now be approximately 4,200,000. Based on our estimate of a 40 percent rise in suburban Black population, 179,000 Blacks would constitute about 4.3 percent of the total suburban population, compared with 3.6 percent in 1970.

Our estimate of a 40 percent increase in Chicago's suburban Black population during the last five years may be somewhat high or low —but the message is undeniable: there has been some progress, but it has been very slow.

This is not to belittle the ongoing major effort to open up the Chicago suburbs. The Home Investment Fund's Chicago Fair Housing Center has assisted minorities to move into about 80 of the approximately 250 suburbs during the last few years. The legal action program of the Leadership Council for Metropolitan Open Communities has fought and won dozens of cases attacking individual instances of racial discrimination in housing. There have been some notable integrated suburban low- and moderate-income housing developments built, such as Marian Park (by the Franciscan Sisters) and Rand Grove Village (by the Metropolitan Housing Development Corp.). And there is a first-year commitment by suburbs, in response to the requirements of the Housing and Community Development Act of 1974, to provide more than 5,000 low- and moderate-income dwelling units, with specific equal opportunity guidelines.

A Housing Agenda

During recent years, when housing was relatively overshadowed as a national issue by other pressing crises, various organizations and interests have struggled to translate antidiscrimination laws into effective action to open new housing opportunities for minorities. A few organizations have been operating on a national level, such as the

168

Washington-based National Committee against Discrimination in Housing, headed by Robert C. Weaver, the first secretary of the U.S. Department of Housing and Urban Development.

Others have operated primarily on a regional level, including the Suburban Action Institute which has backed several important legal attacks on exclusionary zoning practices in states along the eastern seaboard.

There have also been some sustained local efforts, one of which is the Leadership Council for Metropolitan Open Communities (LCMOC), whose central purpose is to achieve a single, nondiscriminatory housing market throughout the Chicago metropolitan area.

The LCMOC was established in 1966 in response to the marches led by Dr. Martin Luther King, Jr., which effectively dramatized the anger of Blacks against prevailing discriminatory and exclusionary housing practices. The organization, directed by Kale Williams, who marched with King, is in large measure backed financially by Chicago's business leadership, supplemented by federal, state, and foundation grants.

A look at LCMOC's agenda for the next few years may be useful to emphasize the magnitude of the problem, and the broad range of strategies necessary to deal with it. LCMOC operates a Comprehensive Fair Housing Program which endeavors to bring under one umbrella ongoing efforts of various organizations, supplemented by some new initiatives. Its chief components are:

1. Enforcement of fair housing laws. Federal fair housing laws provide that individuals encountering discrimination may bring suit directly in federal district courts. The courts hear such cases on an emergency basis and may, if discrimination is proved, issue appropriate orders to enforce the law and may grant damages to the complainant. The LCMOC provides investigators and attorneys. Experience in some 300 cases indicates that this is a prompt and effective method of enforcement.

Although court action in support of the rights of individuals will continue to be the heart of this effort, there are other legal aspects of importance. One is the active monitoring of federal enforcement of its own laws and regulations. For the last several years, builders who participate in FHA housing programs have been obligated to undertake "affirmative marketing" efforts, to attract minorities to their developments. Federal enforcement of this requirement has often been something less than vigorous.

A comparable vigilance will be needed to assure that the "equal opportunity" requirements of the new Section 8 subsidy program are adhered to. Sufficient funds are supposed to be made available to provide rental assistance to about 400,000 lower-income families each year. In the Chicago metropolitan area this could mean about 10,000 additional families assisted each year, about half in the city, half in the suburbs. Along with others, LCMOC will actively monitor the extent to which minorities benefit, both in city and suburbs.

Racial "steering" will continue to receive legal attention; LCMOC has already participated in three suits against groups of suburban real estate brokers. One of these suits has resulted in a "consent" order in which the brokers agreed to desist from the practice of referring white prospects to all-white areas and minorities only to areas already desegregated to one degree or another. This practice brings a threat of resegregation to areas known to be open to minorities while neighboring communities remain virtually all white.

Also, LCMOC brings action to suspend or revoke the Illinois real estate license of brokers who violate antidiscrimination laws and regulations.

2. Making the full housing market effectively available to minorities. A dual housing market persists, effectively excluding minorities from large segments of the housing supply. While whites tend to have access to a market that is metropolitan wide in scope, Blacks and others, particularly in the central cities, perceive a much narrower choice which confines them to their ghetto neighborhoods or nearby "changing areas." The housing market thus operates to perpetuate and reinforce segregation of the races. The program of LCMOC attacks this dual housing market at a number of key points, one of the first being an outreach effort to make minorities aware that housing opportunities for them do exist in a much broader geographic area than they may previously have considered.

Another outreach aspect has been establishment of a relationship with a number of major industries, including some that employ many minority people in their suburban establishments. There are also a number of aspects of this program which deal with the real estate industry, such as working with equal-opportunity committees of realtor's organizations to establish effective programs and gaining access to previously closed real estate boards and multiple listing pools for minority real estate brokers. A new effort has been begun by LCMOC to help establish suburban branch offices for several minority brokers who previously have operated only in the inner city. This is another measure designed to broaden the housing possibilities for minorities whose first contact is generally an inner-city broker.

3. Improving the supply and distribution of low- and moderate-income housing. The Metropolitan Housing Development Corpora-

tion is a not-for-profit organization established by LCMOC to build low- and moderate-income housing in the Chicago suburbs to demonstrate that good quality housing can be produced and successfully marketed on a racially integrated basis. It has completed two such developments, one located close to areas of considerable recent commercial and industrial expansion with a racial occupancy that is approximately 56 percent white, 29 Latino, 13 Black and 2 percent Oriental. A third development would have been completed and occupied were it not for the zoning problem which resulted in the aforementioned judicial decision, *MHDC* v the *Village of Arlington Heights, et al.*

Also LCMOC created the Regional Housing Coalition in cooperation with the Northeastern Illinois Planning Commission and a group of suburban mayors. The coalition (directed by me for the last three years) has developed and sought acceptance of a six-county plan which sets a framework for voluntary local action to meet low- and moderate-income housing needs. The Coalition has been invited to help suburban communities prepare housing assistance plans, to initiate housing need studies, and to explain the workings of housing subsidy programs. Overall, the coalition has endeavored to enhance the political acceptability of lower-income housing in the suburbs and to stimulate the implementation of programs to increase the supply of such housing, with emphasis on those areas which have experienced considerable industrial expansion.

Outlook

There are some encouraging signs that the suburban portions of our metropolitan areas are beginning to open to minorities and the poor. Implementation of the Housing and Community Development Act of 1974, the trend toward mixed-income housing, and action in the courts may combine to make possible some major breakthroughs during the next decade.

But this will occur only if there is sufficient concern and pressure to elevate housing as an issue to one of the top positions on the nation's agenda. It will require action based on the recognition that what happens to housing will greatly influence the possibility of achieving school desegregation, and that what happens to housing will also be crucial in determining whether minorities will have a reasonable opportunity to share in the expansion of employment.

It will require political consensus that opening entire metropolitan areas effectively to the minorities and the poor may well determine

171

the fate of our cities, and that the suburbs cannot prosper without healthy central cities. This political consensus can only be brought about by an overwhelming coalition of business, labor, religious, educational, and civil rights interests.

Despite the signs of progress we have seen in recent years, that progress has, in truth, been painfully slow, woefully inadequate. We can ill afford to be satisfied with a pace of metropolitan-area desegregation which will take many decades to produce a significant impact.

Until the necessary sense of urgency and priority is developed to deal realistically and forcefully with metropolitan housing issues, those having immediate concern with desegregation in education must base their actions on residential patterns much as they exist today. For the changes will occur too slowly to cause any significant numerical alteration in racial residential patterns for many years.

But there should be general awareness that the ultimate solution to desegregation in education is to achieve racial and economic balance in housing throughout our metropolitan areas. Thus it is logical that those to whom desegregated education is of high priority should be in the forefront of the housing effort.

Notes

1. *Newsweek* (December 10, 1973) reported a poll of U.S. citizens which included the question, "What are our biggest problems?" Housing ranked last among the 14 problems mentioned. Education ranked ninth, race relations twelfth.

2. As an example of HUD-established income limits for Section 8 eligibility, the median income for the Chicago metropolitan area has been set at $15,000. For a family of four, the maximum eligibility income (80%) is $12,700; the very low income limit (50%) is $7,950.

References

Kirby, David; Harris, Robert; and Crain, Robert L. *Political Strategies in Northern School Desegregation.* Lexington, Mass.: D. C. Heath Co., Lexington Books, 1973.

Massachusetts Housing Finance Agency. "All in Together: An Evaluation of Mixed Income Multi-Family Housing." Boston, January 1974.

U.S. Congress. Joint Economic Committee. Washington, D.C.: Government Printing Office, April 1975.

The Way I See It: Reflections on School Desegregation by Teachers from Four Cities

Introduction

In the remaining pages, five teachers from four cities present their views of desegregation. Their contributions were invited because we believed that the views of those at the storm center of the desegregation struggle are too often neglected. They are too often viewed simply as the servants of those who are making desegregation plans and those who are opposing them. Teachers, the attitude seems to be, will work in whatever atmosphere we create for them. Their reactions, their sentiments, their informed opinions are of no importance. Perhaps what teachers have to say is, indeed, of no great importance. They must work in the atmosphere created for them, for they are the paid professionals to whom we entrust the classrooms.

Nevertheless, their opinions and their sentiments, their reactions to the atmosphere in which they must work, is crucially important. For only they, in the end, can carry out the day-to-day task of making desegregated classrooms work. Their skills cannot but be affected by their feelings.

It is not particularly astounding to discover, in reading their comments, that these teachers are angry. They are angry at the "system" that has failed to provide them with an atmosphere in which they can use their skills most efficiently. They are, contrary to much received wisdom, deeply concerned about the children they teach. They are passionate in their concern for their schools. They see the center coming apart.

We feel fortunate that these teachers accepted our invitation to be forthright. We hope that their forthrightness will add to the understanding of the issues we all face in the next years as we attempt to find better solutions to the injustices that plague us.

THE EDITORS

SYLVIA FISCHER has taught in the primary grades of the Chicago Public School system for 18 years. Prior to that time, she worked as a social worker for several years. After examining educational changes in England while attending classes at the University of Chicago several years ago, she restructured her classes to conform to the open classroom model community used in England. Recently, she made a trip to China where she examined the schools.

HELEN NICHOLSON has been teaching French and English to high school juniors in the Hattiesburg public schools for 20 years.

MIRIAM W. VANCE has been teaching English in the secondary schools of Mississippi for 22 years. She has devoted a good deal of time to work in professional organizations to improve the quality of education.

FLORENCE C. LEWIS has been teaching English in the San Francisco public schools for more than 20 years. She has published articles and fiction in *Phi Delta Kappan, Changing Education, Teacher Paper, School Review,* and in *Trace, North American Review* and *Playgirl.* She is a member of the Bay Area Writing Project.

NELLIE BRODIS was, for nearly 30 years, a teacher in the Detroit public schools. She specialized in home economics, applied anthropology, and guidance at Western High School where she taught from 1969 until her retirement in 1975. She also served as Director of Home Economics at Wiley College.

From Chicago

SYLVIA FISCHER
Shoesmith Elementary School

In 1950, the Supreme Court ruled that restrictive covenants in housing were unconstitutional. Hyde Park, the neighborhood in which the
University of Chicago is located, which until then had been all white
and virtually all middle class to upper middle class, experienced a
swift change. The eastern boundary of what was then called the Black
Belt of Chicago adjoined the Hyde Park community. With the removal of restrictive covenants, the housing-poor Black community
looked to its closest neighbors for relief. Hyde Park became a "changing" neighborhood.

To the north of Hyde Park was Kenwood, a wealthy community of
manor-like old homes, tree-lined streets, and gracious apartments, an
area that once housed such people as the Swifts and the Wilsons, the
stockyard barons. Its eastern boundary was a street of more modest
dwellings and apartments whose owners gradually used the absence
of effective city restrictions on conversions to turn eight-room apartments into eight apartments. One-room kitchenettes proliferated,
housing for four became housing for forty. New slums began to en-
circle the community.

One public school existed in Kenwood, bearing the name of the
neighborhood. In addition, there were three private schools. Kenwood was a "good" public school. It had an established faculty in an
old three-story building. Its gym doubled as an assembly hall. Its
curriculum was the standard public school fare. Children learned
well, achieved good scores, and graduated to the local Hyde Park
High School, then a top school in scholarship. Kenwood had an active
PTA that did good deeds and held a luncheon of appreciation for the
faculty once each year. The mothers often used their own station
wagons for field trips before this practice was abolished by the Board
of Education. There were few, if any, discipline problems. Parents did
not question the curriculum and there was no challenge to the authority of the teacher. The PTA ladies were a formidable middle-class
group, and the teachers kept at a respectful distance from them. In
the early fifties, before the impact of "change" was apparent in Ken-

wood, the stability of the neighborhood was reflected in the stability of the school.

In the short span of 10 years, the school was transformed from an essentially all-white to an almost all-Black school. For a short period, it was integrated, though the Black children were primarily those of the poor. Middle-class Blacks were still few in number in the community. The curriculum did not change, and the faculty remained stable. But whites began to exit. Suddenly they questioned "educational standards," the "adequacy of the programs." Organized as most schools were at that time in homogeneous groups, their children would continue to receive the best the school could offer. Nevertheless, what had gone unquestioned before now became the rationale for departure. In Hyde Park, the University of Chicago became alarmed at the prospect of becoming a white institution surrounded by a Black community and initiated plans for urban renewal, community organization, and the expansion of its nursery school through twelfth-grade Laboratory School.

The expansion of the Laboratory School helped stem the flight of white families by offering an alternative to the public schools. Many families opted for this rather than other communities. But the effect on Kenwood School was to further reduce the number of white children and, for those families who could not afford the high tuition of a private school or who were commited to public education, the only alternative they seemed to see was the by now all-too-familiar flight to the suburbs.

By 1960, Kenwood was bursting at the seams with children. The almost all-white staff (the gym teacher and one substitute were Black) now teaching an almost all-Black school had difficulty coping. The school became chaotic, and the teachers despaired. There was no help from the Board of Education, just as there was no help from the city for the desperate people in the fringe slums. Hundreds of empty classrooms lay idle throughout the city, classrooms to which children, through redistricting or through busing, could have been sent to protect them from an untenable situation. On the outlying border of Kenwood raw sewage poured out of apartment buildings as the landlords abandoned their upkeep with the knowledge that they would soon come under the wrecking ball and bulldozer. And the city's Department of Public Health steadily ignored the repeated calls by the tenants for the most rudimentary sanitary services. The lack of stability in the neighborhood was reflected in the lack of stability in the school.

To accommodate the white families who remained in the community but who could not or would not send their children to a private school, a new facility was created. A small vacant strip of land owned by a banker in the Kenwood community had been purchased by the Board of Education. This land, however, was located in the very heart of the residential community. A fearful neighborhood, apprehensive about the composition of the school's population, was assured that it would be a small facility, no more than five grades. If the demolition ball and bulldozer did not accomplish their jobs thoroughly, at least the grade limitation would keep the teenage Black kids out, those most feared by the residents. The school was designed by an architect who resided in the area. It was esthetically designed, to be consonant with the neighborhood. Trees were preserved, and, instead of the usual cold blacktop surrounding schools, grass and shrubs were planted. The classrooms, however, were small. They were built to accommodate 25 children when the average class size in Chicago was rarely less than 40 and schools throughout the city were on double shift. (Only in 1975 did the teachers union contract win a class size of 29 for primary grades and 32 for middle grades, 14 long years after this school was built.)

The school, Beulah Shoesmith, named after a successful teacher at Hyde Park High, opened its doors in the fall of 1961. By then, urban renewal had successfully eliminated large pockets of the poor Black community, but not all.

Policies of the Board of Education on Integration

Was there a commitment at that time, by the Board of Education, to the principle of integrated education? Let's place this in historical perspective. This was 1961. A growing resentment on the part of the Black community, supported by white liberal elements decrying the appalling conditions existing in the schools, culminated in a massive boycott of the schools in October 1963. Parents demanded the removal of Benjamin Willis from the office of the superintendent and the institution of a policy of integration of staff and students. Chicago public schools were among the most segregated in the nation. It took three long years plus another school boycott before the Board responded with a new superintendent. What about the demand for integration? In a report of racial segregation in the Chicago public schools, 1965–66, the Chicago Urban League stated, "The response of the Chicago Board of Education to the sustained pressures of the Civil Rights Movement has been to increase what can be considered as *institutional tokenism*. The isolation of white pupils from Negro pupils has decreased. Today a greater number, and a higher proportion of white pupils are attending schools that have Negro students in them. At the same time, Negro students are more racially isolated than they were in 1963–64. A greater number and a higher proportion of Negro pupils are attending segregated schools" (Chicago Urban League 1965).

The Coordinating Council of Community Organizations, an umbrella organization that led the school boycotts and was dedicated to the fight for quality and integrated education, in July of 1965 submitted charges to the Department of Health, Education, and Welfare that "the Board of Education of the City of Chicago ... stands in violation of Title VI, Section 601, of the Civil Rights Act of 1964 ... which states 'No person in the United States shall, on the grounds of race, color or national origin, be excluded from participation in, be deprived of the benefits of, or be subjected to discrimination under any program or activity receiving Federal financial assistance.' ... We hold that the Board of Education of the City of Chicago operates a public school system that is, in fact and by its own statistics, segregated and discriminatory on a racial basis, and that the education offered Chicago's Negro children is not only separate from, but inferior in quality to that offered white children" (Raby 1965, p. 1).

When the Board finally acknowledged that segregation existed, it was attributed to housing patterns, beyond the control of the Board. However, in the case of *Webb* vs. *Board of Education of the City of Chicago, 1964*, it was alleged "that the Board of Education has acted in concert with the Chicago Real Estate Board, which has pursued a deliberate pattern of restriction of Negro residence within the city and ... 'has acted to create racial segregation in the public schools to coincide with residential racial segregation in the City of Chicago' " (Raby 1965 p. 3).

The Chicago Board of Education had also been known to lobby against versions of a bill called the Armstrong Act, which required that school boards not build schools "in such a manner as to promote segregation or separation of children in public schools because of color, race or nationality." In 1959, on March 25, in the proceedings of the Board, it is recorded that the members voted eight to one against that year's version of the Act (Raby 1965).

In 1967, the newly installed superintendent, James Redmond, offered a plan for school integration and improvements. "The immediate short-range goal must be to anchor the whites that still reside in the city. To do this requires that school authorities quickly achieve and maintain stable racial attendance proportions in changing fringe areas. We propose that Negro enrollments in the schools in these changing sections of the city be limited and fixed immediately" (Dunbar 1967). There was no proposal for integrating any other sections of the school community. The totality of the desegregation program in the Redmond-Board report would involve approximately 2 percent of the city's school children while the great multitudes of the children "for the foreseeable future will be attending racially segregated schools" (Dunbar 1967).

This brief outline will place in context the question of whether at any time there existed a commitment to integration in education by the Chicago Board of Education. Thus, "Does integration work?" cannot be divorced from the more significant question, "Was it meant to work?"

How Integration Worked at Shoesmith

When Shoesmith opened its doors in 1961, it was well integrated. Racial surveys were not of public record until 1965, therefore it is difficult to give exact figures. It was at least 50 percent white and possibly a bit more, according to the recollections of members of the community and the faculty. Economically, the school was also "integrated," middle-class whites with a small core of middle-class Blacks, but the preponderance of the Black students were from poor families. These extremes of class was one of the peculiarities of the Shoesmith attendance area. The school was nestled back to back with a block of private homes ranging in value (at present real estate prices) up from $75,000. Private homes to the north and to the west were of similar value. To the south lay a row of more modest but well-to-do homes with the southern boundary a row of luxury apartment dwellings. Directly to the east of the school, beyond a square block of playground which the school faced, was another street of gracious homes. In essence, the school lay in the center of a large square, on the periphery of which was the growing poor Black neighborhood.

During the early years of the school, the method of maintaining racial balance was to gerrymander the school boundary lines. The three public schools serving the surrounding neighborhoods had become almost all Black. There was continuous pressure by homeowners to be included in the Shoesmith area. Boundaries became elastic. As the outer fringes became Black, the district shrank. But average class sizes had to be maintained, so the boundaries moved back and forth across the northern and the western lines. Some children were bounced from school to school. The records of children from the fringe areas reflect the game being played. A child's record often listed three or four schools before he or she had finished two years. It was not unusual to have a child transfer out and back in again as the boundary shifted. Added to the burden of living in housing that was constantly

179

threatened with extinction, many children in these borderline areas never became integrated in the school community, but instead were forced into constant adjustment to a new school, new teachers, and new classmates.

Educationally, the school was traditionally organized with homogeneous grouping. This meant there were all-Black classes and virtually all-white classes. The 1C class, a "readiness" class for children "not ready" for first grade, was not only all Black (with the exception of one white child) but was also composed only of poor children. This was also true of the class for the "retarded" (EMH). Within the school there existed a dual educational system which differed little from the honors system used in integrated high schools and which served to segregate students there. This type of organization within the school continued for three years. To the credit of the administrator, he ultimately responded to the pressure of the PTA and at the close of three years (which coincided with his departure from Shoesmith) organized the school into heterogeneous grouping.

The ability level in the school went from the highest to the lowest. Coping with this wide range was not easy for the teachers. There was no help from the Board of Education. Even after Redmond stated his goal to "quickly achieve and maintain stable racial attendance proportions in changing fringe areas," there was no recognition of the need for programmatic changes or for augmenting the staff with additional personnel. Achieving racial balance was only a statistic to those downtown. The skewed affluence of the Shoesmith attendance area prohibited it from receiving help from the federal government under the Elementary and Secondary Education Act (ESEA). While in neighboring Black communities that qualified for ESEA funds, class size dropped drastically with a pupil-teacher ratio of 20 or less, the average class size at Shoesmith during the '60s never dropped below 32, and an individual teacher often had 36–40 children in a classroom. Eventually the school had the services of one paraprofessional.

Efforts to meet the varying needs of the children had to be assumed by the teachers and the community. In the school, attempts were made to give the individual teacher extra time with slower learners. One such effort was to gather the able readers into the lunchroom each day to work on independent reading while the classroom teacher remained behind with those who needed extra help. The PTA organized after-school study centers to provide tutoring and parents volunteered during school hours to work with individual children.

The burden was too great. In its first few years, Shoesmith had empty classrooms. There was no excuse for not assigning additional personnel to help reduce class size. It was not surprising that the teachers slipped back into homogeneous grouping as the only way to cope with the complex needs of the student body. In their homerooms children of different racial and economic backgrounds sat side by side, but for the bulk of the morning they moved into their reading-level rooms and the composition of the classes looked like it had in earlier years. To the credit of the teachers, those who taught the slower learners gave greatly of their energy to these students. But whether grouping takes place within a self-contained class or in separately organized rooms, the damage to a child's ego is the same. This was compounded for the poor Black children who sensed that the school was not primarily for them anyway.

If we are to believe that Shoesmith was meant to be a pioneering effort in integration, we have to recognize that a primary requisite would be a stable administration. But in a span of nine years, Shoesmith was introduced to four new principals. A small school, with a pupil population of less than 500, it became a steppingstone for new principals. Since they are paid on a per capita basis, it was economically unsound for a principal to remain in the school any longer than the apprenticeship period necessary to make him or her eligible for a larger elementary or high school. This policy of the Board of Education, unsound for any school, was particularly self-defeating to the goal of maintaining a consistent effort toward integrating a school, for above all, such a goal requires the stability of a good administration. Each new principal with new ideas and methods, and differing abilities to cope with Shoesmith's problems, meant a major adjustment for the faculty, the students, and the community.

The Shoesmith faculty was a good stable faculty within the public school system. A core of experienced primary teachers came as a group from the old Kenwood School to form the nucleus of the new faculty. One newly assigned Black teacher and one substitute teacher integrated the staff. The assistant principal was also Black. A desirable school, in a desirable location, made the transfer list into Shoesmith formidable. Within a few years, the staff was augmented by other Black faculty members, thus accomplishing a well-integrated faculty. However, the policy of the Board of Education to maintain a percentage of the staff as substitutes meant that each year one or two classes were assigned to inexperienced teachers who were more than likely assigned the more difficult classes to handle. This procedure is not unique to Shoesmith. It is a poor practice for administrators to favor the established teachers at the expense of the new teacher. As too frequently happens, the substitute may become discouraged and quit. A class may then have a series of teachers before one establishes a place for himself or herself. In the process, the class becomes chaotic and parents become dissatisfied. But, basically, the staff remained stable.

In 1966, only five years after it opened, Shoesmith was given an additional burden. The construction of a new high school in the community placed unusual stress on its facilities. The reasons for the construction of this new high school were almost the same as those for Shoesmith. The local children attended Hyde Park High School, which had not only turned almost completely Black, but poor working-class Black. Once the decision to build was made, Hyde Park's students were immediately transferred into the old Kenwood elementary school, where they would be housed while the new building was under construction. The upper-grade students at Kenwood were squeezed into Shoesmith, necessitating the erection of two mobile units on its grounds. And on the heels of this impossible development, in which a school designed to accommodate children through the fifth grade became a full eight-grade school, there arrived the third new principal. During such a trying time with overtaxed personnel and facilities, the school was not to have the help of an experienced administrator, but one lacking in experience or understanding of the nature of the community.

In 1966, the white population in Shoesmith was 31.7 percent. By the time the new high school was opened and its population returned to normal, in 1969, the white population of Shoesmith had dropped to 27.3 percent. The "delicate balance" of which Redmond had spoken earlier, the anchoring of "white" communities in fringe areas, was apparently no longer of concern.

How involved were the parents in the history of Shoesmith? The "welcome" sign on the door was not an invitation to participation, nor was it a welcome. The public schools have not been known for their warmth toward parents. At the ripe old age of 5, under compulsory, universal education, children are sent by parents who do not question, may not even be aware, that their tax dollars support the school system and that they therefore have a "right" to be involved. Respect and deference to school authorities was an accepted practice in the early '60s.

But the PTA of Shoesmith had always been active, capable, and vocal. They knew how to use influence and exert pressure. The board of the PTA was a reflection of the middle-class community, both Black and white. There was occasional, though much less, involvement of poor parents, too. The PTA traditionally had been a middle-class organization, and as an integrated PTA it still held this class position. While some liberal individuals in the organization made efforts to involve all segments of the population, the gap between the two groups was vast. Meeting on a social basis was not uncommon between Black and white middle class, but it was rare between poor Black and the middle class, either white or Black. This reflected itself in the PTA. Though the school population shifted steadily toward an increased number of Black students, the president of the PTA was always white until 1970. At that time, the school was 70.2 percent Black. The change in racial composition of the presidency of the PTA occurred at the same time that school advisory councils were being encouraged by the Board of Education. The first president of the Shoesmith Advisory Council was white.

In the early years of the school, the PTA worked actively for a more open-door policy. They initiated scheduled parent visitation days and were instrumental in establishing heterogeneous grouping. Like other well-intentioned groups at that time, the PTA set up study centers and tutoring programs to help students raise their achievement levels. Most, if not all, of these students were poor Blacks. But parents did not become involved in the intimate working of the school. It was not until later in the decade, when achievement scores were made public, that parents began to raise questions about what went on inside the classroom.

The spate of books published about the public schools, the deplorable achievement scores of the inner-city schoolchildren, and the impact of the civil rights movement gave a voice to parents who traditionally had not been heard from before. They began to demand to be involved in their children's education, and there arose a demand for community control in the late '60's.

In an effort to handle these demands, the Board of Education set up elected advisory councils in each school, to create an illusion of community control. By so doing, the board not only was able to co-opt those parents but was also able to deliver a severe blow to PTAs that had become militant. There were parents at Shoesmith who really believed that the councils offered them the means to participate in the functioning of the schools that had never been available before. Enthusiastically, they set about "changing" the school.

Conflict was inevitable. Through the years there has always been a standoff between teachers and parents, each feeling very insecure about the other. Knowing this, the board nevertheless made no preparation for this new "alliance" of teachers and parents. Teachers felt threatened, harassed, and distrustful. They felt they were the "professionals" and were leery of council recommendations. The parents demanded changes in organization, heterogeneous grouping, the adoption of innovative programs, participation in selection of new staff people, frequent visitation to classrooms, and a desire to be intimately involved in the functioning of the school. Meanwhile, the recently arrived principal was a former high school mathematics teacher, who came not only from an all-white school and neighborhood, but from a school in which parents had actively resisted integration. Prior to his assignment to Shoesmith, the faculty and the parents of Shoesmith had jointly appealed to have the assistant principal, a Black woman who had been with the school since its opening in 1961, appointed as principal. This request had been turned down. Regulations would have had to be bypassed to do so, and, in the inflexible manner typical of the Board, a request made with the support and unity of both the community and the staff was unwisely disregarded. Bringing integrated education to the school community is at best not an easy job, but when you face it with distrust and perhaps fear of that community, you do not have a prescription for success.

The atmosphere in the school became unhealthy. Suspicion and distrust grew not only between the staff and the community but within the staff itself. If a teacher agreed with the objectives of the parents, she came into conflict with the rest of the staff and the administration. It was a destructive impasse.

In the spring of 1974, the situation boiled over when a group of parents demanded the removal of a white teacher whom they charged with abusive, insensitive, racist behavior. The lack of response by the area superintendent to the parents and the inevitable feeling that there was no avenue for redress of their grievance made the parents take to the streets. The resulting confrontation, with parents and children picketing the school, divided the community. The teachers, the teachers' union, and the board united in defense of the teacher. Four years earlier a similar demand for the ouster of a different teacher had met with the same response. Both teachers eventually left voluntarily after a reasonable time, but the altercations were the excuse some white parents needed to remove their children from a "chaotic situation."

The advisory council at Shoesmith presently exists only nominally. The PTA seems to be reemerging as the stronger of the two groups, with the newly emerging Black middle class in leadership.

The interracial character of the school and its steady decline is reflected in table 1. The figures for the first four years of attendance for Shoesmith are not available, although there is no doubt that the Board of Education knew the racial composition of all of its schools.

In 1975, approximately 400 children were attending Shoesmith School of whom 13–15 percent were white. In 1970, the census figures for the total population of the Shoesmith attendance area was approximately 11,147. Of this number, 6,087 or 54 percent were white, 4,778

TABLE 1

Racial Student Survey, Shoesmith School, 1965–75

Year	Total Membership	White (%)
1965	486	29.8*
1966	631	31.7
1967	623	27.4
1968	608	28.0
1969	384	27.3
1970	393	26.2
1971	394	21.3
1972	376	17.8
1973	394	18.8
1974	427	14.3
1975	385–400†	13–15†

SOURCE.—Data gathered by the Chicago Board of Education and supplied by the Chicago Urban League.

*Percentages based on October 8 attendance for this year, not membership.

†Figures based on principal's estimates, not published reports.

or 42 percent were Black, and 276 or 2.4 percent were "other." The new housing that has been built in the area since 1970 is integrated. If one were to conjecture that there has been a shift toward a higher Black population in these areas, it is still dramatically evident in a walk around the neighborhood that the school population does not reflect the local population. Where have all the white children gone and why? One parent whose son is now at a private school commented, "Shoesmith was a good school. It gave a good solid base, but we wanted more." Another who removed her child during the unrest created by the demand for the teacher's removal and whose child now also attends a private school, stated, "Parents make decisions at our school. Parents must have a strong commitment to the school. The school couldn't last without the support of the parents. We clean the school and make the furniture" (in addition to which they pay $850 a year for these privileges). Perhaps this is one of the answers. When parents, both white and Black in this neighborhood, decide that they have had it with the public school system, it is very comfortable to have the wherewithal, short of moving to the suburbs, to choose an alternative. And what has happened in Hyde Park–Kenwood is that these alternatives are available. They are not only available but numerous. There are at least five alternative schools. There is also a minimagnet public school with racial quotas and a limited class size. At least 68 white children from the Shoesmith attendance area are attending local private schools. If this number of white students, which exceeds the number now in attendance at Shoesmith, were added to its current white student population, this would change the student body to nearly 30 percent white.

As the schools remained unresponsive to the needs of a segment of the population, loss of faith in the public schools developed, all of which stimulated the growth of new facilities. What must be born in mind, though, is that such lack of faith can be translated into action for the parent who can pay for it. And that lack of faith is more evident in the racially mixed schools in the community than it would be if the school were all white. Kenwood of the early fifties was a good school, nothing innovative or dramatically different. When the Blacks moved in, the whites moved out. As a racially mixed school, Shoesmith continued to be a good school measured by the same standards Kenwood had been measured by earlier, but then as each difficulty arose, some white parents chose the occasion to withdraw their children. Those who left could do so because they were financially able to. Obviously, working-class people, whether white or Black, do not have that option.

In the heart of an area dedicated to residential integration, Shoesmith School is becoming segregated. The white community has been "anchored" in the neighborhood, but the white school population has been lost. It is hard to believe that the Board of Education and those who held power in the community ever had integration as an objective for the school. Their objective must always have been simply to maintain a stable white middle-class area by providing a separate school while the Black population of the community was thinned out by urban renewal. To place children of different ethnic backgrounds side by side in the classroom, with different educational achievement and different attitudes, and then to carry on "business as usual" and to call it integration is to invite failure. A commitment to integrate must have as its main component a commitment to educate.

The board never acknowledged the special problems and the special needs engendered by such a diverse population. In fact, it contributed to the destabilization of the school by its personnel policies in the selection of principals, by its inability to resolve teacher-parent problems short of an actual confrontation, and by its disregard of the consequences of overcrowding the school at the time of the construction of the new high school.

The parents of Shoesmith, through the years, have shown greater dedication to the principle of integration than has the Board. Perhaps because of the peculiar nature of the community, which contains a high percentage of liberals and radicals, parents have actively fought to maintain the school as integrated. During the civil rights upsurge and in the height of the anti-Willis campaign, it was they who pressured for the abolition of tracking, recognizing its racist implications. It was the parents who set up study centers and tutoring programs in the hope that they could compensate for the deficiencies of the Board. In spite of these and numerous other efforts by the parents, the school did not work for them.

Now new parents moving to Kenwood to live in an interracial community and have their children share experiences in an integrated school are confronted with a school that does not meet this need. And like the parents who have already removed their children from Shoesmith, they are turning to the variety of alternative schools existing in the community, none of which is segregated.

Ironically, in an integrated neighborhood, where busing is unnecessary to achieve integration and where integration of the school has not caused residential segregation, the school, by virtue of a policy of indifference by the Board of Education, has come to the verge of unacceptable segregation.

References

Chicago Urban League. "Racial Segregation in the Chicago Public Schools, 1965–66." Research report. Mimeographed. Chicago: Chicago Urban League, September 1966.

Dunbar, Ruth. *Chicago Sun-Times* (September 10, 1967).

Raby, Albert. Letter to Francis Keppel, Commissioner of Education, U.S. Department of Education and Welfare, July 4, 1965.

From Hattiesburg, Mississippi

HELEN NICHOLSON
Hattiesburg High School, Blair Center

Yes, in my opinion, school desegregation is still a good idea for the purpose of providing adequate teaching materials and supplies and for dispelling of some of the fallacies usually associated with the races. No, desegregation is not still a good idea from a humanistic point of view.

Before integration of this school system, Black teachers had to provide their own teaching supplies and, for the most part, knew nothing at all about departmental budgets. However, in the integrated system materials are supplied, and major departments have budgets. We may

187

now issue textbooks to each individual child. There was a time when Black students who were either sisters and brothers or friends who lived near each other had to share one textbook.

Physical facilities, in general, are and have been adequate in the entire system. But the classroom I occupy in the now integrated structure is never as warm in winter as the one occupied in the former all-Black school.

Black students were proud of their school, which had its own band and majorettes, its own football team which the entire Black community and some of the white community supported with a certain kind of pride, and its own homecoming queen who was really a "queen" because she had to compete in a contest designed on the format of the Miss America pageant. This contest was supervised by faculty personnel who screened the contestants using certain criteria to be sure the school and student body would be fully represented. The all-Black school also had its annual prom which was the big school social function of the year that involved a majority of the students. The students could only invite school persons (any high school student in the general area) who would adhere to rules enforced by faculty and parent chaperones. But, with forced integration, Black students had to give up and leave buried with the segregated Black school the Black way of doing things. So, from this point of view, forced integration is not still a good idea.

When the local school system was forced to integrate, neither the Blacks nor the whites wanted it. The whites too were proud of their school and its functioning, I suppose. I am sure it was no easier for them to have to share that which they had always had for themselves than it was for Blacks to come where they were not wanted and did not want to come. But, both Blacks and whites met the challenge from a humanistic point of view: school integration was something not desired, but which had to be.

In the beginning both students and teachers who were forced to be together were not relaxed. Most of us worked at making the system work in spite of what we as individuals felt. I believe that the reason the system has worked thus far is because those of us involved—the Board of Education, the superintendent, the assistant superintendents, principals, and assistant principals, parents, community leaders, students and teachers—have honestly tried to make it work.

I also feel that school desegregation is still a good idea because it dispels some of the fallacies related to race, and everyone gets an opportunity "to see for himself" some of the many things heretofore alluded to as "they say." Blacks have learned that all whites are not smart, and whites have learned that all Blacks are not dumb; there are extremes in all racial groups. It is sometimes difficult for some whites to accept the fact that there are some intelligent Black students. Also, Blacks are often labeled as speaking a dialect, but the fact is that there are regional dialects among all races. Nevertheless, nonstandard English is associated only with the Black race. But most times in the classroom where students have been integrated for a year or more no one notices very much difference in speaking.

In the classroom, I have found no evidence that the presence of white students helps Black students learn; but, I do believe that proper motivation and effective teaching help *all* students, Black and white, learn. There are, possibly, some situations where the Black students learn through the presence of white students when the teacher (Black or white) ignores the Blacks and teaches the whites. This, then, is the Blacks' only way to learn, if they learn at all. It is often when the Black child has been ignored that he sometimes demands attention in the classroom by being boisterous or outright rude. Then, of course, he is a "discipline problem" and is often suspended as such. However, "settings for teaching attitudes and behavior essential for dissolving racial tension" have been created to an extent in the classroom. Students do, for the most part, respect anyone who is speaking with no regard to race. We are, after all, human beings brought together for one common cause: Education.

Even now we tend to segregate ourselves by race in the classroom, in the lunchroom, and on campus, not because we are forced to, but because we tend to associate with peers on the bases of race, interest, religion, and social class. For this reason it is my opinion that optimal conditions on which to build an egalitarian multiracial society cannot exist in forced integration. Most especially is this true when one race has to give up its way of doing things, even the good things.

It is hoped that Black students in the future will be given more positive recognition in areas other than sports, and that Blacks will not make up the greatest percentage of students in special-education and remedial-reading classes. We have tried and are still trying to make the system work, and I believe that it eventually will work with less effort.

MIRIAM W. VANCE
Blair High School, Hattiesburg

Black children have not only endured the hostility of white children, of parents and teachers who opposed integration of schools, but have also generated hostility for the same reasons. Integration, however, has given to each group an opportunity to witness Black and white educators cooperate and coordinate their efforts in a spirit of mutual respect.

The Black student who has lost his community school expresses his resentment through negative attitudes, seldom considering the fact that white children have experienced a similar loss. The most difficult task a strong white teacher faces with these students is the student's interpretation of discipline as prejudice, his reaction to correction or criticism as ridicule, and his belief that low grades are an implement of punishment.

The Black student allows racial factors to dominate most student activities. Seldom does he consider the qualifications of the Black and the white candidates beyond the racial factor. In pep rallies and school projects, the Black student does not support the white leaders, but he will enthusiastically back the Black ones. He, in essence, segregates himself in these matters while at the same time demanding understanding and equal treatment.

It is absolutely essential that the Black student and his leaders recognize that the white people also need understanding in their struggle to overcome generations of inbred prejudice. That greater progress can be made toward solving the overall question of integration in the classrooms of our public schools is no mere sociological theory. Teachers—the honest-to-goodness dedicated teachers—do not look at students by color, social position, financial status. A child is an individual in the classroom. Thus time is solving many of the problems of establishing "optimal conditions on which to build an egalitarian multiracial society."

The early days of integration found Black students defensive and hostile. They resented discipline and considered suspension for failure to honor "white" rules of school too radical. In the few protests held, they did not hesitate to intimidate those Blacks who failed to join their crusade.

Stealing increased some 90 percent with integration and the greatest problem for those caught seemed to be the fact that one might be caught. It seemed inconceivable to Black students that teachers and administrators would pursue such a matter until it was solved and punishment meted.

Threatening a faculty member with physical violence, parental intervention, or legal means apparently had been an effective approach to some of the problems in segregated schools. Integrated faculties, however, have been generally very strong and confident and seldom feel such threats to be of any consequence. (This has been a very positive result of integration—the systematic "weeding-out" of weak personnel and the establishment of strong faculties in most schools.)

Distressing also in the early days of integration was the apparent access Black students had to textbook-teacher aids. When tests were given from such materials, poor Black students often scored between 95 and 100 while average and good white students would score under 95.

The years have not changed some problems. Many white as well as many Black teachers and administrators with deeply rooted prejudice remain in the system. Time itself has solved some of the original problems. We have yet to graduate the first class of 12-year-integrated students. But each year brings with it a new group of better-adjusted students who seem eager to learn and ready to accept others for what they are. After some seven or eight years of integration, schools are creating a "setting for teaching attitudes and behavior essential to dissoving racial tension." The final answer how-ever must come from the concentrated efforts of both Blacks and whites to face the remaining problems and to meet the existing needs.

From San Francisco

FLORENCE C. LEWIS
Lowell High School

My story is a story of one city, not two cities or a nation, but I tell you my story because it may point out how much the process we call integration depends upon the careful, compassionate dismantling of walls and prejudice.

As long ago as 1961 the schools of San Francisco were changing their boundary lines. Lily-white schools were showing black and brown faces here and there. In 1964, we had 300 in a school population of 2,700. And the numbers increased steadily. In 1965, one of my colleagues asked our principal to make "these other" kids feel at home. He was dismissed as a troublemaker.

In 1966, I began to discover what it meant to be hated because *my skin was white*. It came as a shock to me because I believed I had never hated a man, woman, or child because his color or religion was differ-ent from mine. In fact, if they had a religion, I always rather envied them because I have none, and I've always been baffled by what other people call "grace." As for color, I was always certain that no pigment has the edge on genius, but that lack of formal education and no money in the bank leads to lack of confidence and alcoholism and prostitution, not necessarily in the first generation but certainly by the second and third and fourth. So I did not hate anybody for his color. I just scorned him. Or I took him for granted. Or I condescended to be nice to him. On occasion I found I genuinely liked a person whose color was different from my own because he or she thought the way I did, cussed the way I did, had the same kind of mothering or grandmothering —and it was always a revelation when I discovered how genuinely decent I was underneath . . . almost like having grace. No, I never hated people. Or, I hated them if they disagreed with me or came late to class or were cop-outs from the classroom like half the staff at Central Office. But hatred for another person's guts, no.

But in 1968, if you asked me to exchange places with a man or a woman whose color was different from my own I wouldn't do it. Why should I exchange comfort and security for the unknown. I repeat. I protest my basic decency. It would be like living with my own immortality! Overwhelming!! So I took comfort in the knowledge that some of my friends and former students were in jails in Mississippi, and then my friends came home from Mississippi and told me that the Black people wanted to be in charge of their own destiny. And then came strange stories about Arabs and the Jews and then came 1968, when we could no longer send a kid on a school errand, lest he come back bloodied . . . and with his teeth missing.

And I found out why.

At rap sessions and community speak-ups, and in the cafeteria where I would walk around at lunchtime eating a hot dog and my heart out, I learned how much I was hated, and my honkie culture, too. And formerly docile Black kids told me and other interested parties that they would no longer tolerate our speaking down to them; nor would they tolerate an attack on a Black brother or sister, verbal even; that they were men now, and women; that their family was united as never before against the common enemy. And Black was beautiful. And white . . . you name it! I recall gasping. And over the years rumbled Willie Powell to haunt me, Willie Powell, who said to me one day, "You think because you're nice to me I have to kiss your feet." Where was I now on the ladder of those who weren't "even" nice to him? Above or below? The venom in this kid had chilled me. Now the hate was wide open. It was everywhere. The ambulance carried it off every day. I repeat, you couldn't even send a kid on an errand—an errand. He didn't come back . . . or you picked up his teeth in the hall. You got a glimpse of another kind of pain, too.

192

"I don't hate you, personally, Mrs. Lewis, but don't hug me when my friends are around."

Or

"I don't have words to say, you know, what I feel inside me. Like a lot of white kids can write, only they don't have nothing to say. Like I feel I got a bomb in me, and I can't get it out."

At a community rap session one day I heard a Black kid speak out. His speech was full of poison against the white establishment. The white man was selling his brothers and sisters down the river to keep them in slavery. The white man was selling them dope and ignorance. And the brothers and the sisters were buying what the white man was selling and buying an image of themselves which all the cries of "Black is Beautiful" could not deny.

"You don't read and you don't think for yourselves," he said.

"You're still slaves 'cause you're ignorant," he said.

"Ignorance is your worst enemy," he said.

The boy was a spellbinder: poised, articulate, dignified. He was a natural orator. I drank in what he said because I was thirsty for some relief of guilt. He was saying what I had said—what Orwell had said. If there was a stronger message beyond the immediate, a threat of more disaster should the Black man and woman ever discover how profound was their enslavement, I didn't want to pick it up. For the moment I wanted to hear that it was not all my fault.

"You don't read. You don't think. You jive."

I didn't say it. He did. I fell in love with him.

Several days later I waylaid him in the hall, and said to him quite simply,

"Why don't you study English with me?"

"I'm graduating," he said.

"Where have you been for three years?"

"Cutting."

He was on his way to math class with my friend Mary Allen who informed me he was, yes, a brilliant cutter, one of the kids who could hit the books by himself, but who lost a lot of the extras that she gave in class and that other brilliant kids gave too, the dynamics of exchange.

What could we do to help him? What could he do to help us? We both decided not to let him hate us. He could hate anybody else he liked. We gave him books to read. We badgered him for his cutting, but our concern and our esteem for him was obvious.

One day Mary asked if Ellis could take a makeup math test in my sophomore English class. We taught next door.

I apologized to Mary and explained that my class was hardly the quiet corner Ellis needed to take a make-up test.

"This is my dump-all class, Mary," I said. "I have 36 separate problems and I'm sitting on a bomb every day."

"Ellis won't mind," she said.

Ellis didn't mind. He strolled in, sat down in a broken chair and proceeded to do his test and watch my class and me carefully out of the corner of his eye.

Sophomore English seventh period—the end of the day: ages 15–17½—reading level, third grade to seventh. Writing: all the way from standing 15 minutes at a pencil sharpener to sitting on a ballpoint pen in class and staring at the paper. Emotional problems grievous and egregious. Hardest hit were the Black kids who couldn't decide to hate Whitey, so they ended up hating themselves and going catatonic like Angie, who sat for a whole period and glared at me. At home she glared at her mother . . . or Princeton, who had to pace back and forth across the room at least twice an hour—just because he had to.

Also hard hit were the white kids who still insisted on using the word "nigger" in my class or thinking it. Even as I scolded them fiercely, I worried for their lives. And I was amazed at how violent my own language had become. "You stupid moron," I called them under my breath, or worse. How convenient to cuss out a kid for his stupidity and ignorance when he wore it so openly and neatly for me to step on him, not on myself.

On a good day, 30 of my 36 kids attended sophomore English. The class that Ellis witnessed was a typical "language day" class. Together we had read a story, dramatized parts of it, cleared up certain problems having to do with the narration and narrator: was the whole story the narrator told a lie? Some of the class wasn't sure. Their generation, raised exclusively on television and the world of sports, still was not sure about a boy who insists he can jump 11 feet without the aid of a pole. Previously he had jumped six feet, without even a running start.[1] Why were the facts so difficult to assess for some of them? Was it ignorance of what goes on in broad jumping or pole vaulting? Only ignorance? Was their own wish for the narrator to succeed getting in the way? Were they being conned? Suckered? Why? Did they want something to happen? A miracle maybe? To take away pain?

After such probing, we would write in class. Our composition? "Why people (some people, all people) tell lies" . . . or "What is a miracle?" . . . and on "language day" we reviewed certain words from the story . . . how to spell them, how to use them, so that we could get ready to write. For example, we would learn what was different about the word "lies" in "he tells lies," "he lies to his mother every day," "he lies around the house on Saturday." How did we know that "lies" was a noun in one sentence and a verb in another? How did we know that one verb derives from the idea to tell a lie and the other verb derives from the idea to recline. What signals did we have? What clues? In a language lesson, barring emergencies like Princeton's needing to pace, we could discuss 10 words easily: their spelling, their parts of speech, their denotation and connotation. What's the relationship between a miracle and a mirage? Why should we bother about relationship between words?

A very basic class.

To get ready for a very simple but earnest composition at home or in class.

To get ready for the major job of understanding why we all love a fairy tale and a happening and a miracle. And lies. To get ready to understand . . . other people, not us.

Ellis left five minutes before the hour ended, and Mary Allen wanted to know what kept him so long.

"I think he was observing the class," I said.

Shortly after (this class), the Black students won their right to organize a BSU. Again, young blood and strong teeth poured down our sinks and into our latrines for this right. I continued to attend a series of rap sessions now devoted to what kids, no matter their color, hated about schools. Two issues prevailed.

The war in Vietnam.

The second was boredom. Over and over again—"Nothing happens in school."

"What's supposed to happen in a classroom?" I asked.

The kids said they had teachers who still gave them chapters to outline in history and biology and *that* was not their idea of teaching.

They had classes that didn't mean anything to them, to their lives —neither their present nor their future. They didn't see what the past had to say to the present.

Math was irrelevant, too.

The Black kids stayed away from these white raps. They had won a little hunk of identity in the BSU, and they still had wounds to probe, and Whitey wasn't welcome at the BSU. He could come, if he wanted to—but masochism has to be somewhat disguised, otherwise it loses its kick. So Whitey stayed away, and the Black kids were happy. Now and then a leader like Ellis would, however, appear at Whitey's rap sessions. He was curious. He liked to listen. Sometimes he participated. He agreed that Vietnam was a vital issue. He also insisted that Vietnam was a way to carry on genocide.

"The Black man is dying in this war and killing his yellow brothers and his sisters."

The white kids listened to Ellis. He was a boy you had to respect.

But always there came the boredom trip. School was boring! Boring! Boring!

I finally exploded: "Learning sometimes requires sitting and listening to a teacher, even outlining. . . ."

Ellis interrupted.

"You remember that class I saw?"

"The day you were taking the test?"

"That's right."

"Yes—"

"That class wasn't boring. I never had a class like that."

"Ellis, maybe you never gave the teacher a chance. You know how much you cut. . . ."

"I mean . . . teachers didn't care . . . they didn't think we could learn."

If you, gentle reader, examine this little story, it may appear to you that I am on a first class ego trip. But what I am trying to make clear is the climate of the sixties—how much injustice the Black kids had suffered, how much they had been left out of a traditionally solid education and certainly the fun of going to school . . . how necessary desegregation was in order to give them a chance because they were the dispossessed. They simply had not counted. What I am also trying to make clear is that kids like Ellis wanted a middle-class education, for that is what I believe Ellis was complaining of when he said he had never had a class like the one he had observed out of the corner of his eye the afternoon he sat taking a math test. He wanted an education that continued, that built on what had gone before, that came to some conclusion, that taught specific skills in the process. I seriously doubt that the schools which he attended, even if he never cut, would have provided him with this fairly routine experience—for a variety of reasons, but among these reasons would most certainly loom teachers who could not teach Ellis or who did not care to. And Ellis was angry. And the girl who said she despised the honkie culture was angry. But Ellis was looking for integration. The angry girl was just looking.

If we now examine the word "integration," I think we can acknowledge the idea that to many people integration still connotes a middle-class education. For if the various parts combine to make a perfect whole . . . what is the whole if not the kind of learning experience which assures the young of reading, writing, arithmetic, and a college education and all the goods and the goodnesses that are supposed to follow? I think we can acknowledge that several in my school were prepared to give Ellis this kind of learning experience, if only he would come to class every day and not hate us openly. We could "integrate" him if only he would "put up and shut up." And Ellis, we believed, would begin to integrate us too, provided that we had learned a lesson or two, that he counted, that he had a past as well as a future. A middle-class education gets kids ready for the good life by keeping them good little kids for a long time . . . but if the rewards are pleasant and everyone has an equal chance and if everyone gets counted once a day, a long childhood is bearable. But Ellis would have to play this game, and playing our game might just be unbearable for him as it was becoming unbearable for kids who felt the system was asking them to die in wars like Vietnam. The civil rights movement and the antiwar movement and the pain of three assassinations had opened us up not only to the pain of the dispossessed but to our own acceptance of a fixed system and a fixed morality that would not even permit charity to begin at home. Our new understanding taught us how to recognize shame and panic behind sullenness and apathy and finally defiance.

But it could not make us understand how much we were hated by Ellis and the angry girl. Could we understand how ugly it was for Ellis to desire this gift of a middle-class education and be forced to play Whitey's game in order to achieve it, to lick Whitey's boots—even though Whitey said he didn't have to, even swore up and down? Could we understand how demeaning it was, how unmanly, to desire this honkie culture when it was Whitey dishing it out? And yet who could do it better? If not Whitey, who then—an Uncle Tom or a Mrs. Uncle Tom who had forgotten what Whitey could never know—the experience, the soul pain? As Whitey, could I be sister or friend—I who had been raised "A Stitch in Time Saves Nine,"—"Early to Bed"—"Save for Tomorrow"—"Duty before Pleasure"? I was verbal, so how could I know what school meant to kids who came from places where no one explained things at the dinner table and on walks; where every day was lived in a closet or else a traffic jam. So how could these kids succeed in school when the ability to verbalize and reason starts with specific questions that the child asks and the generalizations that the adult helps the child make. Home is where it's at—adults reading stories, helping to solve puzzles, drawing pictures. How could these kids fail to be offended by my looks of dismay and wonder . . . And how could they fail to offend me even more by their verbal and physical acting out? How could I not feel violated by their long, sullen looks and their final judgment of me—

"You sh-e-e-t!"

What could they desire from Whitey's school except to tear it down—out of rage, out of frustration, out of sheer inability to cope—or out of sheer unwillingness to wait . . . to overcome.

So where were we with our new understanding?

Right in the middle of our rage and fear and trembling.

Behold! My little story may make clear the meaning of desegregation as the exposition and partial expression at least of rage and hate and bitterness. For historically, dialectically, rage must out, but rage strikes the innocent, just as former cruelty and prejudice destroyed the innocent as well as the strong and left the survivors, in too many cases, as cruel as the executioners. In the meantime, sensitivity to another's pain becomes anesthetized, paralyzed, numb. And teaching the traditional middle-class skills becomes impossible.

Perhaps we can understand integration as the calm that follows the storm or as stasis after stress, or as the new form that force must take—but what is it that the various parts have integrated, what understanding is there after the debris has been cleared away? What is the new form? Out of the painful desegregation process must finally come an examination of why we hate and how we project on others what we hate in ourselves. We hate it when we are called upon to think and feel in new ways. We hate it when we are witness to our intellectual and emotional inadequacies. We hate it when violence is returned for condescension. And, yes, we hate it when we have to live among alien customs, habits, and speech, and when no one welcomes us or makes us feel at home. And, yes, this works both ways. Myself, I know what it feels like to ask a human being a question and have him turn away from me and walk down the hall as if I did not exist. The question is not am I big enough to take this acting out of what others have done to him. The real question is how long can I take it and teach. The question is not whether I am élite enough to put a stop to élitism but élite enough to say—"Look, both of us are wrong if we continue in this fashion." Out of the painful desegregation process must also come a reexamination of some of the idols we have worshiped or the myths we have loved so long. For example, are the following solid structures or simply props which a mean wind can knock over, or an excellent "because" clause? (Try following each of these statements with a good because clause and see where it gets you.)

> That all kids are created equal because
> That they all desire to read and write because
> That their parents desire these blessings for them
> That freedom means doing your thing
> That going to school makes men free
> And brotherhood possible
> And gives men jobs
> That Black people do not "really" have a history
> That white men are by their nature exploiters of other human beings

198

That kids will learn Swahili because it's relevant (two because's)
That kids cannot learn from an authority figure
That only violence can bring about change
That teachers must never go on strike
That the dispossessed and the disenfranchised are purer and less prone to love material gain than their establishment brothers and sisters
That tracking or classes for the gifted is intolerable in a free society
. . . or whatever

The "because clause" knocks the wind out of half-truths, doesn't it? Desegregation has taught us something about some of our pet idols. Are we ready to give up their worship, or do we still adore? What, for example, do most of us know about what the IQ tests *measure* or *do not measure?* How many of us can even begin to think about this question? Without a painful dose of honesty about what is good for certain kids and bad for others, we cannot even be honest about our dismay or our disgust with the way Greater Boston is behaving in the year of our bicentennial. Another Battle of Bunker Hill . . . indeed. What is our part in this hate? For which side are we rooting? Do we still see only Black and white and only one the victim?

If by integration we still mean bringing together separate parts to make up a whole, we had better set limits on that whole. If the whole is forced to produce every single answer for a mixed-up world, then its center cannot hold and things do fall apart. If by integration we mean the instant solution to 50 years of innovation and 300 years of injustice, there can be no harmony. If by integration we desire no acting out of former oppression, no violence either, we had better start talking and backing up our talk. If there are too many separate battles, and the battles all have a rationale—then one part begins to cancel out the other. And the whole? Where is it? What is it?

For some schools and some communities these measures are necessary steps in the desegregation process:

    —Free breakfasts and lunches for kids whose homes cannot provide them with adequate nutrition
    —Pride instilled in little ones that the white man must not put them down
    —Some neighborhood control of school
    —Active recruitment of minority teachers, counselors
    —Sensitivity courses in Black literature, Oriental literature, and Chicano literature in the curriculum
    —Busing

For other schools and some communities these measures are equally necessary:

—Guilt removed from the little ones and the big ones too that they are corrupt because the society is
—Guilt removed that they enslaved others
—Guilt removed that they are more verbal and that they learn with ease
—No forced busing

Can we have a school that attempts to work equally well with both groups? Can we have a school that is not ashamed to provide a program for the gifted so that a boy like Ellis will not be bored to death (my little class would pall on him after the third week)—and a new generation, ethnic, that respects learning? Programs for the gifted learner or the super achiever (we don't have to despise them—do we despise our football stars or our sandlot heroes?) do not necessarily draw funds away from other programs. What they do provide, very often, is innovation in teaching, experimentation, because for one thing you can be sure that in such a class most of the kids will be there, day after day, out of motivation and out of interest, yes, out of desire for a grade too. Can we have a school that provides daily discipline and instruction in language for those kids who come from Vietnam or Hong Kong or the Deep South, without forcing this highly specialized language teaching on teachers who are already meeting the needs of 30×5 or 35×5 or 45×5 kids in literature, composition, and fire drills?

Let me recall to you the story we read in class the day that Ellis listened. It was a story about learning. It taught that learning does not happen by magic—by leaping over a pole without the help of a stick and without days and weeks and months of coming out of practice.

And then it happens—it happens with that leap, that bound, especially after the hard practice, the sweat, the tears.

Perhaps some of us will learn from the desegregation experience how to listen to old needs and new. Perhaps the answer will not be a middle-class education for all, but for some. Perhaps integration will come to mean separate but equal for some . . . once again.

Perhaps we have been trying to jump over a pole, a building, a whole city, a whole century, without the careful work of months and coming out to practice. Perhaps that is why it isn't happening. The desegregation, yes—but not that illusive thing desegregation is supposed to achieve. Perhaps the thing we call integration is the Phoenix that will rise from the ashes.

The past is supposed to teach us about the present, but each present has its own variables, so we do not yet know the shape that our Phoenix will take . . . but it must not be crow—for any, anymore.

Note

1. "That's What Happened to Me," by Michael Fessier, still packs a wallop although the language is dated and sentimental.

From Detroit

NELLIE BRODIS, retired

I have often been accused of being an idealist, and a naive one at that. This aspect of my personality combined with more than two decades of public school teaching convinces me that our dream of peaceful integration can become reality. But two decades in the public schools of Detroit have also convinced me that, while the children can easily accept integration, they will do so only if we can find ways to change the attitudes of their parents and the school people. It will not just happen; specific things must be done to help them overcome their resistance. Therefore, I would like to offer some guidelines that I believe are needed and would be effective to unite Americans in their efforts to build an integrated school system.

I need to add, before I go on, that I have, in these opening words, been talking about integration, implying that desegregation and integration are synonymous. They are not. But I believe that desegregating the schools will in time accomplish their integration. I should also add that I do not believe that desegregation can occur in our present circumstances without busing. So, in the following pages, I will be including, when I say desegregation, busing for desegregation. The legal requirement that the schools desegregate, to be accomplished by busing children out of their neighborhoods, has caused great damage to some children and parents. I believe that the guidelines I am about to propose can avoid, in the future, the problems we have witnessed in the past. What I want to suggest will help us avoid:

—Division among adults who had not previously been divided
—Confusion in children about values, standards, and whom to emulate

—Loss of respect for our laws, for those who enforce them and others in authority
—Bewilderment and disenchantment with school that result from the disparity between what can be observed and what is taught

The mandated dissolution of dual school systems and racially identifiable schools emanated from idealists who were strong supporters of our Constitution, loved America, and believed that quality education for all was a moral issue and school segregation was morally unjust.

The idealists envisioned the elimination of racially identifiable schools and of a learning environment which would encourage, challenge, and instruct all children. As a result each child would improve and develop cognitive and affective strengths consistent with his innate capacities. They believed in the possibility of a curriculum that would provide the opportunity to acquire social, emotional, and intellectual competencies, attitudes and habits necessary for harmony and success in a multiethnic society.

These goals can be peacefully accomplished if we are willing and able to benefit from the expertise and resources of what Lippett, Watson, and Westley (1958) refer to as a change agent, a resource person called in to help improve conditions while working with the people or community involved. These kinds of skills are required because those people involved in the desegregation process must be capable innovators. They must be able to handle the resistance that they will inevitably encounter; to understand the customs, habits, and values of people from all socioeconomic classes; to plan classroom methods based on the favorable and unfavorable elements of the environment; to realize that the problems of desegregation are problems of group ethics which often evoke emotional reactions which require that innovators govern their responses by professional ethics and knowledge of racial differences and individual learning capacities; to understand that some people benefit from the existing system of social and racial inequality; to understand that the complexity of parent-child, teacher-school relationships that influence performance in school become intensified in a changing scene. Indeed achievement in an integrated school is doomed to failure unless one understands that the teachers themselves are "change agents" and as such must bring to class special competencies to introduce change.

Loud demands, unruly demonstrations, and violence are often methods of remediation. Therefore, court orders for desegregation should require that all the professionals involved take courses in methods of introducing social change. Such courses should include information about cultural differences so that those involved can understand and anticipate the reactions of communities who reject, for example, the concept of busing. Such understanding could then be used as a basis for the selection of appropriate techniques for the penetration of personal, interpersonal, and intergroup barriers.

This training period should be about a month long and should be presented before the implementation of busing particularly, so that those who oppose busing can at least begin to unlearn these attitudes.

But behavioral change does not depend upon attitudinal change if the sanctions for nonperformance are great enough. The current economic situation, the surplus of teachers, and the general paucity of jobs in other fields could be combined with accountability of school personnel in such a way that few educators could refuse to meet the requirements of their jobs.

For most people, the loss of economic security is too great a price to pay for engaging in antibusing behavior.

Assisting the teacher.—Directing the students' learning activities is one function of a teacher. This function is largely a matter of human relations, concerned with guiding, overseeing, securing cooperation, and maintaining good interpersonal relations. While the teacher function is always the most crucial one, it becomes even more important in a classroom that is undergoing social change. The teacher needs help, both in human-relations training in the workshops I've proposed and also in the curriculum planning.

Academic as well as extracurricular programs should be examined to determine whether they are providing opportunities for building equal status, shared interests, and guides to interracial understanding. Planning should provide opportunities for outside speakers, role playing, demonstrations, field trips, films.

Required resources.—Desegregation can be facilitated if the following resources are made available: access to individuals who have been successful in their attempts to integrate; professional consultants; seminars and films on human relations and human development; personal reports, letters, interviews with parents, teachers, and students who are in systems where busing is already occurring.

Beginning early.—It is crucial that desegregation begin in the very early years, with kindergarten. It is in the primary grades, beginning with kindergarten, where fundamental attitudes, habits, concepts, and orientations toward learning and classroom behavior are learned.

In the beginning years children learn to achieve, often out of fear of failure or a desire to please. As they reach adolescence, they begin to examine the validity of the concepts, values, attitudes, and behaviors of the significant adults in their lives. If they are confident in their own value orientation, comfortable with people of differing backgrounds, they will be more capable of maintaining their own independent perceptions and judgments. If however, they are fearful, or have not been exposed to alternative ways of "living and relating," the probability is infinitely greater that young people will accommodate to the attitudes and behaviors that are safe or familiar.

Many children fail in school not because they lack ability but because they have not acquired the skills and habits that are necessary for success. When this kind of child is placed in a classroom that requires, perhaps, more cooperation than might be required in a segregated classroom, these problems might be considerably alleviated if imaginative programs are included in the curriculum in all grades. In the elementary grades, the emphasis could be on social behavior: how to behave, what to do, how to do it. In the junior high and high school, emphasis should be on increased understanding of psychological processes; their primary goal should be the enhancement of understanding of the psychological bases of family interaction, of desirable child-rearing practices, of understanding of the demands and expectations of society, and on the development of a desirable self-concept. Free mandatory workshops should be given all teachers of these courses whose education is not recent. Workshop leaders should be authorities in the field. Classes for parents—adult education sponsored by the community and available in the evening—would provide similar understanding and awareness. This should be a cooperative effort of the community and the school.

In addition, committees should be set up for discussions and problem-solving sessions in churches, YMCAs, block clubs, YWCAs, PTAs, chaired by professional people. Television stations and newspapers could play an instrumental and supportive role in facilitating desegregation. Universities and colleges can contribute. They might offer fieldwork credits to students for working in areas involved in desegregation. Last, but not least, civic organizations have a variety of resources and manpower. They could offer awards to school personnel, students, communities, "the best story award," or the best "TV coverage." They could use their skills in promotional methods, fund raising and organizing to motivate individuals and communities to get behind projects. They could gather volunteers and solicit the help of celebrities, business people, and politicians to support school desegregation. They are an important part of the "power base" which should not be overlooked.

Some may say these guidelines for peaceful desegregation are merely the dreams of an idealist because there are too many hurdles —economic, social, and psychological—to be jumped before they can be implemented. But the same things were said 25 years ago about the desegregation of public transportation and other facilities in the South. Today this ideal is a reality. There is a strong similarity between the attitudes and actions of whites in Boston and Louisville today and those in Little Rock and New Orleans 20 years ago. The initial opposition in 1954 to desegregation has thawed. Since a country divided cannot prosper, pragmatists have adopted the stance, with the idealists, that the United States will not destroy itself by continuous disregard of its Constitution, its amendments, and Supreme Court decisions. Idealists say all people are required to obey laws of our country, which were designed to protect, provide, and ensure equal rights and justice to all. Pragmatists devise, promote, and engage in endeavors that cause these ideals to become realities. These guidelines, if followed, will stand the test of time.

Reference

Lippett, Ronald; Watson, Jeanne, and Wesley, Bruce. *Dynamics of Planned Change.* New York: Harcourt Brace & Co., 1958.

Index

Academic social science, character of, 3, 31; constraints of, 34; limited utility of, 37; methodological traditions, 36; technical difficulties, 35
Achievement patterns, 115–18, 126
Adams v. *Richardson,* 102
Advisory councils, 183–84
Allport, Gordon W., 127
American Educational Research Association, 46
American institutions, racist legacy, 95
Anrig, Gregory, 9
Arlen, Michael, 86, 88, 93
Armstrong Act, 178

Bell v. *School City of Gary,* 107
Better Communities Act of 1974, 135, 139
Black pride, 188
Black schools, control of, 26–27; inferiority of, 26, 58
Black students, and hatred of whites, 191–93; negative attitudes, 190; positive recognition, 189; self-segregation, 190
Black Student Union, 195
Black-white achievement gap, 37
Bond, Julian, 140
Bosco, James, 52, 53
Boston School Committee, 9, 10
Braxton, Mary V., 128
Brown v. *Board of Education of Topeka,* 1, 7, 39, 85, 97, 100, 105, 106, 109
Brown II, 1955, 105, 106
Bullock, Charles S., III, 126, 128
Business cooperation, self-interest, 11
Busing, 3, 10, 49, 52, 201; and parental rights, 55–56; as acceptable procedure, 58; as phony issue, 9; cross-district, 48, 167; opposition to, 47, 58, 65, 67, 101; superficial issue, 23

Cataldo, Everett, 33
CBS News, 47
Change agent, 202–3